THE BUSINESS OF ART

Second Edition

Lee Caplin

*Published in cooperation with the
National Endowment for the Arts*

PRENTICE HALL
Englewood Cliffs, New Jersey 07632

Prentice-Hall International (UK) Limited, *London*
Prentice-Hall of Australia Pty. Limited, *Sydney*
Prentice-Hall Canada, Inc., *Toronto*
Prentice-Hall Hispanoamericana, S.A., *Mexico*
Prentice-Hall of India Private Limited, *New Delhi*
Prentice-Hall of Japan, Inc., *Tokyo*
Simon & Schuster Asia Pte. Ltd., *Singapore*
Editora Prentice-Hall do Brasil, Ltda., *Rio de Janeiro*

© 1989 *by*

PRENTICE-HALL, Inc.

Englewood Cliffs, NJ

10 9 8 7 6 5 4 3

Library of Congress Cataloging-in-Publication Data

The Business of art/ [edited by] Lee Caplin.—2nd ed.

p.   cm.
"Published in cooperation with the National Endowment for the
Arts".
Includes index.
ISBN 0-13-091653-6.—ISBN 0-13-091646-3 (pbk.)
1. Art—Economic aspects.   2. Art—Marketing.   I. Caplin, Lee
Evan.   II. National Endowment for the Arts.
N8600.B875   1989
706'.8—dc20   89-15978
                                                                                    CIP

ISBN 0-13-091653-6

ISBN 0-13-091646-3 {PBK}

PRENTICE HALL
BUSINESS & PROFESSIONAL DIVISION
A division of Simon & Schuster
Englewood Cliffs, New Jersey 07632

PRINTED IN THE UNITED STATES OF AMERICA

Preface to the Second Edition

This edition comes after a span of six years, during which time *The Business of Art* has established itself not only as a best seller, but has generated considerable monies which the publisher has donated to the National Endowment for the Arts as an "unrestricted gift" for artists' grants.

The first edition addressed a condition that has not changed: most artists and students of art participate in a "calling" that can also become a "profession." However, tools for the "professional" aspects of the artist's career still are not a standard part of the artist's education.

This condition is more critical today than it ever has been. As more people become affluent, so the desire to partake of the finer things of life leads them to purchase more art for the home and office. Financial opportunities for the artist exist today as never before, but serious attention is necessary to transform these opportunities into sufficient income for a lifelong career. The artist Philip Pearlstein notes that "there is a real drop-out rate among artists over the age of 30" and that there are "hardly any artists over the age of 50." Apart from the issue of whether or not an artist has creative ability, Mr. Pearlstein's observation may reflect the artist's difficulty in mastering the "business" of art.

In the new edition of this book, every effort has been made to address changes that have taken place in the last six years, while concentrating on broader, more generic issues. Thus, each chapter concentrates on the "evergreen" nature of the information included: the relationships between artists and dealers, what gallery owners look for in adding artists to their rosters, how to prepare a slide portfolio of artwork, the concept of planning for the professional artist. Nevertheless, certain parts of the book are always subject to change: tax and other legislation, the state of the gallery scene in general as well as in specific cities, and where to look for particular grant applications and other documents.

An unexpected audience for the first edition of *The Business of Art* has been the art-collecting public, who use the book as a reference tool. Art collectors and buyers are fascinated to know what business-related issues are of concern to artists. The book provides a basis for new areas of mutual involvement beyond the artwork itself. Moreover, the chapters concerning corporate art collecting and art commissions suggest that there are additional topics that could benefit both artists and their public. As a result, this edition introduces chapters on buying and selling art—the rather exclusive world of professional art advisors, and auction houses specializing in the fine arts. For the first time, advisors for such diverse clients as Sylvester Stallone and Citibank give insights into acquiring and "deaccessioning" art for pleasure and profit. While such information is vital for collectors and would-be collectors, it is also critical for artists, if only to further demystify the process by which art is bought and sold.

Finally, the new edition touches on the "politics" of art. Initially, politics suggests the role of Congress in funding the National Endowment for the Arts and other art-related agencies. Since its inception, the Endowment has battled each year for more public funds to assist the arts in America. While the amounts requested are tiny compared with other budget items, there still remains a portion of the Congress that does not believe in the government's role as arts patron. Fortunately, sufficient political power exists to ensure that public funds are available to keep the Endowment and its sister agencies alive. But artists, apart from selling their work, are well advised to look beyond the Endowment for support. Hence, there is a new chapter on grantsmanship in pursuing funds from foundations and arts councils.

In analyzing what elements go into the successful pursuit of career support, the issue of "politics"—in the broadest sense—emerges as a factor to be considered. Superstar-artist Julian Schnabel reveals events leading to his rise from art student to selling a painting for $350,000. One sees that Schnabel is keenly aware of the people dotting his landscape; he exudes self-confidence and singlemindedly has positioned himself, from day one, as a part of the art world to be reckoned with. As a final commentary, this new edition contains excerpts from the CBS cable television show "The Great American Art Game": many of the art world's well-known figures express their views on the role of "politics" in the making and breaking of artists' careers.

At the time *The Business of Art* was conceived, the home video industry was in its infancy. However, detailed videotapes were produced of all the artists who participated in the federal lecture program. For the first time, a 60-minute distillation of those historic lectures is being made available as an adjunct to this book. Artists such as James Rosenquist, Larry Bell, Sylvia Stone, Robert Graham, and Philip Pearlstein speak about being artists, and how to cope with the "business" side of their life's work. It is hoped that the video program will lend an additional sense of reality to the large body of information in this new edition of *The Business of Art.*

Lee Caplin
Los Angeles, 1989

Acknowledgment

The author gratefully acknowledges the invaluable assistance of Miss Elsie Walker in the preparation of the First Edition; and Walter Slocombe, Esq., a partner in the Washington, D.C. law firm Caplin & Drysdale, in the preparation of the Second Edition.

Foreword

by
Livingston Biddle, Chairman
National Endowment for the Arts
1978–1981

One of the ironies of history is the position which artists have occupied in society. While revered and respected for the works they produce, many artists—if not most—are unable to support themselves wholly from the creations they provide for our enrichment. This is especially the case in times of fiscal restraint. Artists need to develop maximum avenues for support. Methods developed by the business community can be very helpful to artists in making their creations known and better appreciated by increasing numbers of people.

This book grew out of the continuing efforts of two federal agencies, the National Endowment for the Arts and the U.S. Small Business Administration, to offer technical business assistance to individual artists.

To test how to present information in this complex area, 4 pilot conferences were held in different cities across the country. Since then, more than 50 have followed, and the opportunity now exists for artists in all states and territories of the United States to have access to this type of valuable information.

Many of the perceptions of the conference panelists—artists, dealers, lawyers, and business experts—are included here. Their opinions are diverse and reflect the unique experience of the world of the visual artist. One idea that emerges is that there is no one path for artists to follow in approaching the arena where artworks are bought and sold. At the conferences, several artists emphasized the statement: "All the clichés are true, and the rules are made to be broken."

Nevertheless, many concepts are vital to understand and useful to apply. This book is an attempt to state the concepts clearly and concisely so that more artists will have the opportunity for self-sufficiency and will be able to organize the business side of their lives in such a way as to allow more time for the creation of their art.

I am privileged to express gratitude for the special initiatives taken by Joan Mondale and by Vernon Weaver, former administrator of the Small Business Administration, in beginning these significant collaborative efforts, and I express particular appreciation to the present SBA leadership, for carrying them forward toward expanded goals.

The Creation of a Federal Program for Artists

Lee Caplin

LEE CAPLIN created and directed the Federal Program "The Business of Art and the Artist" while serving as Special Assistant to the Chairman of the National Endowment for the Arts in Washington, D.C. Mr. Caplin currently produces feature films and television through his company LEE CAPLIN PRODUCTIONS in Los Angeles, California.

Between September 1979 and May 1980 over 4,000 artists gathered together in Los Angeles, Chicago, and New York City, where, for perhaps the first time, two federal agencies combined forces in four major events to assist art in America. Blue jeans and paint-stained windbreakers merged with three-piece suits, and an air of lively curiosity and expectation filled the auditoriums at L.A.'s and Chicago's Museum of Science and Industry and New York's American Museum of Natural History. After 18 intense hours at each location, artists were still talking, listening, taking notes, exchanging names.

The events were conferences, co-sponsored by the U.S. Small Business Administration (SBA) and the National Endowment for the Arts (NEA), to give artists basic business and marketing information.

This apparent unlikely pairing has a rational basis embedded in the purpose and philosophy of the two agencies involved.

The National Endowment for the Arts is the federal agency that is charged with giving support to all aspects of the arts in America. It not only supports the arts through grants but also supports artists and arts groups through technical assistance—helping them to be better organized and to get on their feet financially. NEA also has been involved in advocacy efforts to try to get members of the private sector to become involved with supporting the arts. One segment of the private sector has been the business community.

The business community at large has primarily been active in supporting the arts as a patron—purchasing art for office buildings, giving support to symphony orchestras, dance companies, museums, and theaters. However, the business community also possesses the practical knowledge of how business affairs are run—knowledge potentially very valuable to artists or arts groups in managing their own affairs—and in making the most of opportunities to earn income.

Each year as the Endowment's budget is reviewed by Congress the questions inevitably come up: "Are artists hooked on the federal dollar? How much do they really help themselves?" The NEA/SBA joint project seemed like an ideal opportunity to start answering those questions in the most positive of ways.

The Small Business Administration offers a variety of assistance projects for the small businessperson. It makes loans and loan guarantees and gives technical assistance to individual entrepreneurs or businesses. However, there is one major distinction between the purposes of the Arts Endowment and of the SBA: SBA gives direct support only to groups or individuals who are trying to make money, while NEA gives grants only to individuals or to art groups which are tax exempt and therefore primarily not engaged in making a profit. However, indirect or technical assistance to individuals is ground common to both agencies.

SBA brings to this new partnership a widespread "delivery mechanism" for technical assistance. It has field offices in all 50 states and territories that give business training sessions to all aspects of the small business community. While SBA does not have programs that deal specifically with artists, artists occasionally have found their way to SBA training conferences on accounting or establishing business operations. Nevertheless, SBA has previously given no specific attention to the arts. And most of the arts community is unaware that SBA gives technical assistance applicable to the arts.

The National Endowment for the Arts realized that it could help SBA develop a mechanism to train artists in business and marketing affairs that would respond to some real needs in the arts community. So with SBA to purvey technical information, and NEA to help develop that information, the two agencies began their task of putting together a training program for artists.

The development of this partnership received interest and support from the wife of the vice president of the United States, Mrs. Joan Mondale. As hononary head of the Federal Council on the Arts and the Humanities, Mrs. Mondale saw the NEA/SBA alliance as embodying the goal of the Federal Council—that the Council should act as a catalyst in involving other federal agencies besides the Endowment in assisting the arts. With Mrs. Mondale's strong endorsement, the project was off to a fine start.

NEA's Visual Arts Program—dealing with individual painters, sculptors, printmakers, photographers, and varied craftspersons—was chosen as the most practical area on which to focus this first program. Since the area of visual arts is so broad, subject areas dealing with art marketing and specific problems of artists are best addressed both by practicing artists who have "made it" in the financial sense and who understand the business aspects of their activities, and by accountants and lawyers who, in the course of their practice, handle artists' affairs.

In its training activities, SBA traditionally uses lecturers picked from its "service corps of retired executives" (SCORE) and an "active corps of executives" (ACE). These experts are business executives who donate time to SBA to assist in training and advising small businesspeople. While such resource people often do not have familiarity with the arts community, the Arts Endowment found them especially receptive to tailoring their remarks to fit the artists in the audience. With an array of experts from both the arts and business communities, NEA and SBA felt that the subjects would be fully addressed.

Three pilot conferences, in Los Angeles, Chicago, and New York, were planned. These cities were picked because of the size of their arts communities and because of the quality of SBA's district offices. The key to the success of these conferences was identifying and engaging local conference co-sponsors. Such co-sponsors would take part in the planning and execution of the conferences and would continue to be available on the local level for future artist training efforts by SBA. The Los Angeles co-sponsor was the California Confederation of the Arts. In Chicago and New York, co-sponsors were both the state and the city arts agencies. An additional cosponsor in New York was the Foundation for the Community of Artists. These organizations gave unselfishly of their time and resources to supply the essential support so critical to a successful program.

The response was amazing. Whereas SBA's past experience in training led it to believe that no more than 200 applicants would attend each conference, about 1,000 artists attended in each city. In Los-Angeles, there was such an overflow crowd that there had to be last-minute closed-circuit TV coverage in an adjoining auditorium. In New York an entire second conference was scheduled to accommodate nearly 1,000 additional artists who were unable to fit into the auditorium during the first New York conference.

During the course of the four two-day conferences, over 80 panelists appeared. On the first day artists talked about planning; an artist's accountant talked about arts accounting problems; and experts explained the intricacies of insurance, retirement plans, money-lending sources, banks, credit, tax, and the law in relation to the arts. Monona Rossol, of New York's Center for Occupational Hazards, described health hazards facing artists and art buyers from the materials used in making art. The second day was all about marketing. Successful artists from various corners of the arts community, experienced in traditional or alternative marketing possibilities, spoke on such subjects as galleries, museums, alternative spaces, and commissions. Dealers who were involved as brokers, middlemen, or direct sellers of art, spoke about marketing art in those settings. According to the evaluation forms and other responses the Endowment has received, artists found the program format ideal. Certain areas, such as law and accounting, are so complex that they deserve specific attention if they are to be explained fully. However, NEA and SBA simplified their presentations within a larger context, sensitizing artists to the need for legal and accounting advice, and devoting more time to some of the specifics of *where* and *how* artists go to sell their work.

Surprisingly, some artists who were approached to serve on panels were at first skeptical about the program. They feared such a conference might emphasize elements antithetical to art. But ultimately all agreed that artists could generally benefit from exposure to business and marketing basics.

Despite the practical purpose of the conferences, it was far from a simple "How to" program. The basic philosophy of those who make their lives in the arts was explored thoroughly by the artists on the panels. As these artists later unfolded their stories it was evident that they wanted to make certain that people in the audience, who call themselves artists, were not putting the cart before the horse; art is not so much a business as it is a calling and it is not so much the manufacture of products for sale as it is a matter of producing something because one is obsessed with producing it, and only then wondering, once the art is produced, what should be done with it. On the one hand, artists who had developed formulas for success did not want to reveal their formulas to the audiences. In many ways such formulas were unique to those artists. On the other hand, some of the speakers did not care to admit that there are any business-oriented steps that artists could or should take. Painter Ed Moses suggested, "There's art, there's stuff that looks like art, and there's stuff that just looks good. If you're into the last two, you're into business." The point being that "if the art is good, it will speak for itself." In the words of sculptor Bruce Beasley, however, "If you hide your light under a bushel, nobody will see it, but first you must be sure there's a light."

Several of the artists' presentations were discouraging, in their hesitancy to validate a business element in "getting one's art out." Painter Philip Pearlstein urged that each artist ask the question, "Do I have talent?" He said that the drop-out rate of artists over 30 suggests that many *are* asking themselves that question. "There are very few artists over 50," Pearlstein said.

Other panelist-artists, who are adept at promotion and marketing, made the assumption that everyone in the audience had work that he or she was proud of, and therefore it was valid to probe the extent to which business techniques were adaptable to the professional structure surrounding the making of art. They were able to identify means by which artists could go further in promoting and selling their own work.

A significant point was made that in all instances there is a quotient of "luck" and a quotient of "quality" involved in any success by any artist. Painter Joan Snyder called hers a "Cinderella story." Larry Bell was unable to explain what he had done to promote himself other than by doing his work, observing those he admires, and "emulating their style" in handling their own affairs. Most subscribed to doing only what is comfortable in terms of self-promotion. What may be easy for one artist, such as shaking hands at gallery gatherings, or setting a market value on a price of art, may be anathema to another. Sculptor Sylvia

Stone admitted that she tended to undervalue her work and preferred to let her dealer establish the prices. Conceptual artist Newton Harrison even advised his fellow practitioners, with some humor, to cultivate the "appearance of incompetence" for the purpose of conducting business affairs, since any attempt on their part to compete on an equal footing with other business practitioners would only lead to greater exposure and susceptibility to the various government rules and regulations.

Artist June Wayne suggested that government agencies lack sophistication about the unique business problems of the arts. To those who draft tax legislation, an artist's overhead looks suspiciously large compared to the slim profits or repetitive losses the artist's tax return may reveal. Because Congress assumes that the only credible reason for pursuing any business or profession is to make taxable profits, the persistence with which artists pursue their unprofitable activities greatly puzzles and vexes both our lawmakers and our enforcers. As a result, for an artist to fit into the tax laws is, according to Wayne, "for an eagle to fly while wearing an ox-yoke."

The traditional rules of business do not always apply in the business side of the arts. Gallery owner Ivan Karp stated that he chooses the artists he represents on the basis of how he responds to their work—not on the work's marketability.

One theme of conflict recurred and was never fully resolved: some artists felt that planning was essential in having a professional career as an artist. Other equally successful artists felt that any plan is out of place—that it stifles one's creative instincts. Painter Jim Rosenquist gave his view by quoting President Eisenhower: "A plan is nothing, planning is everything." On balance, however, everyone seemed to profit by some aspect of the conferences. Few expected to be given a list of "ten easy do's and don'ts" for becoming a successful painter or sculptor. But despite their individualism, most artists share many of the same problems and needs. As they listened and asked questions, artists were able to arrive at a balanced view of the various options available to them in marketing and promoting their work.

Certainly the gatherings themselves were significant events apart from the valuable information conveyed. Many of the artists in the audience had never seen or heard dealers such as those on stage. Many had never been in the company of artists of major reputation, such as appeared in the three cities. There was great value in the audience's listening to sculptor Fred Eversley, on the one hand, showing clear knowledge of how to market art work or Bob Graham, on the other hand, suggesting that there is little an artist can do in marketing artwork; that his work somehow seemed to sell almost by itself. On a human level, it was reassuring to encounter colleagues of one's own discipline or geographic surrounding, who attended the conferences to get the same information, and to be able to communicate with these people afterward at the receptions that were held.

The Endowment, for its part, certainly does not advocate treating art as a business or artworks as commodities for sale. Rather, its main role in participating in the project is to make available as much technical business and marketing information as possible, so as to offer the broadest range of choices to artists pursuing their callings as professionals.

As a result of the pilot program "The Business of Art and the Artist," the Endowment and SBA produced a documentary video tape and a conference organizer's manual to be used in presenting workshops throughout the country.

This volume can supplement these workshops and is a useful introduction to the business side of art for all those who have not yet received such technical assistance. The material presented here is not meant to be inclusive, nor is it supposed to supplant courses in business and marketing. Rather, it is a first step toward understanding many aspects of "survival" for artists in a commerce-oriented society. The artists, dealers, and business professionals who have contributed their thoughts in producing this book hope it will help you discover the types of questions you ought to be asking either yourself or those whom you enlist to help you. They hope that their views on the professional side of art will illuminate and demystify many seemingly technical and complicated details that might seem burdensome to those who just want to make art. Their ideas apply to all forms of visual arts and crafts. Whether the topic is sculpture or the Los Angeles art scene, the information can be generally useful. Artists as a group are less eager to share "techniques" that have worked for them. Dealers, too, sometimes are reluctant to be candid about their colleagues and the practices they use. But for the first time, gathered in one place, a composite of the art scene is depicted by what is said—and what is left unsaid—by the authors of this book.

Larry Bell once stressed that each of us is responsible for the best and the worst of what happens in our careers. What you won't get by reading this book are any "Ten Commandments" for becoming a successful artist. What we hope you will get is a better sense of what you really want from your art and how far you are willing to go to achieve your goals. If you can place all the elements of your art and the business of art in perspective, you will have achieved a lot, especially in terms of being responsible to yourself as an artist and as a professional. For some there may be a period of time when fame and fortune are a reality. For others, there may be a perpetual obscurity. In between are many variations on the theme, as well as behavior patterns ranging from the promiscuous to the recalcitrant. Sylvia Stone made a keen observation when she said that "making art is one of the true areas where we have a kind of independence and serve our own sense of morality. It is one of the free activities still left to some of us. And I say; 'Use it. Use it and enjoy it.' "

Contents

Part Two PROTECTING

Part Three MARKETING

Part Four   EXHIBITING

Part Five   BUYING AND SELLING

Part Six   THE POLITICS OF ART

Mary Boone · Sidney Janis · Leo Castelli · Arnold Glimcher · Paula Cooper · William Rubin · Patterson Sims · Hilton Kramer · Peter Schjeldahl · Richard Brown Baker · Nathan Cummings · George Segal · Jennifer Bartlett · Chuck Close

PART ONE

PLANNING

The first thing you have to decide is whether you have talent. It's a hard decision to make but alot of people seem to make it. There's a big drop-out period when people reach 30. There are very few artists over 50.

Philip Pearlstein

1 An Artist's Way of Life

James Rosenquist

JAMES ROSENQUIST is an artist and a former member of the National Council on the Arts.

The question I ask myself when art and business are discussed together is, "Has art grown into a desk job?" I started drawing in 1949—or even before that—but I arrived in New York in 1955. The Third Avenue El was just being torn down, the Colosseum wasn't built yet, and the Whitney Museum was still on 54th Street. At that time the art world was very small. The number of galleries was few, and I would say the number of people who collected avant-garde art—which meant that it had come from young living Americans—was perhaps less than a dozen.

While art, historically, has always been related to communication, in 1955 in New York many famous underground artists lived within a few blocks from each other but did not know each other, had never met each other. In the 1950s, Jim Harvey—the man who designed the Brillo box—who used to travel to the Middle East, brought back slides of his travels and invited the whole art world to come and see the slides down at Coentie's Slip. So everybody and his brother showed up, and I was surprised to find that people did not know each other. I met Ad Rinehardt—one of America's most famous artists—for the first time. Major artists were not in close contact. In the late 1950s, American artists such as Baziotes, de Kooning, Gottlieb, Guston, Kline, Motherwell, Newman, Pollock, Still, Rothko, and others had tremendous underground reputations. They had worked for years—some of them, like Franz Kline, in the WPA programs—yet they hadn't had one-man shows, and they were already in their late forties or older. Some of them would get up at the Friday Night Club and broadcast their art. They'd talk about it, be assertive about it, defend it, and they were, I would say, very self-conscious about their work. They talked among themselves. They would try to establish the work; in other words, they were not cool about it. They were *hot* about it compared to the next generation, called Pop Artists, of which I was a part.

When I arrived on the art scene, the art audience had already begun to increase. In 1958 de Kooning had a show, and one of his paintings sold for the highest price for a living American artist—$14,500. Just after that, Jasper Johns appeared on the scene. He seemed to be a reactionary to a style in painting sometimes described as drips and splashes. Actually it was called "abstract expressionism." His style resulted in critics trying to group artists in a "movement," but they were not all alike.

4

At that time in New York, Ivan Karp, Henry Geldzahler, and Dick Bellamy would prowl the streets, going to artists' studios to discover new talent. They actually went from door to door to find out who lived in each loft. I think this was the first time artists were solicited. Young unknown artists felt they didn't have a chance to show their work when they saw someone like de Kooning walk down 57th Street in an old Levi jacket and bedroom slippers, looking very poor. If *he* wasn't doing well, how could a lesser known artist expect to do well?

One day in 1960 I ran into Bob Indiana. He said, "Guess what I saw, Jim. I saw a dirty new collage of Bob Rauschenberg's behind a big glass table on Park Avenue! Let's go out and have a drink and celebrate!" So we celebrated Bob Rauschenberg's breakthrough. At that time artists supported themselves any way they could. Some did commercial art jobs, some worked on construction jobs, and some sold coffee in Madison Square Park from the coffee stands. I painted billboards and created window displays for Bonwit Teller and Tiffany. Rauschenberg also did window displays for Bonwit Teller. We all had to make a buck.

When Henry, Ivan, and Dick started looking for people, Henry was a curator at the Metropolitan Museum, Ivan was at the Castelli Gallery, and Dick was about to open his new Green Gallery. Dick asked me to be in his gallery. I knew I could make a living at that point, so I quit my commercial artist's job just to paint. I was very happy. I lived frugally, and was able to live on very little. I could eat breakfast for 25 cents at the Seamen's Institute! I found it a tremendous luxury to be able to live in a cosmopolitan city and not have to deal with it except to dream. The dealers urged me to hurry up and have a show as fast as I could, but I was happy just to live with my pictures and simply let things happen. My paintings were like my companions, and I wasn't consciously trying to sell them. But then Dick sold some of them to Bob Scull, the Tremains, Dick Baker, Jan Streed, Morton Newman, and others, for prices ranging from $350 to $1,100.

In the 1950s you could walk into the Whitney Museum annual exhibit and buy almost anybody's painting for a thousand bucks. Then things started to heat up. People became interested in art—I don't know why. Leon Menuchin bought practically a whole show for Brandeis University. People followed his lead. Harry Abrams, who had been buying French Impressionism and Old Masters' works before that, saw what Leon had done and began buying young artists' work. John Powers saw what Harry and Leon bought, and he bought what they bought. So collectors of young unknown American artists began to proliferate.

ART AS A BUSINESS

I've been asked, "How does an artist relate to business?" and "Can I plan a career as an artist?" As for planning, Eisenhower once said, "A plan is nothing. Planning is everything." Being an artist, whatever that is, involves constant questioning of everything. It is very difficult to set out a plan in a businesslike manner because a happy accident could happen and someone might like your worst work.

Artists work in unknown territory. If it were known, they probably wouldn't be artists. This is difficult for an artist to realize, but it's also more difficult for an audience to understand. However, when an artist is through with a work, then strange things can happen, like people wanting to be near it, people talking about it, and people wanting to own it. When this happens, artists usually don't know what to do.

My first experience in relating to business was like building a better mousetrap. I never had to ask my friends or potential buyers to visit me. One day Barbara Durkee visited me. She told her husband Steve about my work, and he told his dealer Alan Stone. Alan told Ileana Sonnabend, and she told Bellamy and Karp, and they told Leo Castelli. Jasper Johns even asked to come to my studio. He said, "Where did you learn to paint like that?" People beat down the door to my studio. Artists, then, were usually indifferent to galleries; they didn't expect much money, only the possibility of having their work on view in a neutral space. Before I had any reputation, I never had to schlep my paintings anywhere. That's how it happened with me. Other people's introductions to a gallery and to business happen differently. Frank Stella just walked into the Castelli Gallery, and Leo asked him, "What do you paint?" Frank said, "I paint. I just paint, man." The artists of the 1960s and the 1970s were a little luckier because they didn't have to solicit their art. In the 1980s there is an entirely different situation. There are many more artists living in New York City, and there are many more galleries. I like it that way; there is more to look at, more to investigate.

All through the 1960s my daily routine was waking up with a hangover about ten o'clock, painting all day, at five o'clock renting a tuxedo from Silver's Tuxedos, going up to 57th Street to an opening, going up to the Jewish Museum to Rauschenberg's opening, or somebody else's opening, or my own opening, then going out, staying out till one or two in the morning, waking up with a hangover, working the next day, renting another tuxedo at Silver's (or keeping the same one), going out again—every night of the week! Sometimes I was invited to three dinners at a time. Life was fast and fun.

But getting back to that planning thing: planning is like looking for your wallet under a street lamp when you didn't lose it there in the first place. When I started planning, I wanted to be a mural painter. I tried to go to school where they would teach me mural painting. All these men teaching had read books about it, but they had never done it. I looked around and I saw billboard painters painting, and I thought, "Gee, those guys can handle any kind of space. They must know how to handle paint and brushes." So I went right into billboard painting as a master billboard painter—no apprenticeship, no nothing. I learned a great deal from my helpers: David Mishnick, a sculptor who had come from Russia in 1927 and had shown his work with Arshile Gorky; Solly Schnee, Harold Bernstein, who had a lot of knowledge about paint. These old-timers were like teachers to me. They told me what *not* to do. It was like going to school—but it was a tough commercial business.

Successful artists as well as businessmen use creative thinking to get from point A to point B. The attempt to repeat an approach or a style that has been successful in the past in order to achieve new success can lead to a dull result. Creative, successful artists and businessmen rarely approach the same thing in the same way twice. Art isn't really done for any reason other than a means of the artist's self-expression. Business, on the other hand, is traditionally done to make money.

Now art may not be done to make money, but that doesn't rule out its value. The problem for any artist has always been either having money and no time or a lot of time and no money. The ideal life for an artist would be to live in a cosmopolitan city and be free from the burden of having to make a living. And, however one accomplishes it, that freedom from "making a living" could be essential to being an artist. I think a problem comes when an artist does start to sell something, for then he becomes connected with business and his life is no longer free from that involvement.

For myself, I don't have the slightest idea of how to allocate time between art and making money except on a case-by-case basis. I really have no plan at all. The reason I work, the reason I make things, is to illuminate physically some feelings I've had. Then they exist outside of myself in some kind of form, so when I am old and gray I'll be able to look at them and realize that I was alive at a certain period. I really regard it almost like a philatelic thing. When I'm dead, that's outside the human condition and I don't care any more about the works.

There's a whole new crop of young artists who grew up surrounded by materialism, as I did, but who try to plan their art careers like the climb up a corporate ladder. I can't imagine an artist's life being as steady as that. People who don't know what an artist does ask me, "Are you doing pictures for magazines now? What are you doing this for?" My answer is that I'm not doing art for anyone but myself. The reason *why* is that if I did art for somebody other than myself, I wouldn't know what to do. I don't have to paint something this color or that color because of someone else's reason. I can do anything I please. And that's the lovely, scary thing. It's challenging to go into a room with a canvas and know that you can do anything you want to do. This is probably a Far Eastern attitude about learning. You confront yourself totally, whether you're able to work or not.

So, getting back to the idea of planning, to an artist's mind there are no holds barred, no barriers. The only thing that stops you is the old Catch 22 thing, the financial problem that you just don't want to deal with. Yet you have to face it.

When I began painting, James Michener came to my studio and said, "I want to buy that painting." I said, "I'm sorry; it's already been sold. Richard Bellamy sold it." He said, "I'd like one just like it, or something like it." I felt that the look of my art wasn't like anything else being done at that time, so I was very reactionary, and I said, "No, I can't possibly do that." Now if he hadn't said what he did, I might have made four more paintings similar to that one, or studied it further. But I viewed his request as an interference. I was very sensitive then!

Just a few years ago it wasn't fashionable to want one's son or daughter to be an artist. Now sons and daughters are encouraged to study art because it could be possible to make a handsome income from it. I can't think of art as a desk job. Avant-garde artists still face hardships in spite of a current government attitude that art is alive and well in the United States. Artists have a hard time getting credit, getting hospital care. Their work is sold, and resold quickly for high prices in a short time, and the artist gets only the first piddling commission from a dealer—or may not get paid for years. Artists can't contribute their work to museums for a tax deduction as art collectors can, because the government says the only value coming from an artist's work is the cost of the materials! Back in the 1960s, when it was lawful, the art dealers' association carefully scrutinized donations, so there were very few overvalued works. The person possibly most responsible for stopping contributions was former President Nixon, who donated his writings for an unrealistic deduction.

Artists' heirs are often stuck with a huge inheritance tax on unsold works and have to sell them off cheaply to be able to pay the taxes. There are a great number of artist problems pertaining to business and taxes. If the speed of thinking of the IRS and the government could accelerate at the same rate as the speed of artists' and inventors' thinking—that is, linked with communication—I think we could get away from a guns or unemployment society and get into space without bringing war with us.

During the time I've taken to write this, the current acceleration of the change of events regarding government support for the arts, business support for the arts, and the fate of the National Endowment for the Arts under the new administration has changed drastically. The new government senses a need for extreme budget cuts in every area except military spending. In *The New York Times,* during the height of the Vietnam conflict, the annual government military contracts to major corporations were published. If one added up the cost of all the arts activities in the United States for the same year, including dance, music, museums, theater, and even large Hollywood films, it wouldn't be a drop in the bucket compared to the enormous military expenditures for Vietnam.

On a television program on Sunday, April 28, 1981, the panelists seemed to agree that art should become a business in order to be able to make it on its own. Mr. Herb Schmerz, of Mobil Oil, stated that art groups should be able to function and survive as a business. Mr. Schmerz was happy to announce that art finance should be left to the private sector and will happily be taken over by big business. One panelist said that art in America is alive and healthy, and always was, despite government support. Another panelist suggested that viewers should send their ideas to their congressmen.

I remember a time not long ago when art barely existed in New York. And the future of art in America doesn't look good now. In this great country of ours, let's encourage the arts and humanities, and new forays into visual art. Let's build one or two fewer missiles and provide the National Endowment for the Arts—with its history of a hands-off attitude—with a healthy, growing budget. Let's not let large corporate control lead us into *1984.*

2 | Practical Planning

Bruce Beasely

BRUCE BEASELY is a sculptor with works in the permanent collection of the Museum of Modern Art, the Guggenheim, and the Musée d'Art in Paris, among others. His large sculptures can be seen in public places such as the federal courthouse in San Diego and the San Francisco International Airport.

I have been asked to address the rather vague area of planning in regard to a career in art. I am not sure what this encompasses, but I know for certain that I did not plan to be an artist. It just happened just as falling in love happens.

Although I myself cannot imagine being anything but an artist, I do not believe in soliciting others to follow me in this field. Art is a joy too precious—and painful—to proselytize. Therefore, I extend my sympathies and, of course, my warmest feelings for anyone who has the art monkey on his or her back.

I am asked what can be expected when you have been bitten by the art bug. You can expect challenge, the joy of expression, exploration, and sometimes exploration that leads to exhilarating accomplishment. You can expect frustration, self-doubt, and loneliness. You can also expect damn little practical support.

THE ESSENTIAL DILEMMA

There is much known history about artists and money problems, and a lot of it is true: Michelangelo fighting with the pope over payments, Van Gogh writing his brother for more money. The stories are endless, and they point to a terrible historical dilemma: an artist must have money to live and to make art. But the motives for making art are not financial. This puts artists' needs in direct conflict with their motivation. In fact, artists are economic victims of their own aesthetic, which of course is not news to anyone who is an artist.

The purpose of this chapter is to shed some light on this dilemma. Perhaps the reason I was asked to address this question is that some years ago I made a decision to throw myself on the world of galleries and sales of my art for my sole livelihood. I am therefore supposed to know something about it.

I am not sure this is true, nor am I sure that I know any more about it now than I did when I made the decision. However, in looking back on that decision (which at the time was made more in passion than in logic), and also in observing and sharing the lives and careers of friends who made both similar and dissimilar choices, I have thought of some things I have learned which I would like to share. Maybe they will sound simplistic and obvious, but they have been lessons to me.

MAKING CLEAR CHOICES

Basically, I would say that the artists I have known who have had rewarding and successful careers are those who have been able to make very clear choices about their priorities and expectations. Once these priorities were selected, they wasted no emotion on the other things they gave up.

I want to make it clear that when I refer to a successful artist I do not necessarily mean financially successful. To me a successful artist is one who continues to make art and is not more than 50 percent bitter about the rest of life.

If you teach for a living, the pay per hour is good, but for some it is aesthetically draining; if you drive a cab you have to put in more hours, but it's less complicated. If you work in California you don't have the New York scene; if you live in New York you can't work outside as you can in California.

To cast in bronze is expensive. If you work in plaster, people won't pay as much for it. If you work monumentally, you can do only a few pieces per year. If you work small, you can't be in the shows of monumental work.

These trade-offs are endless, and in addressing the specific and terrifying question of how one can make art and also make a living, there are myriad answers, and all of them have a good part and a bad part.

My most sincere advice is to take a hard look at your desires, your abilities, and your temperament, and then pick the solution that is the least repugnant.

I purposefully put the phrase as "the solution that is the least repugnant," not as the best, because that is how I see it. The best part is the art you are going to make. The negative part is that somehow you have to get some money in order to do it. And believe me, there are no perfect solutions.

BE AWARE OF DRAWBACKS

If you are rich to start with, you and others will wonder if you could have made it on your own. There are the same and even greater doubts about marrying for money. If you teach, there are time constraints, and for some there are aesthetic drains and the general diversion of your time and energy that university involvement demands. For many, selling their art has its drawbacks also. It requires the drive to sustain a regular output even at difficult times. Some have difficulty in letting the work go once it is finished. It requires that your prices be set by what the work will really sell for rather than by what you think it should be worth; this often requires facing painful realities. Some artists find the whole business aspect of galleries and sales to be unpleasant.

My decision to try to live off my work and cut the bridges to teaching in the early days involved my acquiring a mechanical skill to fall back on when nothing sold, and also being willing to live very cheaply for many years. I do not mean to go into a long lament on the suffering and starving artist, but there is more than an element of truth in the cliché. If you are going to depend on the sales of your work as your means of livelihood, you must expect to go through a period of very real deprivation. This may mean forgoing a family, living in genuinely inadequate conditions, and, in every material sense, living a lousy life. On the other hand, this will also be a period of great excitement and reward as you hit a stride with your work that was previously prevented by the demands of school or regular work.

There is, of course, no guarantee that your learning the elements of business will produce any financial success in your art. After all, we are not talking about earning merit badges or getting into heaven.

It is hoped that you will have found out your work capacity, discovered the depth of your ideas, and produced a good body of work.

For myself it has been a good choice and one that I would make again. It is not, however, as good as it often looks from the other side of the fence. I am under constant pressure to produce and exhibit. I must actively seek out and enter into competitions for sculpture commissions that are often time consuming and unrewarding. Aside from the actual making of the art, it is a rather practical life—full of details of crating, shipping, photographs, installations, and so on. And there is, of course, no certainty that because things sold this year they will sell next year. But I am not complaining. I made my choice, and when the payoff isn't worth the pain, I will make another choice.

But it would be a critical mistake to eat myself up with bitterness about the bad part that came automatically with the choice I made. If I am going to live off my work, I must pay more attention to the business part than if I had another source of income. It is just like sweeping up the studio or changing the oil in the air compressor; it isn't interesting or aesthetic, but it is reality that has to be dealt with.

KNOW YOURSELF

So, basically, what I am saying is this: pick where you want to be and go there without looking over your shoulder, without looking back. If you are gregarious and good at self-promotion, do it. If you are not, do as much as you can stand; realize that you are making a choice not to do more, and don't be bitter about your not being better at it.

If you love working in the mountains, great. But don't badmouth the New York "conspiracy." If showing in public is painful, don't show. If you can't manage a variable income, get a secure job.

These are a lot of don'ts, but I also have some do's: do make art; do make good art; and do make it all through your life, because, really, that is the only reward you can expect.

Selling your art is nice; public acclaim is nice; but it's like the warmth of a sunburn. It's superficial and shortlived.

Be practical but only about practical matters. Expect damn little, but expect a lot from yourself—because finally your relationship with the art you make will be the major source of joy and sorrow in your life.

3 Setting Up Business

Harvey Horowitz

HARVEY HOROWITZ, former chairman of the board of the Volunteer Lawyers for the Arts, is a partner in the law firm of Squadron, Ellenoff, Plesent & Lehrer, of New York City. Mr. Horowitz is a member of the arts and entertainment committees of the City Bar Association of the City of New York and is Adjunct Professor for Performing Arts and the Law at the City University of the City of New York's Graduate School.

SELECTING A BUSINESS ENTITY

When an artist or a group of artists sets out to undertake a business venture, several types of business entities can be utilized. However, to determine which form of entity best suits a particular need, various factors should be considered. Among them are tax considerations, record-keeping obligations, formalities necessary to establish a particular venture, whether federal tax exemption will be sought, what legal liability the venture and its individuals might be exposed to, and, in general, the impact on conducting business that the structure would have.

Depending on particular needs, one or more of these factors may have greater significance than the others. It is almost impossible to generalize what should be foremost in the minds of artists beginning a business in terms of selecting a structure. Even if circumstances would not warrant a highly structured business entity, it still is useful to have a working knowledge of these various formats since interaction with them is almost a certainty if one begins conducting a business.

STARTING OUT AS A SOLE PROPRIETOR

The simplest and most direct manner of starting out is to conduct a business individually under one's own name. Under such circumstances, the business itself has no separate identity legally or otherwise from the person conducting the business. The individual is liable for commitments made and is personally liable to pay taxes on any income the venture produces. No separate tax returns have to be prepared for federal income tax purposes. Items of income and expense are reported on Schedule C to the individual's Form 1040 federal income tax return. There are no formalities necessary when starting a business under an individual's own name. Very often, if the type of business does not warrant any further formalities, an individual should not seek to overstructure the activity. Therefore, doing business under one's own name should be seriously considered as an initial step.

CONDUCTING BUSINESS UNDER A
TRADE NAME OR AN ASSUMED NAME

A slight variation from conducting business under one's own name is individually conducting business under an assumed or trade name. The tax and legal ramifications of conducting business under a trade name are substantially identical to those attaching to conducting business under one's own name. The business is not a separate legal entity for liability or tax purposes, and, again, the individual conducting business is personally responsible for debts and taxes on income earned. Similarly, no separate federal income tax return is required to be filed. The added formality necessary to conduct business under a trade or assumed name is that in most states the individual would have to file a form of certificate disclosing the true identity of the person conducting business, and the trade name being assumed. Most states also require that a copy of the certificate be displayed at the place of business, and most banking institutions require a copy of the certificate for the purpose of opening a bank account in the trade name. Although conducting business under a trade name does not differ from conducting business under an individual's own name, some persons believe the assumption of a trade name adds a certain cachet to the business venture. There are opposing opinions on this point, but both have validity. In some instances, it is possible that the use of a trade name might make the business venture appear more substantial. In some fields, however, it might be important to establish the reputation of the individual involved, in which case it would be preferable to conduct business under an individual's name. As was noted, the formalities of conducting business under a trade or assumed name are rather minimal, and the costs, including filing fees and photocopies, of a business certificate should run under $50.

FORMING A PARTNERSHIP

When two or more individuals set out to conduct business, usually some structure is required. The most common form when two or more people come together is a general partnership. Just as with a person doing business under an assumed name, the general partnership does not have a legal or tax identity separate and apart from the individual partners. Accordingly, partners are liable for debts incurred by the partnership, and taxes must be paid by the individuals on the income earned by the partnership. Even though taxes on partnership profits are payable by the partners, the partnership is required to file a separate partnership tax return reflecting the financial activity of the partnership and the identity of the partners. State and local partnership returns may also be required. A partnership is a consentual arrangement between two or more individuals to conduct business together. It should be noted that the agreement to conduct business as partners can be a tacit as well as an expressed agreement. In most states, the agreement need not be written and an oral partnership agreement might suffice to constitute individuals as partners. While it is recommended that individuals desiring to form the partnership do so under a written agreement, it is important to note that an oral or tacit understanding can give rise to the partnership status. This is significant because of the legal rule that each partner can legally bind the partnership and each partner is legally responsible individually for all of the partnership's debts and obligations. Accordingly, if two people set out to conduct business, and one of the individuals orders supplies or enters into a lease, the other individual could be held liable for these obligations if it is later determined that the partnership status was created by tacit agreement between the parties. In forming a partnership, it is generally useful to have a writing setting forth the rights and obligations of the parties to each other. For instance, one party who may be contributing more time or funds to the partnership might desire a greater participation in profits. Also, if there are several individuals involved, the parties might wish to delegate responsibilities for certain matters among various partners. However, it is important to note that no matter what the agreement is among the partners, as far as other individuals and entities are concerned, each partner is fully liable for partnership obligations. Consider, as examples, two persons entering into a partnership arrangement and (1) deciding that one individual would have a 90 percent partnership interest, while the other has a 10 percent interest, or (2) agreeing that each shall have an equal interest in the partnership. Notwithstanding the fact that either of these agreements would be binding and valid as between the partners, if one of the individuals in either partnership example signed a partnership lease, then the other partner would be fully liable for the lease obligations.

As a point worth considering, it is possible for a person to "accidentally" fall into a partnership with another party without so intending; if two or more individuals *act* as if they are a partnership, they may be treated as one in the eyes of the law, despite an internal understanding that a partnership has not been formed. This raises all the potential liability problems discussed in the section. An affirmative statement that a partnership has *not* been formed may not be enough to defeat the finding of a partnership by a court or other entity; caution is therefore advised in becoming involved in a situation susceptible to the partnership interpretation.

THE PARTNERSHIP AGREEMENT

The formalities for setting up a partnership usually include a partnership agreement, which can take the form of a rather simple letter of understanding signed by the partners and the subsequent filing of a certificate of partnership with a state or county office. Again, the requirements for filing vary from state to state. But, in general, a certificate of partnership is filed, and copies are needed for the purpose of opening a bank account. Also, most states require that a copy of the partnership certificate be displayed so that the public knows the identity of the individuals involved in the partnership venture. The cost for setting up a partnership, including filing fees and photocopies, is usually under $50.

SETTING UP A CORPORATION

The most structured form of doing business is the corporate form. All states have adopted some form of corporation law which contains the requirement for establishing a corporation. Again, as was the case with a doing business certificate and a partnership certificate, the requirements vary from state to state. Generally speaking, however, the corporation is formed by the preparation and filing of a charter or certificate of incorporation. Unlike the situations with persons conducting business under an assumed name or as partners, a corporation has a separate legal identity from that of its stockholders, officers, and directors. Accordingly, a corporation is responsible for its own debts and obligations and is liable for taxes on income earned by the corporation. Most states permit at least two forms of corporations, the first being the business corporation or stock corporation and the second, the nonprofit or not-for-profit corporation.

ESTABLISHING A NONPROFIT
CORPORATION

Usually the requirements to establish a nonprofit corporation are greater than those required to establish a business or stock corporation. For the most part, the nonprofit corporation mode is adopted where the goal is ultimately to obtain some form of tax exemption that is needed for the purpose of soliciting contributions or receiving grants from federal or state agencies. To be able to qualify for nonprofit status in most states, the organization must be established to serve a public, charitable, or educational purpose rather than pursue a purely business or commercial goal. As an example, nonprofit corporations have been established to run art schools, to award fellowships, or to conduct training or educational programs. Since most artists are pursuing their profession with a view toward financial gain, it is unlikely that they would select the form of doing business as a nonprofit corporation as their primary business mode. Accordingly, there is intentionally excluded a fuller discussion on the requirements for establishing a nonprofit corporation and the requirements for securing tax exemption. In all events, it is advisable to consult an attorney if you are considering such a move.

STRUCTURE OF A CORPORATION

In most states, a business corporation may be established by one or more individuals to pursue any lawful commercial or business goal. Most states allow one person to incorporate, although some states may require a greater number of individuals to be incorporators. A business corporation consists of the individuals who own the corporation and who are denominated as stockholders. Stockholders usually elect a board of directors to manage the affairs of the corporation. The board of directors in turn elects officers to carry on the day-to-day business management of the corporation. Directors of a corporation need not be stockholders, and officers are not required to be directors or stockholders. A corporation's charter or certificate of incorporation usually does not contain a lot of detail regarding the operation of the organization. Accordingly, it is customary for a corporation to adopt bylaws at an early stage of its existence to set forth the procedures for operation. The bylaws usually contain procedures for stockholder voting, convening of meetings, and election of directors. Bylaws also include similar provisions for conducting meetings by directors.

While the procedure for establishing a sole proprietorship and partnership is quite simple, the procedure for establishing a corporation is more complicated. Accordingly, while it is possible in most states to form a corporation without using a lawyer, some consideration should be given to whether legal advice should be sought. The filing fees for establishing a corporation are approximately $100, and legal fees can range from $250 to $500. Additionally, most states require the payment of an annual franchise tax or corporate fee tax, even if the corporation has had little or no activity.

TWO OTHER BUSINESS STRUCTURES:
LIMITED PARTNERSHIPS AND TRUSTS

Thus far, we have briefly reviewed three forms of business structure: (1) the sole proprietorship (whether under an individual's own name or an assumed name), (2) a general partnership, and (3) a corporation. These three categories are the ones most likely to be considered when one or more persons sets out to conduct business. However, to complete this presentation, mention should also be made of two other forms of legal entities—a limited partnership and a trust.

Limited Partnerships

A limited partnership is a hybrid form of entity having some characteristics of a general partnership and other characteristics of a corporation. A limited partnership is generally utilized where investments to the business venture are being sought and certain tax benefits and profit distributions are contemplated. In the cultural and arts community, this vehicle is most frequently used in the theatrical field when money is being raised from investors to produce a play. A limited partnership consists of one or more individuals or corporations who are called "general partners" and one or more individuals or corporations who serve as "limited partners." (In this regard, it should be noted that certain state laws may prohibit a corporation from being a general or limited partner or limit its power to become such. As is the case with other forms of doing business, the rules applying to the formation and operation of a limited partnership are governed by state law. Accordingly, these laws may differ from state to state.) The general partners of a limited partnership, like the partners in a general partnership, have full liability for partnership debts. Limited partners, however, have only limited liability for partnership debts. This limitation is usually an amount equal to the money invested in the limited partnership. To this extent, the limitation of liability for limited partners is somewhat analogous to the limited liability of corporate stockholders. As in a general partnership, taxes on the income earned by a limited partnership are the responsibility of the partners. The allocation of profits and losses for the purpose of computing taxes is governed by an agreement of limited partnership. Establishing a limited partnership requires more formal steps than is the case with the general partnership. Usually a certificate of limited partnership has to be filed in a state or local office and notice of the formation of a limited partnership published. Since it is a somewhat complex form of business venture, it is suggested that professional advice be sought before establishing a limited partnership.

Trusts

The other form of entity is a trust. Trusts are usually established by a deed or instrument of trust or by a last will and testament. Trusts are not frequently utilized as a vehicle to conduct business, and it is unlikely that anyone pursuing a business career in the arts would opt for this mode of doing business. A trust is a separate legal entity and consists of one or more trustees who manage the trust and one or more beneficiaries who are entitled to receive the benefit of income generated by the trust. Because it is highly unlikely that the trust mode of business would be used, no further discussion on this legal entity is included.

CHOOSING THE RIGHT BUSINESS
STRUCTURE

As stated earlier, the three modes of doing business most frequently utilized are sole proprietorship, general partnership, and corporation. The decision as to whether to conduct business as a sole proprietorship or as a partnership is more a result of necessity than of choice. Clearly, if more than one individual is involved in a venture, but those individuals do not want to incorporate, the partnership mode of business results directly from the decision to associate with others and conduct business. Accordingly, the primary issue to be considered when starting a business, is the question of whether or not to incorporate, since (1) in most states an individual can incorporate; (2) a corporation is permitted to have only one shareholder, director, and officer, and (3) self-evidently, more than one individual can form and operate a corporation. In this regard, the individuals should assess the financial, practical, and tax considerations adherent to incorporating.

From a management point of view, operating a corporation imposes an additional burden in terms of record keeping and reporting. At the early stages of operation, a certificate of incorporation or charter has to be drawn, bylaws prepared, and officers and directors elected. Since a corporation is a separate legal entity, it is required to file tax returns annually, and the entity will pay taxes on corporate profits.

An exception to this rule is the "Sub-Chapter S" corporation. Provided that conditions and requirements contained in the Internal Revenue Code are met, stockholders of a corporation can file what is known as a Sub-Chapter S election with the Internal Revenue Service. In such a case, from a tax point of view, the profits and losses of a corporation are picked up by the stockholders on their personal tax returns. In such a case, the individual stockholders would pay taxes on the profits of the corporation rather than the corporation paying taxes directly on such profits. Since the tax rules for Sub-Chapter S elections are specialized, it would be advisable for individuals considering such an election to seek professional tax assistance.

SELECTING A CORPORATE NAME

Additionally, when setting out as a corporation, it is necessary to select and clear a corporate name. The purpose of clearing a name is to determine whether the corporate name selected is substantially similar, or the same as, the name of an existing corporation. If the name is similar to an existing corporate name, most states will not allow it to be used for fear of causing confusion in the minds of the public. Most states have a rather simple procedure for checking or clearing corporate names. The fees are usually modest for this service. However, it is important to realize that official state clearance for a proposed corporate name does not necessarily mean that the name is not being already used by an unincorporated business within the state or a corporation in another state; some suggest a trademark search on a national/international level prior to spending much money on a logo, stationery, advertisements, and so on to avoid building up goodwill for a name which may ultimately be unavailable. Another practical consideration relates to banking arrangements. Since a corporation is a separate legal entity, banks often require corporate financial statements for a corporation if a loan is being requested. Very often, a bank might also request the personal guarantees of stockholders before making a loan to corporations. In addition, banks require the filing of certain corporate resolutions which designate the names of individuals authorized to sign checks on behalf of the corporation. Additionally, corporate meetings of stockholders or directors may be required in connection with substantial business transactions such as leasing space or equipment. The reason for such corporate action is that landlords or suppliers of equipment usually require written evidence that the stockholders or directors have authorized the corporation to enter into the contemplated agreement. Most organizations that request corporate resolutions, be they lending institutions, landlords, or equipment suppliers, usually have their own form of corporate resolutions which they will supply to a prospective lessee or bank customer.

DIVIDENDS AND COMPENSATION TO STOCKHOLDERS

Another practical consideration relates to the way in which funds can be distributed to stockholders. These procedures primarily concern the tax effect on withdrawal of such funds. The only manner in which corporations can distribute funds to individuals is by way of compensation or salary for services rendered, or as dividends. Most states require that dividends can be paid only out of corporate profits. Accordingly, when a dividend to stockholders is declared, the corporation is required to pay a tax on the profits that generate the funds for the dividend. In addition, the individual stockholders receiving the dividend must pay income tax on the amount received. The corporation is not entitled to take a deduction for the amount of dividends paid to stockholders. Compensation or salary for services rendered can be paid by the corporation out of any funds and constitute a corporate business deduction for tax purposes. The amount of compensation paid to a stockholder can be reviewed by the Internal Revenue Service which has the authority to question the amount paid if the IRS feels the amount is excessive for the services performed. If the IRS determines that the amount of compensation paid to a stockholder for services performed is unreasonable, it can disallow the deduction the corporation has taken for the payment of compensation and treat the amount as a dividend. In such a case, the corporation would be required to pay tax on the amount distributed. Generally speaking, the test for determining whether an amount paid as salary to a stockholder is reasonable or unreasonable is based on the particular factors and circumstances involved. What the IRS generally does is examine to see what the prevailing salary for similar services would be in the particular field of operation. It is only when the amount in question is considerably in excess of that prevailing rate or where in actuality very few, if any, services have been performed that the IRS will find the salary is unreasonable.

ADVANTAGES OF THE CORPORATION

While it is apparent that some problem areas exist in terms of doing business in the corporate mode, there can, on the other hand, be substantial benefits. The most significant of these benefits is that the stockholder is protected from liability for corporate debts and obligations. Accordingly, if the corporation borrows money from a bank and is unable to repay it, the bank has no recourse against the stockholder. Additionally, if the corporation owes taxes, the individual would not be responsible for these taxes. (At this point it should be noted, however, that certain officers may be personally responsible for the failure of a corporation to pay withholding or FICA taxes or, under some circumstances, local sales taxes.)

The second benefit is that the corporate existence can continue in most states for an indefinite period of time. Accordingly, if one shareholder should die or decide to leave the corporation, the corporation could still continue in existence. In the case of a partnership, the retirement or death of a partner usually leads to the termination or dissolution of a partnership.

The third benefit is the ability to spread tax liability over fiscal years different from the reporting years for the stockholders. Additionally, there might be a tax benefit in having the corporation pay taxes on profits, because in these situations, the taxable rate on these profits might be lower than the taxable rate payable if an individual had earned profits in a like amount.

The final consideration also may be a financial one. When individuals start in business, they may need most of their financial resources to carry on that business. Accordingly, the payment of corporate filing fees and perhaps legal fees might create an additional financial burden on the venture. In addition, the costs of operating through a corporate vehicle are somewhat higher since annual franchise tax fees are payable even if the corporation has little or no profit.

The ultimate decision as to which mode of doing business is most suitable can be made only after all of the preceding factors have been weighed. The information presented here is intended as a summary of the factors to be taken into account and should be assessed in terms of the business venture.

4 | Understanding Everyday Finances

Robert T. Higashi

ROBERT T. HIGASHI is a certified public accountant with the firm of Robert T. Higashi, an accountancy corporation, in Los Angeles, California. Many of Mr. Higashi's clients are artists.

Struggling to survive can be disastrous to your work. I believe that economic freedom, the ability to work and live where you want to and not where you have to, is dependent upon economic success.

Once achieved, however, economic success creates other problems. Tax rates rise as high as 45 percent in our society. The state may add 11 percent to this startling figure. On another level, too much success, or "too many toys," as the saying goes, can cause a maelstrom of budget problems, and that is an equal distraction. To the person faced with these facts, financial planning becomes imperative. Generally it encompasses tax and investment planning. It may also lead to retirement and estate planning.

But don't be turned off by these words up front. It's not just bookkeeping, taxes, and being prudent we're discussing here. More than that, it's an understanding of certain basic concepts that enable you to create and become more productive as an artist.

UNDERSTANDING "ACCOUNTING"

First, let's demystify the term "accounting." The techniques of business are not as complicated and sophisticated as you might think. Once understood they are easy to apply, not only by multinational corporations but also by individuals struggling to survive.

Everybody has a different idea about what accounting is: it is a set of books, financial statements, invoices, and receipts. Accounting encompasses much more than any one of those things, but it's simple to understand. Accounting is nothing but the recording, classifying, and summarizing of economic data, a science of economic transactions. These data are usually rendered in terms of dollars and cents, but it can also be used in terms of "units," that is, a number of paintings or sculptures.

I find many times that artists are not aware of the real help and assistance this business tool can bring to them. I can't express strongly enough to you my feeling that accounting is of value to the artist who has passionate dreams of creating, of making something new and unprecedented. Artists are always asking, "Why does the businessman have all the money?" The answer is that the artist often does not recognize and adopt the tools used by shrewd, wise, calculating businessmen. That may be a large part of why even some successful artists are behind in this area of economic achievement.

Yet the need to feel self-sufficient and create a proper environment seems paramount among artists. So I think it does us no harm to regard art as a profit-making venture, a way to make money and to sustain yourself and your work.

CASH PLANNING

One of the most fundamental principles of accounting is budgeting, or "cash planning." This is a very helpful tool because it enables you to predetermine your cash needs. At the same time it helps monitor your economic performance. Basically, cash planning is the system of comparing your estimated cash flow with your actual cash flow, both in and out. To write a budget you simply design a calendar that shows perhaps a 6 or 12-month period. Then you take into consideration all the financial ingredients of your life, the cash you require and your fixed obligations—studio facilities, equipment, helpers, supplies and research, automobile expenses and insurance, good food, drink and laughs—whatever makes up your life. When you total the cost of all these things you determine your financial needs.

Next, you determine your cash flow from the sale of art, lecture fees, grants and loans, perhaps teaching salaries or royalties. You determine when you can expect this money to arrive, and you mark it on your calendar. Now you have a comparison of the cash required and the cash expected, and from that you can make sound financial decisions.

As things happen and conditions change you simply reorganize the figures. You update your plan for the next month, week, or year. When you revise your plan as the need arrives, you become better at it, falling closer each time to that "bull's-eye" which is your desired financial situation. That opens up all kinds of interesting possibilities.

Suppose in the beginning you wanted only a kiln and a glazer. In time, you decide to make your studio more useful. It needs more ventilation for ovens, more electrical power, a skylight to provide natural light, shelving, a wall taken out. These things cost money, and if your budget projections suggest that such studio additions could really happen, you will undergo changes in the way you approach your work. Thus, budgeting becomes a tool for personal and professional growth.

There are other benefits to consider. A budget compels you to coordinate various aspects of your life. A budget determines just exactly when you will be short of cash, which gives you ample time to arrange financing from a bank, dealer, agent, relative, or friend. Perhaps most important, a budget places you in positive control of your financial future. After all, if you're experiencing a shortage of money, you are hardly a rarity. And yet you don't have to be a victim of circumstances if you use this tool of foresight.

That's a simple description of how a budget can work for you. Now let's view a more complicated use of it.

BUDGETING IN ACTION

I was once assisting a sculptor who experiments with color and light. His needs include expensive materials and a $100,000 piece of equipment which produces the desired effect of light and color.

The sculpture he wanted to produce was a large piece. Labor and overhead were added to the budget. However, without sophisticated accounting techniques we couldn't devise a reasonable, accurate projection of the cost.

The way of most artists is to wait for a commission before they begin a large work. "I will create a work, present the work, and I will get my money." While this is a safe approach to budgeting for doing a large work, it certainly was not productive in the mind of my client, who couldn't wait for that to begin. He had the inspiration then, and the probable cost to him was phenomenal, including a projected payroll of $6,000 per month for the four months he estimated were necessary to create the work. That was a lot of money to pay toward something which he might or not be able to sell. He had no guarantee someone would purchase the sculpture for the high price he planned to ask.

The large financial risk involved was, to him, worth taking. It was even exciting, because to him, belief in himself made it important that he take a risk. If an artist is really good, it would seem natural that people would help him fulfill his creative power and passion. Often this is exactly what happens.

The first step in the artist's conception of the plan should be the budget. How much will it cost? Where can the money come from? A sound budget is a conceptually complete blueprint for action.

In the case of my client, the work was eventually sold to an important art collector for a substantial amount of money. And I will return later to the creative financing which helped this project. First, however, let's discuss another basic, important accounting tool.

KEEPING RECORDS

Record keeping, or bookkeeping, is essential to your operation. It tells you whether you operate at a profit or loss, and how much of a profit or loss.

You have two basic reasons for keeping records: (1) for your own edification as you keep track of your affairs and (2) for your obligation to statutory authorities—the federal, state, and city governments.

The Internal Revenue Service is the most imperative reason for keeping records. The IRS requires that you keep "adequate books and records," to substantiate the income and expenses declared on your income tax return; the responsibility of satisfying them with the legitimacy of your claims rests entirely upon you.

No one has ever really formalized a definition of adequate books and records. As far as the IRS is concerned, if it can follow your records, then your records are adequate. The IRS presumes that every person in business opens a bank account, so generally, the basic foundation of books and records consists of bank statements and canceled checks.

The bank keeps records of your monthly statements, cash receipts, and canceled checks. At the end of the year some banks, for a fee, can also give you a computer printout of all your checks. All of these are individual documents of the funds you've spent. The bank records them for you, and all you need do is compile and classify the various documents. Now you have a whole financial picture, a record of how you spent money. You could sit down with that and summarize a year's activity in a few hours.

In addition you should keep any invoices, bills of sale, receipts of various kinds, and any business documents. The sum total of all these documents will constitute adequate books and records. A clear picture of your financial history will greatly assist your projections for the future.

Bookkeeping systems vary from keeping receipts and invoices in a shoe box and tabulating them once a year, to your own microcomputer which produces monthly financial statements and other financial reports. In between these extremes are manual, pegboard, and computer service bureau systems. Depending on your particular circumstances and needs, any one of these systems may be appropriate. The wide range of systems may seem confusing to you. I recommend that you hire a certified public accountant to help you choose and install the right system.

ACCOUNTING SYSTEMS

Cash-Basis Method

The simplest type of accounting system is called the cash-basis method of accounting. This system records income when it is received in cash and expenses when they are paid in cash. It is the most commonly used method of accounting because of its simplicity.

However, the cash-basis method merely tracks the cash through your business. It doesn't tell you how much people owe you, how much you owe others, or what you have in inventory.

Accrual Method

To obtain this information for your records you should adopt the accrual method of accounting. This is a more complete method of reporting economic transactions because it recognizes income when you earn it and expenses when you incur them.

Suppose you owe your welders $20,000. You haven't paid them yet. But at the end of the year, you can record an expense of $20,000 based on the accrual system, thereby allowing yourself a deduction for the sum of money you owe. Conversely, if you shipped an art piece to a customer and billed him $40,000, but you haven't been paid yet, then this transaction must be recorded as income under the accrual accounting method. But you also can report and deduct the expenses incurred.

The accrual method proposes to tell you what really happened in an economic transaction. That's a closer picture of the truth than the cash-basis method of accounting.

Records are just as important for your own personal reasons. You should keep an accurate, detailed record of all the artwork you produce and the location of each work, whether it's in your studio, a gallery, a museum, or a private collection.

INVENTORY YOUR WORK

You should take periodic inventories to determine whether your artwork is all physically accounted for and located. This documentation of your total output is of great importance to you. There are cases of art either lost or misplaced by galleries and museums. Such institutions handle the work of many artists. Through the passage of time and a lot of activity, a work may become mishandled or misplaced, damaged, or lost. An agreement must be reached that the galleries and dealers will inform the artist when a work has been sold and to whom. This way you will know when your share of the sale is due.

Suppose you consign 15 paintings to a gallery and six months later that gallery sends you a statement which says they have only 13 of your paintings. Where did the other 2 go? Maybe those 2 paintings represent $15,000 each in total sales, and to you maybe they represent, net after commission, $21,000. Could you possibly be out $21,000? If your records are not meticulous and accurate, you could run into big problems. You have no effective means of representing yourself, and that leaves you at the mercy of someone else, which is where you don't want to be.

Before you send your work on consignment, you should obtain a written agreement with the gallery as to who is responsible for insuring the goods. Many times a work is damaged in transit, or while being unpackaged and handled by a gallery. If there's no prior agreement you may be subject to loss, and at best there may be an argument as to who is responsible and who gets the tax write-off.

Suppose you have an exhibit. Besides this *certificate of insurance* you should obtain a *written agreement of responsibilities.* This should be a clear-cut agreement as to what exactly this artist must provide and what the gallery must provide in terms of the kinds of space, the kinds of help, and the kinds of expense reimbursements. If these matters are not resolved in advance, they may later become the subject of disputes, not only with both parties, but with the IRS too if it reviews your early income and expense record to verify the correctness of your income tax return.

These matters are the general conduct of business, a system which says that before you have an exhibit, and before you transact any major business, you should prepare a list of things which must be resolved. Contrary to being a lot of added work, this attention to organization and good record keeping pays off in many ways. It contributes to your creative output and productivity by furnishing you with timely information about the cost and expenses of your work. It relieves the anxiety of "not knowing." It eliminates the lack of effectiveness which always accompanies disorganized business.

PLANNING YOUR TAXES WISELY

The subject of "taxes" is very broad and stimulates a great deal of thought and a lot of questions. A complex network of taxes raises money for the government. Tax laws are complicated, dynamic, and ever changing. By giving special concessions to various segments of society, Congress uses tax legislation to effect desired social results. In effect, what government does do is give certain groups more money through tax incentives, thereby avoiding the need to have a special congressional appropriation of money for the same purpose.

Tax is a euphemism for money. A tax break is less open to criticism. It is more disguised. So when we talk about taxes, we're not talking just about a painful obligation, but also about a way to obtain more money or preserve the money you have. The situation is not hopeless, as some people think. You are not entirely a victim of circumstances. Our system of taxation is a system by self-confession in that you are left to confess your income and expenses. That leaves you in control of the situation. You must remember that you can minimize your taxes by arranging your affairs in the most tax-advantageous manner with the aid of a skillful, creative tax planner.

FEDERAL TAX

"The government" represents federal, state, county, and city governments. Federal and state income taxes are the most important because they're by far the highest—up to 55 percent. To a lot of people, including writers, musicians, and artists, tax consultation is vital to their livelihood. Artists, I feel, are among those most needing assistance. They often don't make as much money or do as well economically as other professionals. The artist is a true small businessperson, albeit somewhat oblivious to making money.

Most states have income taxes. Each state has its own individual rates and laws. The various state rates reach as high as 11 percent. In rare instances some cities such as New York have income taxes.

The stakes are high with the 1988 federal rates including self-employment taxes going up over 40 percent.

STATE AND LOCAL TAXES

The next major tax to consider is a state, county, or city sales tax. Each state governs its own rates and laws. Most states assess a tax ranging from 2 to 7 percent based on the sales price of goods and sometimes services. This tax may be passed on to the purchaser in some states or assessed against the artist. In either case, accurate records must be kept of the sales and sales taxes collected and paid. The artist must check with his or her own state or municipal authorities to learn what he or she must do to comply with the law.

Say you're an artist living in California. You sell a painting for a thousand dollars to a collector who walks into your studio, and you neglect to add the 6.5 percent sales tax. You sell another painting for a thousand dollars to a friend. Because you want to give this person the best price possible, you again leave off the sales tax. Now you owe to the State of California a bill of $122, which comes out of your sales price.

In my experience many artists have unknowingly failed to charge sales tax on art sold directly out of their studio. The sales tax people, as a result of subsequent audits, have assessed these artists the uncharged 2 to 7 percent plus penalties and interest. This assessment comes long after the money has been spent, and results in a real hardship. What you must do then is file for a resale license, qualifying yourself as someone who is in business and incurs sales taxes, and charge the appropriate sales tax as any other merchant would.

OTHER TAXES

There are other taxes to consider. Each city usually charges a business license tax, generally based on gross receipts. You should always keep adequate records to compute these taxes. Moreover, there are penalties that are levied when these taxes are neglected.

There are federal and state payroll taxes, with each state having its own individual laws. When an artist hires employees, he or she is required to withhold federal social security and income tax deductions from their pay and remit to the government as required. Most states also have a state payroll-withholding requirement. Quarterly and annual payroll tax returns and year-end W-2 forms must also be filed. The combined rates are usually no more than 10 percent of the gross payment. However, here again the reporting of payroll requirements is very precise, and violations result in substantial penalties.

Many states have personal property taxes. Those are assessed by the municipalities. Unlike all the other taxes previously mentioned, personal property taxes are not computed and reported by you. The state or county sends you a tax bill for payment.

The tax laws are numerous and complicated. They require a certified public accountant to help you interpret them, and to understand what is required of you by law.

I once represented an artist who, when he came to me, hadn't paid any taxes for years. Furthermore, he had no notion of how much money he had made each year. With this client, I sat down and wrote a story—the story of his life based on the last few years. In this way, we tried to piece together his sources of income.

When asked what his activities had been in a given year, he said, "Oh, that year I had an exhibit. The rest of the year I didn't work. I just went to Africa." Later, however he presented me with a tattered bundle of notes. It turned out to be statements of bank deposits totaling $40,000, which he had "kept for some reason." I asked him, "Where did all that money come from?" to which he replied, "I don't know, Bob, it came from all over."

The reason he hadn't kept track of his income was either that he didn't know it was his responsibility or he didn't accept it as his responsibility. Explaining where the money went to was not so difficult. We had canceled checks. Some of them qualified as deductions. But the sources of the bank deposits were a problem. The consequences were that the government said that unless he could prove otherwise, that $40,000 was income.

DEDUCTING BUSINESS EXPENSES

Expenses are a basic concept in taxation. All business expenses are deductible against business income. Business expenses are defined as those that are ordinary and necessary to the conduct of your work. The definition is broad, and yet it specifically excludes all expenses of a personal nature, such as food, shelter, clothing, and entertainment. It includes the cost of your work: your supplies, facilities or studio, employees, utilities, rent, telephone bills, auto expenses, travel and promotion, and anything further that relates to your work—including your accounting and legal fees.

Travel and expenses to out-of-town exhibits and dealers are often incurred. Also, most of the cost of the meals and lodging during that time are deductible. Since many of these expenses are paid by cash, the IRS requires that a "concurrent" diary or daybook be kept to substantiate the cash expenses. You can use this diary for all other cash expenses during the year. If the diary is properly documented, actual receipts are needed only for those expenditures over $25.

If your studio is in your home, you may be able to allocate a portion of your home as your work area. Special rules apply that should be reviewed with your accountant. A part of your utilities, maintenance costs, and all other work-related concerns are deductible.

TAX LAWS THAT APPLY TO ARTISTS

The Tax Reform Act of 1986 has had a profound effect on artists, writers, photographers, and other creative people. The new law allows a creative artist to deduct his or her business expenses only when income from a project begins to be realized. This section of the new law is called Uniform Capitalization Rules. This provision of the new tax laws met with sharp criticism. As a result of widespread criticism of this provision, in May 1988 the IRS released a decision to allow artists, authors, photographers, and others who incur expenses in producing creative properties, a "safe harbor" method of deducting these expenses. This "safe harbor" method allows the taxpayer to deduct 50 percent of the expenses in the year incurred and 25 percent in each of the second and third years. The IRS suggests that taxpayers may amend their 1987 returns to take advantage of this "safe harbor" rule.

This new ruling may be short-lived. Bills are pending in both the House and Senate that would restore the pre-1986 tax law's treatment of expenses incurred by writers, artists, and others who produce creative properties.

Artists often receive prizes and awards, or fellowships and endowments. The

1986 Tax Reform Act now requires the entire amounts to be reported as income. However, a candidate for a degree may still exclude from income a scholarship or grant used for tuition, books, and supplies.

But some tax laws do not work to the benefit of artists as much as others. There's the concept of donating art to a charitable organization. If a collector donates art to a museum, she can deduct the full market value of that work. But if an artist donates her own work of equal value to a museum, she can deduct only the actual cost to her of its production, that is, the cost of "paint and canvas." This often seems negligible to the artist.

The concept of "taxable income other than cash" is another tax matter that relates particularly to artists. Take the example of one artist selling his painting to another artist, who in turn gives his own painting to the first artist. In other words, they exchange artworks. Under the IRS Code you can deduct as a business expense only the cost of your painting—the price of the "paint and canvas." If that cost was $50 and the painting is worth $1,000, then your reportable taxable income on that transaction is $950. Another example of "income other than cash" is the case of the artist who receives services as payment for his work. Suppose a dentist pays you for an art piece with $1,800 worth of dental work. The law requires that you report the value of this service as income.

These are some of the tax laws that particularly relate to artists. There are other more intricate laws to consider, which are more complicated and require more than a simple explanation. But the four that I have mentioned—uniform capitalization rules; fellowships, awards, and prizes; donating art to charity; and taxable income other than cash—are basic to your understanding of the tax obligations.

CORPORATIONS AND TAX-DEDUCTIBLE RETIREMENT PLANS

A "corporation" can be utilized by artists as a means of tax saving. Under such a format, the artist does business as a corporation. The corporation is a legal taxpaying entity. The corporate form of doing business is used by many "high-earning" professionals such as doctors, lawyers, CPAs, architects, and so on. The major advantage of using the corporation is the ability to "shelter" otherwise taxable income in a qualified profit-sharing or pension plan. Presently the maximum tax-deductible contribution into a qualified "defined contribution" profit sharing and/or pension plan is $30,000.00

A very successful artist may be able to adopt a special retirement plan called a Defined Benefit Plan that given the appropriate circumstances could require a tax-deductible contribution into the plan of double the maximum deductible contribution of the defined contribution plans.

The contributions to the plans are then reinvested in stocks, bonds, savings accounts, T-bills, and so on. The income from these investments of plan assets are "tax free" until such time as the beneficiary withdraws the assets.

The plan assets are available to the artist upon his or her retirement. The plan assets are held in a trust, with either an institution such as a bank, or the artist himself or herself serving as the trustee.

As you can see, there may be tremendous tax advantages from the use of corporations and qualified profit-sharing and pension plans. Great care and planning must be taken in utilizing these tools. A CPA and an attorney who specialize in these corporations and plans must be retained to assure compliance with all the complicated laws and regulations.

NON-CORPORATE RETIREMENT
PLANS FOR THE SELF-EMPLOYED

There are two types of tax-deductible retirement plans available to artists who are individuals not operating as corporate entities.

The first plan is called the *Keogh Plan.* This plan is simply a qualified plan maintained by a self-employed individual. The rules that apply to Keogh Plans are now virtually identical to the rules applicable to corporate qualified plans.

The second type of plan is the *IRA,* an Individual Retirement Plan. This plan is limited to the lesser of $2,000 or the amount of compensation including salary-type income. The deduction may not be allowed or may be severely reduced if the taxpayer or spouse is an active participant in an employer-maintained qualified retirement plan.

CREATIVE BUSINESS—OR KEEPING
THE MONEY YOU MAKE

Now you have a basis for studying your obligation to the various tax laws and also some methods of preserving your income. If you progressed financially at the same rate as you read this chapter, you now have some money. Since *some* money is rarely enough for artists with large dreams, we can proceed with the more creative aspects of business.

One dream you can't afford is the illusion that someone will just walk down the street, recognize your genius, lift it out of obscurity, and drop it into the audience's consciousness. Dreams should be well thought out and realistic if we expect them to come true—but that's not saying they have to be small and insignificant.

Let's recall my client artist who experimented with light and color. This individual's art involves a large need for space, high technology, and expensive materials. It's obvious the artistic process is costly. If his business had not been creatively well planned and well managed, it couldn't even have begun. But it did begin, and it continues to happen for this artist, because of the ingenuity necessary to make it happen and the foresight to see that it could.

In the beginning I assisted this artist in obtaining an interim business loan based upon using a blanket lien on his own finished inventory. In other words, the bank had a legal ability to take art pieces and sell them if the loan was not repaid. Banks often won't agree to such a loan, but in this case we were able to persuade a local bank by relying on the importance of the artist and his work. Creative business evolves from an artist's need to create. The creative energy from one feeds the other.

Many creative ways of making money were born out of desperation. A thoughtful plan may be part of the process, and yet the act is still triggered by desperation. Usually, when pushed to that point, you find you must put other aspects out of your life, unfortunately including your creative work. What we are really talking about in this chapter is how to avoid distraction by this all-consuming effort to make money. What you must do, then, is construct a financial plan for the future. Let's call it an "action plan."

Obviously, before you commence with your plan of action, you need a professional consultant to assist you. You need to rely on someone, just as you need a doctor for what hurts you. This business is too complicated for you to master it all and then administer the medicine yourself.

Hire someone who is reliable and qualified. Obtain referrals from people you have confidence in, and whom you respect. Ask yourself if this individual truly understands what your needs are and can articulate them back to you. No matter how technically qualified this person is, if he can't communicate with you he won't be able to help you. What it takes from you is a personal awareness that this person truly feels and understands your needs. If your consultant has your best interests in mind, then the two of you working together can accomplish a great deal. A good business consultant can bring new skills to an artist, as well as an application of these skills. Once an artist discovers this for himself he also discovers a new arena for his creativity.

RISK VERSUS RETURN

Investment planning is a highly creative endeavor. How can you best posture yourself for keeping the money you make? Consider the money that you don't immediately need to live on and to conduct your business with. That is the residue you use for investments, such as your work, your studio, real estate, stocks, and bonds.

Everybody wants to make money with money. In business there is one thing to keep in mind: the concept of risk and return. The more chance there is of making money, the larger the risk. Many people who profess to know a lot about business lose sight of this concept. And yet you can't expect to make a lot of money unless you are prepared to take a lot of risks. An expectancy of high returns brings high risks, and low returns should involve low risks.

ESTATE PLANNING

Estate planning is the thoughtful planning of how to preserve your estate from death taxes, both federal and state. It also provides for the orderly distribution of your assets. My first question to a client concerned with estate planning is this: "Is it necessary?" Death is something we should provide for, but estate planning should be looked at in its proper perspective. Although it is necessary, it should not have undue attention placed on it. Be concerned with living, not with planning for death.

SUMMARY

If the article provokes your thinking, clarifies some concepts that you've heard but never understood, it has accomplished something. The relationship between creative output and supportive business concepts is tied closely together. Think of this chapter's numerous concepts as being a complement to your artistic activities.

5 Preparing for Taxes and Other Atrocities

Ira M. Lowe
Paul A. Mahon

IRA M. LOWE and PAUL A. MAHON are partners in the firm of Lowe and Mahon, specializing in art law. They are members of the Washington, D.C., New York, and Massachusetts bars.

The authors wish to acknowledge the invaluable assistance of attorney Betty Battle of Washington, D.C., and the expertise of Frank Williams, CPA, of Glen Falls, N.Y., on the earlier edition.

The media called it "the inheritance of the century." Pablo Picasso had no will when he died at the age of 91 in 1973, leaving more than $250 million in artworks stored in three villas in the south of France plus $40 million in other assets. Instead of writing a will, he chose to leave his heirs to struggle over the estate in a fractured family version of "Guernica." It is remarkable that they were able within four years to reach agreement on the division of nearly 40,000 works of art.*

The Picasso "family" resembled one of his cubist works. His widow Jacqueline and his son Paulo were the legal heirs at the time of Picasso's death. The remainder of the family, all alienated from Picasso, were three legitimate grandchildren, offspring of Paulo (Pablito, Marina, and Bernard), and three illegitimate children (Maya, Claude, and Paloma), offspring of mistresses Maria Thérèse Walter and Françoise Gilot.

Intestacy laws, in the absence of a will, govern designation of heirs and the amounts they receive. Only after the French government in 1972 enacted a new law which gave inheritance rights to illegitimate children and applied it to this case, did Maya, Claude, and Paloma become eligible as heirs. Each was allowed half the share of a comparable legitimate heir.

Before final settlement of the estate, son Paulo died of alcoholism, and Pablito and mistress Marie Thérèse committed suicide.

The French law (*dation en paiement*) which permits estate taxes to be paid in works of art (or assets other than cash) saved the estate from having to borrow money or to sell quantities of art through forced sale at depressed prices. The most important works were painstakingly selected by the French government to satisfy estate taxes and are displayed in the new Picasso Museum in Paris.†

---

* Specifically, 1,885 paintings, 7,089 drawings, 3,222 ceramic works, 17,411 prints, 1,723 plates, 1,228 sculptures, 6,121 lithographs, 453 lithograph stones, 11 tapestries, and 8 rugs.

† *Dation* was also cited recently by the French Finance Ministry to select 464 works from the estate of Marc Chagall. The estate of Joan Miro relied on a similar principle to satisfy Spanish estate taxes.

Had Picasso died a resident of the United States, the outcome would have been substantially different. There is no *dation en paiement* for payment of federal estate taxes and cash is due nine months after death unless an extension is granted on a showing of reasonable cause. There also are immediate obligations to pay state death taxes, funeral costs, administrative costs, and support for family members. And where would these funds come from?

If he had died without a will (intestate), the historic collection could not be given to a museum to qualify for a charitable deduction to decrease estate taxes, nor could the taxable estate be reduced by any other form of gifts.

In the absence of a will, the estate would be divided according to the laws of intestacy, which vary from state to state. Generally, the surviving spouse receives the first $50,000 plus one-half the balance and the other half passes to surviving issue (linear descendents), or if none, then to surviving parents, or if none, the entire estate passes to the spouse.

In the event that there are no surviving spouse, descendents, parents, or other relatives, the estate passes (escheats) to the state.

WHAT CONSTITUTES AN ESTATE?

Your *gross estate,* for federal tax purposes, includes the value (at date of death, or six months thereafter, at the election of your executor) of all property owned by you at the time of death. It also includes the value of many types of interests in property short of outright ownership.

Most interests in property are easy to identify: a car or house in your sole name, or print portfolios and lithographic plates in your studio. It is more difficult to identify your interest in an employee pension plan or the right to income from a trust (benefit rights), the unrestricted right to name beneficiaries of a trust fund (a general power of appointment), or the right to borrow money on a life insurance policy (an incident of ownership). The values of all these interests in property are includible in the gross estate for federal tax purposes.

Property may be tangible or intangible. Tangible property includes such physical property as real estate, household goods, personal possessions, works of art, stocks and bonds, savings certificates, bank accounts, and pension and profit-sharing plans. Intangible assets include patents, copyrights, trademarks, interests under a lease, accounts receivable, and debts owed to you.

From your gross estate are subtracted certain expenses and deductions, such as funeral and other administration expenses (including dealer's commissions and fees for selling artwork to raise cash to satisfy taxes and probate expenses), debts and claims against the estate, unpaid mortgages, and net losses during administration. This new figure comprises your *adjusted gross estate.*

All property given to your spouse since 1982 and at death passes without federal estate tax. This is called the *unlimited marital deduction.* On your spouse's death, however, his or her estate includes all of his or her own property together with the property you have transferred. As the tax consequences of this second estate can be staggering, estate planning should provide for your spouse's estate as well as your own.

All property given at death to art museums, foundations, charities, and other qualified tax-exempt organizations also passes without estate tax significance. A provision in your will providing for placement of your works in important public collections achieves both historic recognition as well as estate tax benefits.

Your *taxable estate* is the adjusted gross estate less any marital deduction and charitable contributions.

HOW THE FEDERAL ESTATE TAX WORKS

You may transfer a total of $600,000 in value tax-free during your lifetime (by gift) or at death (by inheritance or by will). Any transfers above $600,000 are taxed. Gift and estate taxes are unified so that the same rate is applied to property transferred over this $600,000 threshhold, called the *lifetime exemption.*

In addition, an important way to minimize federal taxes is to make annual gifts of $10,000 to your relatives or friends which are gift tax free. If you are married, you and your spouse may make joint gifts (called *split gifts*) totaling $20,000 per year per recipient gift tax free.

Assets held by you in trust for the benefit of another are not included in the taxable estate, but it does include assets held by another in trust for your benefit if you have the power to control disposition of the assets by will. Interests held by you only for your lifetime are not included because the interest terminates upon your death. However gifts you give may be included in your taxable estate if you retain a lifetime interest.

Also excluded from the taxable estate are individual retirement accounts, Keogh plans, qualified pension and profit-sharing plans (under certain conditions), social security benefits, workman's compensation awards payable to the survivors but not to the estate, and wrongful death benefits. In general having a joint interest will not keep property you buy out of your taxable estate. The taxable estate excludes only that share of joint property which was purchased with funds of the co-owner.

In six western states (Arizona, California, Idaho, Nevada, New Mexico, and Washington) as well as Texas and Louisiana, special rules are applied under their community property laws. In general, one-half of the property acquired jointly by husband and wife while under the jurisdiction of community property state is included in the estate of each. These laws vary between states and should be reviewed for particular application to your situation.

After the estate assets have been valued, the total amount of lifetime gifts in excess of the annual exclusions is added to the taxable estate. The tax rate is then applied, beginning at 37 percent for amounts over $600,000 with a maximum rate of 55 percent on taxable estates in excess of $3 million, to yield the tentative tax due.

State death taxes

This chapter deals with federal estate and gift taxes because of their importance to estate planning. Most states also have transfer and death taxes, many of which are treated for federal estate tax purposes as a credit against federal tax due. The majority of states have estate taxes which mirror the federal scheme, and thus estates under $600,000 are not taxable. Above this amount, state death taxes are calculated based on the highest amount federal law allows as a credit against federal estate tax. Because approaches vary from state to state, familiarity with your local regulations is a necessary estate planning consideration.

WITH—OR WITHOUT—AN ESTATE PLAN

Consider the case of Aida, a serious painter showing at an important gallery in her city. She lives with two teenage children, 13 and 15 years old, in a rented studio loft and is divorced from a photographer who is remarried and struggling to support a second wife and small child. Aida sells four or five major canvases each year and has an annual income of $35,000, which includes dividends from $50,000 of inherited IBM stock and $8,000 annually from part-time teaching activities. Her studio and storage contain most of her life work, approximately 150 paintings and 226 drawings. As a result of a recent gallery exhibition, which received favorable reviews, several large works sold for $6,500 and a number of drawings brought $400 each. Fifteen years ago, an uncle left her a beach cottage on Martha's Vineyard, then valued at $80,000. She uses the cottage on weekends, lives there in the summer, is indifferent to the appreciation in value of the waterfront property, and wants it to be kept for the children to use in future years. Last year Aida purchased a $50,000 ordinary life insurance policy through the art school where she teaches, naming her estate as beneficiary and hoping that the proceeds would provide for the children's support and education in case she dies prematurely.

Without an Estate Plan

What if Aida dies unexpectedly? Her estate, which includes artworks valued at $532,700, computed on 50 percent of retail sales price, real estate appraised at its current value of $270,000, life insurance of $50,000, IBM stock of $50,000, and $20,000 in cash and personal property, would total $922,700.

Without an estate plan, federal estate taxes would be over $96,000 and estate expenses (funeral, administrative costs, local estate taxes, and legal expenses) as much as $50,000, requiring that the IBM stock, life insurance, and available cash be used immediately to pay these obligations. In addition, at least $25,000 in artworks must be sold within the nine-month period after death to fund the balance due. It may be unrealistic to depend on sales of that amount within such a short period.

Even a one-year extension may be inadequate. Her executor may argue successfully that there is a reasonable justification to extend payment of tax over 14 years, with the first five annual payments consisting of interest only, because the artworks were part of a closely held business. An extension would partially solve the problem of satisfying the taxes. But Aida's intention for the life insurance to provide for her children's education, let alone their immediate and future support needs, was not achieved.

With an Estate Plan

What steps could Aida take to protect the estate for her children?

- *Annual Gift Program.* She could make annual tax-free gifts to her two children of artworks for five years, amounting to $100,000, which would remove this amount from the value of her taxable estate and would also provide assets which the children could liquidate from time to time for emergency use.
- *Assignment of Life Insurance Policy.* She could assign ownership of the existing life insurance policy to her children (giving up all control over the policy) and even continue paying the premiums, thereby removing $50,000 from her taxable estate.
- *Additional Life Insurance Policies.* She could purchase an additional $50,000 term life insurance policy (extending over the ten-year period of greatest need for education and support expenses) in the name of her children, give them ownership in the policy, and make successive annual

gifts to the children to cover the cost of premium payments. Or she could purchase an additional ordinary life insurance policy and assign it to an irrevocable trust outside the estate, making annual gifts of premium payments to the trust to benefit the children upon her death.

- *Charitable Deduction.* She could make charitable bequests in her will of 60 paintings (appraised at 50 percent of the sales price of $6,500 each), deducting $195,000 from her taxable estate.

After removing $345,000 from her gross estate through the foregoing suggestions, Aida would have no federal estate tax due—the $577,700 remaining value of her estate is less than her $600,000 lifetime exemption. The IBM stock could be sold to pay immediate estate expenses, and the children would have immediate access to life insurance proceeds (outside the estate) adequate for their support and education.

Although this illustration is simplified, careful estate planning can ensure maximum security with minimum reduction of assets.

ESTATE PLANNING GOALS

There is more to planning an estate than writing a will. Your primary goal should be to facilitate maximum enjoyment and use of your property during lifetime; your secondary goal should be to provide for the smooth transfer of your assets at death according to your wishes and with the least diminution in value and burden to beneficiaries. Tax considerations are of major concern to the planning of an estate, but they are not the only considerations. There are others involving personal needs and human relations which are paramount.

Much depends on when you begin to plan the estate and on individual personal and family needs. A photographer just five years out of school with a spouse and two small children will have different objectives than will the single older artist whose inventory includes over a thousand works and whose paintings sell for over $10,000.

Goals are determined by analyzing your unique situation. Ask yourself these questions:

- What will happen in case of serious illness or incapacity? Or premature death?
- What if your spouse dies first? Or if both you and your spouse are killed simultaneously in an accident?
- Who will take care of the children? Are there funds for their support and education?

- Should assets go directly to the children? Or to a trustee for their benefit?
- Is a change in marital status likely? If so, might your spouse remarry? Might your spouse have another family?
- Is your spouse competent to manage the inherited assets and likely to pass them on to your children? What if the surviving spouse remarries and chooses to pass the assets to another family instead?
- Does your spouse have separate property which, when your inheritance is added to it, will cause unnecessarily high taxes and reduction of the second estate? Will the surviving spouse receive more income than is necessary for a lifetime?
- Is the core collection of art of sufficient value and interest to warrant establishing a foundation or trust to preserve and place the art in appropriate institutions?
- Will your beneficiaries maintain and preserve the artworks in accordance with your wishes? Will they maintain the integrity of the artworks, preserve the physical condition, and exercise care in offering the art for sale or placing it in museums to protect the historical value of the body of work?
- Should the core collection of your work be donated to a museum? Now? Or on death?
- Should gifts be made now to family members, friends, or museums?
- Have circumstances changed since you drafted your will or created a trust? Should changes be made?
- How will the assets be valued and distributed at death?
- How will the estate pay taxes and estate costs without an unfavorable forced sale of works of art?
- Who will be executor of your estate? Legal guardian of your children?

ESTATE PLANNING ADVISORS

If you were selecting a doctor, you would seek a specialist who has experience with your particular illness. You should seek estate planning advisors with the same care, inquiring as to their professional expertise, sensitivity, and knowledge of your special problems.

An attorney is essential to many aspects of handling estate matters. Only an attorney familiar with estate planning should draft a will or trust or advise on drafting certain contracts. He or she should be selected with the same care exercised in choosing an executor of your estate. A certified public accountant or tax consultant should be brought in to prepare financial statements and income tax returns and to assist with accounting matters. An appraiser may be needed to value assets. And a life insurance specialist may be needed to advise on and arrange for purchase of a policy suited to your needs. The optimum result will be obtained if these efforts are coordinated; the attorney is in the best position to undertake responsibility for the overall estate plan and to call in the other advisors.

ESTATE PLANNING STRATEGY

Thomas Hart Benton at the age of 80 described the problem of estate taxes on the large number of his unsold works:

> It actually has become so bad that they seem to penalize my heirs by my painting a picture. . . . The Feds have got it now so that just by comparing me with market values they make me a multimillionaire on paper and I have got to pay taxes for which I have no money . . . the best solution would be to destroy all unsold works before I die.

New Mexican artist Ted DeGrazia actually burned 100 paintings in the early 1980s which he had valued at $1.5 million, claiming it would be too expensive for him to die.

Of course, there are other ways of creating a zero estate for tax purposes without destroying your legacy. If your taxable estate is valued at less than the $600,000 lifetime exemption, there is no estate tax to pay because the tax credit exempts this amount from tax. Although a simple and enjoyable method of estate planning is to consume everything above $600,000, there are more considered alternatives. For example, if married, you may pass unlimited amounts to your surviving spouse tax free through the marital deduction.

One way to escape tax altogether on estates over the exempted amount is to bequeath the excess to a qualified charitable institution. This may or may not be the approach your heirs would prefer.

Estate planning strategy should be tailored to your personal lifetime goals and particular wishes for the transfer of your assets at death. At first glance it may appear ironic that one's goal in life may be to work hard to build an estate of growing value to provide security for dependents, but to accommodate estate planning best, it may be wise to reduce the value of the taxable estate. These ideals are not contrary if effective estate planning observed.

The following are important concepts basic to estate planning which are described in more detail in this chapter. They apply to any artist's estate regardless of size and value:

- Maintain an accurate *inventory* record of artworks to assist in identifying, locating, and valuing your assets. Include the cost of materials and fabrication with each item.

- Include in your inventory an estimated valuation which you believe is reasonable for estate tax purposes.

- Consider structuring your artistic activities to qualify as a closely held business.

- Reduce art inventories by selling works and using the profits to fund the purchase of *life insurance* to provide the liquidity for tax obligations and family needs in the period after death.

- Avoid inclusion of life insurance proceeds in your estate by assigning all ownership rights in the policy to a beneficiary. It is better still if the beneficiary takes ownership in the policy in the first place.

- Fund life insurance premium payments made by the beneficiary with annual gifts, taking advantage of the *$10,000 annual gift tax exclusion.* Or reduce the size of the estate before death by making annual tax-free gifts of up to $10,000 in artworks to each family member and other beneficiaries.

- If you are married, take advantage of *gift splitting* which allows a spouse to join in passing an additional $10,000 tax free each year to each recipient.

- Take advantage of the *unlimited marital gift tax deduction,* but consider the impact on estate taxes and other costs in the second estate when the surviving spouse dies.

- Take advantage of the *unlimited marital estate tax deduction,* but avoid overloading the second estate.

- Consider the advisibility of establishing a special-purpose *trust* to manage assets and distribute income to your beneficiaries.

- Choose your beneficiaries carefully. Consider direct bequests to children above what your spouse will need or want. Consider appointment of a guardian for your minor children.

- Reserve a selection of artworks from each type and period of your work, building an *historic collection* to represent your life work.

- Consider the advantages of a charitable bequest of artworks and make arrangements during lifetime for transfer at death of a part or all of the historic collection to a museum or other charitable institution. A *charitable donation* of the historic collection excludes it from estate taxation and assures its preservation.

- Do not overlook the advantages of medical insurance, social security, employee disability, retirement plans, and death benefits and the possibility of establishing your own self-employed retirement plan (either a Keogh or an IRA).

THE FIRST STEP—AN INVENTORY OF ASSETS

Value the Estate

It is understandably difficult to place a dollar sign on your work. It is, however, a practical necessity in dealing with the value of potential estate assets. Until you have an accurate idea of the value of your estate, with awareness of what constitutes your estate, you cannot intelligently make plans for its disposition. Too often artists fail to consider the potential value of art in the studio or in storage, or fail to realize the appreciating value of forgotten or rejected or even unfinished works. In many notable case histories, only a small part of an artist's inventory has been sold prior to death, followed by startling appreciation in value thereafter.

Maintain an Accurate Inventory and Document File

By developing careful habits of clearly identifying, signing, and dating each work, and by keeping an inventory with accurate descriptions as to size, media, date, exhibitions, insurance value, sales price, current location, awards, and any facts relating to provenance, you can assist in reducing the administrative burden of handling the estate. Photographs of artworks facilitate identification and are a valuable part of the inventory record.

All legal documents are of prime importance to settlement of the estate. These include income tax returns for at least the five preceding years, bank statements, records of bank deposits and safe deposit boxes, certificates of investments, stock and bond certificates, life insurance policies, birth certificates, marriage certificates, documents of title, deeds of trust, trust documents, mortgage and loan documents, business records and contracts (including sales contracts, dealer contracts, loan exhibition contracts), and current will.

Review Assets for Liquidity, Change of Title, or Form of Investment

Once the approximate present-day value of the entire estate is determined, you should consider which items provide liquidity to meet cash requirements in case of emergency, disability, or estate obligations. Stocks, bonds, savings certificates, life insurance, and death benefits are ready sources of cash, but artworks are not always readily salable and produce no income until sold. Consider, as well, the form of title in which the asset is held to determine whether it can be assigned (a life insurance policy, an annuity), whether a joint tenancy (real estate) should be severed, and whether certain assets should be sold and converted to cash or other form of investment.

JOINTLY OWNED PROPERTY

When Morris Louis died in 1962, his wife claimed ownership as the surviving joint tenant of the 577 canvases mostly rolled up in the basement of his Washington, D.C., home.

Few paintings had sold during Louis's lifetime. The artist relied almost entirely on his wife's income from teaching activities as a source of funds for materials and studio, and she therefore provided "consideration" sufficient to substantiate joint ownership with the artist in his works. By law joint tenancy assets pass directly to the survivor outside of probate and the laws of intestacy, but are subject to taxation.

Consideration Test

It may be surprising to learn that jointly held property is included entirely in the taxable estate of the first co-owner to die except to the degree the survivor can show individual contribution to its cost from separate funds. Failure to provide evidence to the Internal Revenue Service of the survivor's contribution may cause the entire value to be included in the decedent's estate.

However, in the event the survivor is the spouse, there are no tax consequences owing to the unlimited marital estate tax deduction since 1982.

Advantages and Disadvantages

The creation of a joint tenancy limits the donor's ability to transfer the property and, as a practical matter, requires the consent of the co-tenant to sever title in order to sell it or to make a gift to a beneficiary, third party, or trust. It can be conveniently used in small estates to assure continuity in ownership of a family residence, a family car, and similar property and has the advantages of avoiding probate and the accompanying costs. Thought should be given, however, to other forms of title for assets in larger estates.

Tenants in Common

The treatment of joint property does not apply to an interest in property held as tenants in common in which each holds an undivided interest and can freely sever his identifiable share and transfer it to a third party or to beneficiaries.

An interest in a tenancy in common is included in the estate of the deceased only up to the value of his declared share. This permits a wife to will her share as a tenant in common to a child upon death and allows the surviving husband to retain his share as before.

Life Insurance

For estate tax purposes, if you purchase an ordinary or term life insurance policy on your life and if the policy permits you to change beneficiaries or to borrow on the cash value of the policy, or if it is payable to your executor or estate, the entire proceeds of the insurance will be included in your taxable estate at death. Also includible in your estate is any policy owned by another which is required to be paid to your estate or to the executor or designated to be used for payment of your estate taxes. A life insurance policy in which you hold any such "incidents of ownership" is taxable in your estate. "Incidents of ownership" refers to the holder's right to affect or enjoy any economic benefits of the policy, for example, the power to alter beneficiaries, to revoke assignment or transfer of title of the policy, or to borrow money on the policy.

Ownership in an existing policy can be assigned and given to a spouse or other beneficiary and thus remove from your estate the appreciation over the cash value at the time of the assignment. As with any other gift, the assignment of a life insurance policy is taxable on the value at the date of gift, approximately the cash value at that time. To determine if your existing policy is assignable, it is necessary to read the fine print: to succeed in removing it from your estate, it is necessary to transfer all "incidents of ownership." The smallest thread of control or benefit from the policy will bring it back into your taxable estate.

An insurance policy can be given to a lifetime trust which is funded with the proceeds upon your death, with benefits flowing according to your instructions to a surviving spouse or children or other beneficiaries. A designated individual, many banks or trust institutions will act as trustee for such a trust, holding the life insurance policy for a nominal fee until your death and receiving annual gifts from you to cover the cost of premiums using the $10,000 annual exclusion.

If a new policy is being purchased, consider the advisibility of having someone other than yourself as the owner, for example, your spouse, who can be a beneficiary, or you can designate the children as beneficiaries.

VALUATION

Your artworks may be the main part of your estate. The problem of how to value these works has plagued artists, dealers, appraisers, insurance agents, lawyers, judges, and tax collectors for years. Each may claim a different value, depending on the objective of the valuation.

The lawyer for an artist's estate may claim in the estate tax return a low value, the IRS may claim a high value, and the tax court judge may choose a value in between. On the other hand, one appraisal may be high for purposes of a charitable contribution and deduction, while the IRS may challenge that amount and insist on a lower figure.

The artist can deduct for income tax purposes only the cost of materials when giving a work of her own creation to a tax-exempt institution, but once she dies, the value of her art is calculated at fair market value on the date of death or six months thereafter, at her executor's option. Fair market value is defined by estate tax regulations as "the price at which the property would change hands between a willing buyer and a willing seller, neither being under any compulsion to buy or sell and both having reasonable knowledge of relevant facts."

This definition leaves considerable room for appraisers to differ in their estimation of value.

Factors determining fair market value include the quality and period of the work, recent comparable sales, costs of selling, preparation for exhibition, framing, shipping and transportation, terms of sale, time and place of sale, and any unusual circumstances that affect price all should be considered in reaching an appraisal. Any sudden increase or decrease in value of a work requires justification.

The executor of the estate bears the burden of supporting the estate's valuation, and he may be assisted by records kept by the artist prior to death. In some instances, the IRS has actually accepted the artist's own valuations. Simply by distinguishing between "finished" and "unfinished" works, an artist can assist her executor in making these valuations.

IRS regulations require an appraisal by an expert or experts, under oath, of works of art with a value over $5,000 to be filed with the estate tax return. This must be accompanied by an affidavit of the executor as to the completeness of the list of property and as to the disinterested character and qualifications of the appraiser(s). The expert must be qualified to appraise the particular type of art object, and the IRS is free to challenge his or her qualifications and employ its own appraiser.

To assist in this difficult area, the IRS has an Art Advisory Panel of 25 members divided into three subpanels specializing in Painting and Sculpture, Far Eastern and Asian Art, and Primitive Art. The panel members include representatives of museums, universities, and dealers, who meet twice each year to review and evaluate appraisals. The panel reviews appraisals where the total collection exceeds $20,000. When this total amount is reached, the panel may evaluate appraisals for works with even a minimal value within the collection. Collections or individual works valued under $20,000 are generally handled by the IRS district offices.

The most recent Annual Summary Report of the activities of the Art Advisory

Panel indicates that the panel reviewed 1,636 items with an aggregate valuation of $118,205,000. The panel recommended acceptance of only 33 percent of the appraisals. In 64 percent of the valuations reviewed, the panel recommended total adjustments of $27,131,000. Valuations for charitable gifts, which are usually overvalued to achieve a maximum income tax deduction, were reduced 56 percent. Valuations for estate taxes, which are usually undervalued to escape increased taxes, were increased 136 percent.

Selection of an appropriate appraiser is crucial to obtaining acceptance of the appraised value. The appraisal of an expert whose reputation is respected and who is established as a specialist in the particular field will be given more weight by the IRS and the courts than will the appraisal of one who is less well known or less experienced. The Tax Court dismissed the valuation of one expert because he impressed the court as "a cynical person with flexible scruples."

It is important to inform the expert that the appraisal is for submission to the IRS for tax purposes so that he or she can comply with the requisite formalities. Also, the executor should be careful to select an appraiser who will not benefit personally from the appraisals or have other conflicts of interest. If the work is being valued for a charitable donation to Museum X, the appraisal by Museum X officials would not be reliable. Similarly, an appraisal from the dealer who sold the taxpayer the artwork in question is considered unreliable. If the appraiser's fee is based on a percentage of the appraised value of the property, it will not be a qualified appraisal.

Finally, the deductibility of selling costs, including dealer's commissions of 25 to 50 percent, transportation, insurance, and other charges, is permitted "if the sale is in order to pay the decedent's debts, expenses of administration, or taxes, or to preserve the estate, or to effect distribution."

VALUATION CASE STUDY: ESTATE OF DAVID SMITH

While the IRS may claim the highest market value for works of art, the David Smith estate tax case provides striking proof that lower valuations may be successfully argued. David Smith's executors contended that if an estate were forced to sell valuable artworks in bulk in order to pay estate taxes and related costs, the market value would be reduced considerably.

Sculptor David Smith sold fewer than 80 sculptures during his lifetime, and at his death in 1965, the main body of work which comprised his estate consisted of 425 pieces of welded sculpture. The executors computed a value of $714,000 for the art and paid taxes totaling $244,495. In 1969, one week before the three-year statute of limitations would have precluded any further claims, the IRS revalued the estate at $5,256,918 and claimed additional taxes of $2,444,629.

The executors challenged this assessment, and in its decision the U.S. Tax Court conceded that the impact of a simultaneous offering for sale of a large number of artworks would reduce substantially the return on the hypothetical value. In addition, the Court considered the fact that Smith's stature had not been fully recognized before his death, that the bulk of Smith's work was located inaccessibly at his studio at Bolton Landing in the Adirondack Mountains in upstate New York, and that the size of the sculptures (many over 10 feet in height) were all factors influencing marketability and value.

As finally determined by the Tax Court, the Smith estate was valued at $2,700,000, an amount midway between the executors' and the IRS's appraisals of the sculptures and was based on the discounted amount a bulk sale would obtain. Additional deductions were allowed for (1) costs incident to the sale of those sculptures required to be sold in order to pay debts of the estate, (2) other taxes, (3) administrative expenses, and (4) expenses necessary to preserve the estate and to effect distribution of the estate, which constituted most of the costs. Deductions were not allowed for selling costs attributed to sales not considered necessary to pay debts, taxes, and expenses.

As finally assessed, the estate had to pay only an additional $69,944,* resulting in a total estate tax of $314,439 rather than the $2,689,124 sought by the IRS.†

The David Smith case has been utilized as precedent for valuations of artwork in other estates, including those of Georgia O'Keeffe and Alexander Calder.

THE $10,000 ANNUAL GIFT TAX EXCLUSION

The ability to give to any number of individuals up to $10,000 in value each year gift tax free is one of the most important and effective estate planning tools. This tax-free gift may be in a variety of forms including cash, artwork, forgiveness of a debt, or even payment of someone else's tax obligations. It can be made to a spouse, a child, or any other individual or entity.

By making regular annual gifts to family members, a donor can transfer a substantial portion of his or her estate. For example, a gift of $10,000 a year to

---

* Tax rates determined by the then existent Internal Revenue Code.

† Furthermore, the increased fair market valuation at the date of death to $2,700,000 raised the basis for computation of estate income taxes from postdeath sales of sculptures, entitling the estate to an income tax refund of approximately $400,000 with a net gain, resulting from the Tax Court suit, of about $330,000 for the heirs. The executors' original evaluation of approximately 3,000 Smith drawings and paintings at $15 each was left standing.

each of two children for ten years permits a tax-free transfer of $200,000. If you are married, this benefit is doubled if your spouse joins in so-called "gift splitting." Thus in this example, an additional $10,000 can be passed to each child annually, or $400,000 altogether passes tax-free over ten years. Additional gifts under this provision to grandchildren, other family members, and friends can increase this tax saving.

IRS regulations also provide for an unlimited exclusion for gifts of certain medical and educational expenses. There is an unlimited gift tax exclusion for payments made after 1981 on behalf of any individual as tuition to certain educational organizations or as payment of medical care to any person or institution providing medical care with respect to that individual. Payments must be made directly to the educational institution or medical care provider to qualify for this exemption.

For a gift to be legally valid, though, the following requirements must be met: (1) you must intend to make the gift (to give up complete ownership and control rather than just a loan), (2) the gift must be accepted by the recipient (the recipient must know of the gift and agree to receive it), and (3) you may not retain any dominion or control over the subject matter of the gift. If these three requirements are not met, a gift has not been made, and no tax exclusion will be allowed.

A gift may, however, be for only an interest in property and not for the entire property itself. Thus a gift of "one-fourth of my sculpture 'Brooklyn Bridge' " is valid, provided the gift was intended, and accepted, and the donor gave up control of that one-fourth interest.

Apart from the mechanics of a valid gift, the major limitation on the $10,000 exclusion is that it cannot be a gift of a future interest—an interest in which possession or enjoyment does not begin until a future date. Finally, for gift tax purposes, the gift must be made in the year claimed and cannot be retroactive.

ADVANTAGES OF LIFETIME GIFTS

Aside from the personal satisfaction of gift giving, there are important estate planning benefits involved in making lifetime gifts. One of these advantages is that appreciation in the value of property is passed on to the recipient. Thus a gift of stock five years ago worth $10,000 may have a present value of considerably more. Had the property remained in the estate, the tax burden to the estate would have been greater.

A gift, though, carries with it the donor's basis or actual cost, and the recipient takes the gift with that basis. If the donor had acquired the stock for $1,000 and the recipient sells it for $31,000, he must report income of $30,000 on the sale.

When an artist makes gifts of his own work, the artist's basis in these works is limited to the cost of materials, exclusive of his own labor. In the hands of the artist, his work is "inventory" and is subject to ordinary income tax on any profits from sale. When an artist gives a work of his own creation to a charity, he can deduct for income tax purposes only his minimal cost basis in the painting—the cost of canvas, stretchers, gesso, and paint. When the artist gives his artwork to another, the recipient assumes the same low basis and is subject to ordinary income tax on profit when it is sold.

Contrast this with the collector who purchases an artwork. The collector's basis is the purchase price (his cost), and he may deduct the full fair market value (cost plus appreciation) if he gives it to a museum or charity.

If the artist, rather than giving his own work, dies and the work passes either by will or intestacy, the recipient does not receive the artist's minimal basis. Rather, on the artist's death, all assets in the estate, including artworks, receive a "stepped-up basis" equal to the fair market value on the date of death. The recipient of property by will or inheritance gets the benefit of the market value basis and clearly fares better when he sells an inherited work than when he sells a work received as a gift.

While this is true from the recipient's viewpoint, the estate planner must consider the estate tax implications of retaining the appreciation in the estate. For smaller estates, it is more desirable to hold art assets until death so that the stepped-up basis is passed along to the beneficiaries. There may be additional advantages in retaining the art as a core collection for donating to a museum after death.

One approach used by both Harry Callahan and Aaron Siskind, the photographers, involved the donation of a collection of their negatives and archival materials to the Center for Creative Photography at the University of Arizona to take place after their deaths. In this manner, Callahan and Siskind could make the donation and still enjoy use of the property during their lifetimes.

The decision whether to give artwork during life or at death involves weighing and balancing a number of personal and financial considerations. Since passage of the Tax Reform Act of 1986 which substantially reduced income tax rates, the maximum 28 percent rate is more favorable than the minimum 37 percent estate tax burden, suggesting that income tax on apprecia-tion of gifts may be preferred to estate tax on assets retained in the estate. However, be aware that taxable gifts in excess of the annual gift tax exclusion will be added back into the total estate for calculating estate tax, so you should maintain accurate records of all gifts to avoid later disputes with the IRS.

CHARITABLE GIFTS

If you choose to make gifts to tax-exempt organizations during your lifetime, you will realize an income tax deduction. However, you should ascertain whether the intended recipient is a public or private charity, or a private operating or distributing foundation. Depending on the status of the organization, your own income for the taxable year and what it is you give, there are limitations on the amount of tax benefit you will achieve from your gift. Gifts unrelated to the charitable purpose of the institution receive a reduced deduction and, depending on the nature of the property given, only 60 percent appreciation in value may be deductible. Charitable deductions against income tax can only be taken in the year in which the gift property is actually transferred to the institution or the artist relinquishes control.

Although the requirements for charitable deductions from income tax are strict, in certain cases you will maximize tax savings by giving now rather than in your will. If you give property other than artwork you created to charity during your lifetime, you are entitled to deduct up to the full fair market value of the property for income tax purposes. This advantage, though, does not apply in the same way to gifts of your own artwork. You would only be able to deduct the cost of materials for gifts of work which you have created.

There has been an increased legislative awareness of the disparity between the small deduction the artist receives for donating his own work to charities and the full deduction received by the collector. Three bills introduced in the most recent session of Congress restore a fair market value charitable deduction for works given by an artist to a charitable organization. It is not clear whether these bills have sufficient support to be enacted.

Although a small tax benefit may be derived from a gift of your artwork, other benefits of charitable donations include placement of your work in important public collections and satisfaction from supporting charitable causes. Robert Rauschenberg established a foundation called Change, Inc., with a prominent Board of Directors involved in the arts, which assists professional artists in need of immediate small grants. Financial assistance is awarded in situations recognized by his Board as an emergency, such as fire, medical catastrophe, and utility turn-offs.

If you do not wish to make gifts, you may want to consider lending art works to museums during your life on an indefinite loan basis. By including in your will bequests of specific artwork to these museums, your estate will receive the charitable deduction of the fair market value at the time of death.

MARITAL DEDUCTION

As discussed earlier, gifts and bequests between spouses are tax free under the unlimited marital deduction. However, consideration should be given to the tax consequences for the estate of the surviving spouse.

TRUSTS

Although "you can't take it with you," you can make arrangements to control the management and distribution of your assets for as long as the life of your beneficiary plus 21 years. You can establish a trust for special purposes, whether it is to manage assets for minor children or an extravagant (or marriageable) spouse or to bypass estate taxes on the death of the first beneficiary.

The trust vehicle is a simple arrangement whereby one person (the trustee) holds title to assets (the trust corpus) for the benefit of another. Trusts can be created which accomplish the dual purpose of providing professional administration of financial assets or other property as well as permitting maximum savings of income and estate taxes and probate costs.

Most important, trusts provide peace of mind to their creator who has made arrangements to provide for the needs of his beneficiaries long after his death. A common trust provides for specific assets to be managed by a trustee who distributes all income for the benefit of one individual for his or her life, and on that person's death, the trustee distributes the corpus to a second individual or group of individuals. Thus a trust document may state: "My trustee is directed to distribute the income to my husband for his life and upon his death the trust corpus is to be divided equally among my children then living." Trustees may also be empowered to distribute principal of the trust, rather than simply income, at their discretion for a beneficiary's support, health, education, and welfare, among others.

A living (inter vivos) trust is one which is set up during the lifetime of its creator. It can either be changed during lifetime (revocable), or it can be permanently established (irrevocable). While a revocable trust sometimes shields assets from probate and accompanying costs, your gross estate will include the entire revocable trust assets for estate tax purposes. The estate of the life beneficiary, though, avoids estate taxes on the trust.

An irrevocable trust which is established during your lifetime and in which you have placed the assets completely beyond recall by you will not be included in your gross estate. There may be gift tax consequences if your transfer to the trust exceeds $10,000 per year ($20,000 for joint transfer) for each beneficiary of the trust, but both probate costs and estate taxes will be avoided. Thus you may transfer $30,000 ($60,000 for joint transfer) a year to 3 trusts benefiting each of your three children tax free. The irrevocable trust requires that you permanently give up ownership and control of the assets during your lifetime, a limitation many are reluctant to accept.

Because of the complicated tax consequences of gifts and bequests to trusts, careful consideration should be given to assure the validity of the trust under your state law. Should the trust be invalid for any reason, those assets you attempted to transfer will be included in your estate and will be distributed according to your will or the intestacy laws, possibly achieving a result you did not intend. Also, these assets will be fully taxable. An attorney skilled in drafting trust documents should be consulted to ensure your intentions are achieved.

Trusts are extremely flexible instruments, and there are numerous types of trusts to accomplish as many purposes. Thus a trust for a minor may be desirable where there is no surviving parent who can competently manage assets for the child's support or education. Trusts for minors are also used to pass assets directly to children on the death of the first parent so that estate taxes are saved on the surviving parent's death.

The Tax Reform Act of 1986 changed the way income on certain trusts is taxed, making it much less beneficial to create a trust in which you have retained some valuable interest. The income generated from assets in a Clifford trust, so named after a court case, passes directly to the beneficiary for a ten-year period, usually someone in a lower tax bracket than the grantor. At the end of ten years, the property reverts to the grantor who has successfully avoided income tax for ten years at his higher tax rate and has also passed the income along to someone else without giving the property up. The new tax law does not allow this income to be shifted and taxes it as if the grantor had received it, rendering this type of trust undesirable.

The new law has, however, made other special trusts more attractive. Grantor-retained income trusts (or GRITs) are esoteric devices which achieve estate tax savings on the theory that a gift in the future is worth less than a gift now.

Small changes in the tax law may have a devastating impact on elaborate trust schemes, many of which dart in and out of fashion for the moment. The 1986 Tax Act has eliminated most ways to shift income to lower brackets.

A trust is not for everyone. Unless there are income-producing assets of at least $200,000, many trust institutions and banks are reluctant to act as trustee. Trust management fees can consume as much as 6 percent of the annual income. Institutional management is traditionally conservative in placing investments and usually prefers lower-yielding securities and certificates to more glamorous (and risky) higher-income investments.

Trustees should be sensitive to your personal wishes, to the trust purposes, and to the needs of the beneficiaries. Choose a trustee as carefully as you choose your executor. In some cases it may be the same individual.

BEQUESTS TO CHARITABLE
INSTITUTIONS

Mark Rothko engaged in estate planning. The results filled the press and art journals and dragged on for three years after his death through seven court cases. There are lessons to be learned in studying what Rothko intended for his estate and what went wrong with the plan which he apparently approved.

Rothko sought in his will to reduce estate taxes by leaving almost his entire estate, valued at $43 million, to the Mark Rothko Foundation, a charitable organization established under New York law with the purpose of giving financial assistance to mature artists. In his will, Rothko bequeathed $250,000 and the family residence and its contents to his wife, and the entire residue of the estate was left to the foundation. No provision was included for his two small children if his wife survived him. Rothko's widow died only six months after his death and his two children contested the will. Under New York law, a disposition to a charitable organization was valid only up to one-half of the estate if challenged by a spouse or child with a claim to the estate. The challenge was upheld by the courts and the children were awarded their share of the estate. The legal conflict involved other important issues, most notably the conflict of interest of some fiduciaries.

Rothko's intention to pass artworks or the proceeds thereof to a charity was clear, and this bequest successfully accomplished tax savings as a charitable contribution after close scrutiny by the IRS and the courts.

Charitable contributions have long been recognized as an estate planning device for the rich, but there may also be considerable advantages for the not-so-rich in donating property to a tax-exempt institution. For the artist, charitable bequests by will are fundamental to estate planning. Aside from the marital deduction, available only to spouses, and use of trusts, which should be funded with a certain amount of income-producing assets, no other concept provides such substantial impact on minimizing estate taxes. Charitable bequests reduce the taxable estate and at the same time provide assurance to the artist of maintenance and preservation of a selection of her work.

For charitable contributions to museums, the artist should select the institution with care. The museum will also be exercising care in selecting the artist: many institutions have wall space for as little as 5 percent of their collection. The artist should, therefore, be realistic. A consultation should be held with an appropriate staff member before the will is drafted to determine whether the bequest will be accepted and whether conditions or restrictions concerning exhibition, reproduction, insurance, loan of the work, deaccessioning, or any other special concern may be stipulated. The artist should obtain a copy of the IRS letter verifying the museum's tax status. A separate agreement with the institution should be prepared to recite the understanding. Alternate organizations should be specified in the will in the event circumstances change and the preferred institution is unable to receive the bequest.

You might consider establishing your own nonprofit corporation or foundation set up for your special purposes, either during your lifetime or in your will, as Rothko did. The Adolph Gottlieb Foundation ($4 million) has been making direct grants to mature artists since 1976, and Lee Krasner established the Pollock-Krasner Foundation ($20 million) which has been in operation since 1985.

Your attorney and accountant can advise you as to whether the value and nature of your assets justifies creation of a new foundation and whether it can be structured to qualify as a charitable organization under existing laws. If so, you should provide instruction on how the funds are to be utilized and/or distributed.

FOUNDATION CASE STUDY: ANDY WARHOL FOUNDATION FOR THE VISUAL ARTS

Andy Warhol's will left $250,000 to his longtime friend and business manager, Fred Hughes; $250,000 each to his two brothers, John and Paul Warhola; and the remainder of his estate to a Foundation for the Visual Arts. The will directed the executor, Fred Hughes, to create and run a foundation along with the initial board of directors consisting of himself; John Warhola; and Vincent Freemont, the chief administrator of the Factory, Andy Warhol's studio and business headquarters.

To fund the foundation, the estate was required to sell off Warhol's vast possessions. Sotheby auction catalogs were sold in popular bookstores for $95, and intense curiosity fed the Warholmania, ultimately sending auction prices soaring for commonplace items. Preauction estimates were considerably below the $25.3 million raised during the ten days of the event.

Other property remains to be sold, including *Interview* magazine founded by Warhol (estimated at between $7 million and $14 million), unsold paintings by the artist, and real estate in Manhattan, Montauk, and Aspen, Colorado. In order to exploit other avenues to raise funds for the foundation, the estate has sold rights to Warhol's artistic and literary properties, including merchandising rights in Warhol's works and name that may appear on such varied goods from perfume to a fashion line. Warner Books purchased Warhol's diaries for $1.2 million.

In all, the foundation is expected to receive an estimated $75 million to $100 million, making it perhaps the largest artist-created foundation in existence.

Notwithstanding this huge sum, Warhol's will was silent on how the money was to be spent. The will merely directed the executor to create a foundation for "the advancement of the visual arts" and gave the foundation's board complete discretion to disburse these funds.

DRAFTING THE WILL

Having completed an inventory and tentative valuation of assets, decided on beneficiaries and executor(s), reviewed joint property and life insurance, considered setting up a trust or charitable foundation, and negotiated with a charitable institution to receive charitable bequests upon your death, you are now ready to draft or redraft your will.

Should you die with no will or an invalid will, your state's intestacy laws dictate the distribution of your estate, most likely in a way you had not intended and contrary to your wishes. Each state's law governing intestacy is different, but in general the surviving spouse would receive up to one-half the estate, with the remainder distributed to surviving children. If there were no spouse, your surviving children would inherit everything, and if there were none, then your estate would pass to their lineal descendants (your grandchildren) or to your collateral relatives (brothers and sisters).

A spouse, including one who is separated but not yet divorced, has inheritance rights and, if dissatisfied with what is left by the will, may claim a statutory marital share (or dower or courtesy rights) up to one-third or one-half the estate, depending on state law. This marital share will be paid first out of your estate, and the beneficiaries under your will will have their bequests proportionately decreased. Children born out of wedlock may, in some states, be ineligible for any share.

No matter what size your estate is, it is preferable to direct the disposition of your assets by will. A will is your opportunity to direct how your artwork is to be managed and cared for during the period of administration and afterward: who is to do what, how and when they are to do it, and under what conditions and limitations.

Proper drafting of a will requires the expertise of an attorney, to avoid unnecessary burdens or expenses to the estate. The inclusion or omission of key phrases can affect whether your property is divided as you intend it to be.

This chapter does not offer a detailed discussion of will drafting. There are, however, several points to be considered by the artist beyond those generally applicable to others:

- Unless there are special reasons for making a bequest of a specific item in the estate, a particular work of art, for example, it is preferable to give your executor discretion to make an equitable distribution of such items among clearly identified beneficiaries. If a specific bequest of an artwork is indicated and it has been sold or destroyed prior to death, the gift cannot be made unless an available alternative is specified in the will.

- If you desire to leave artwork to a tax-exempt organization, it is advisable to consult the institution in advance to be certain of their willingness and ability to accept a bequest. Alternate beneficiaries should be named in the event the organization may no longer exist.

- You could direct your executor to reserve major works for certain museums or charitable donations, or such decisions could be left to your executor's discretion.

- Include provision for administrative expenses in connection with maintenance, storage, shipping, and insurance of artworks in the hands of the estate. The residuary estate—the amount left over after specific gifts have been made—will be charged with these costs unless you direct that recipients deduct the costs from their inheritance.

- Provision should be included to authorize your executor to sell works of art as needed for payment of tax obligations, administrative costs, legal fees, and family expenses and to allow deduction from the gross estate of the costs of selling artworks, including fees and sales commissions.

- Include a clause which specifies disposition of copyrights to all bequests of artworks or other copyrightable assets. Copyrights extend 50 years beyond the creator's death and are transferred separately from the artwork itself. If no special provision is included for transfer of copyright, it will pass to whomever receives the residuary estate.

- You should designate one or more individuals who are familiar with your artwork to be art advisors for your estate. Your executor would be directed to consult with your art advisor on the timing and prices for the sale and/or placement of your work, as well as other matters which benefit from a detailed knowledge of your inventory and sales experience. You may want simply to name one of these persons familiar with your work as your executor.

COPYRIGHTS AND THE WILL

Pictorial, graphic, and sculptural works are eligible for copyright protection from the moment of creation. The duration of copyright is for the life of the creator plus 50 years. The new copyright law emphasized the distinction between ownership of the material object (a work of art) which is copyrightable and ownership of the copyright itself or of one of the exclusive rights under copyright: the right to reproduce, the right to prepare new works based on an earlier work, the right to distribute copies, or the right to exhibit works publicly. Sale of an artwork created after January 1, 1978 does not include the sale or transfer of the copyright. Only by written agreement or a transfer in writing can the entire copyright or one of the exclusive rights under copyright be transferred.

A will may provide for the bequest of a specific painting to a named beneficiary, but if nothing more is said, the copyright on works created after January 1, 1978 will be retained by the estate and passes to whomever receives the residuary estate. It is therefore important to include in the will specific provision for transfer of copyrights to the beneficiaries of your choice or a direction that the copyrights shall pass along with the works of art.

While you may bequeath a sculpture to a museum and the separate copyright to an individual, you should be aware of tax technicalities concerning the donation of your artwork to charities which do not have a connection with the arts—a donation to your church rather than to an art museum. Where use of the artwork is not related to the charitable function of an organization, you may be required to transfer both the work and the copyright to receive the most favorable tax treatment. You should consult your lawyer if you are considering such a gift or bequest.

It is equally important not to overlook the question of transfer of copyrights when making lifetime gifts of artworks. While the gift may be completed by merely handing the artwork over, the copyright on works created after January 1, 1978 is still yours and will remain in your estate unless it is transferred in writing.

You should think of your artwork as having two identities: the actual physical work and the exclusive rights under copyright. The purchaser or recipient of the gift owns the artwork, but, unless otherwise transferred in writing, you retain the right to reproduce that artwork.

DEALER CONTRACT

Franz Kline provided in his will a bequest to his friend Charles Egan of two paintings to be selected by Egan "prior to the disposition of my works by my executrix." After Kline's death it was discovered that the two paintings selected by Egan had been sold, one to the Art Institute of Chicago, the other to Kline's dealer, Sidney Janis. The court found that neither sale had been consummated prior to Kline's death because the dealer, whose consignment contract had terminated, no longer had authority to sell the paintings. The beneficiary was given the paintings according to the wishes of Kline.

Unless the dealer's contract specifically extends a dealer's "agency" status beyond the lifetime of the artist (as in the case of the David Smith estate), the contract terminates immediately on the date of death of either party. The dealer cannot negotiate sales or continue to represent the artist's estate without specific authorization in writing, either by the original contract or by subsequent agreement with the executor.

A provision in the dealer's contract which may greatly facilitate estate matters as well as meet the need for immediate liquidity is one obligating the dealer to advance an amount of cash to the estate while continuing to hold certain artworks for sale. Where the artist has a long-standing dealer relationship and profitable sales record, it may be possible to include a buy-out agreement in case of the artist's death. In exchange for a favorable bulk price as specified by the artist, the dealer would agree to purchase within a limited period of time a certain number of works consigned to the gallery. The cash received by the estate would be available for administrative costs, taxes, and immediate family needs. This has the advantage of liquidating part of the estate without necessarily forcing public sale of artworks under unfavorable conditions. Also, the price for those pieces sold is established for valuation purposes.

The dealer may agree to purchase life insurance on the artist's life payable to the gallery to provide liquidity for purchase of a specified number of artworks on his death. This could be a term policy, renewable as long as the artist and dealer continue their relationship. The policy should be structured so that it is not taxable in the artist's estate at death.

PAYMENT OF TAX

If the gross estate does not exceed the lifetime exemption (including taxable lifetime gifts), there is no requirement to file a federal estate tax return. Where valuation of artwork is involved and the estate is near the exemption limit, executors should consider filing a return even though tax is not due. This is advisable because the three-year statute of limitations for the IRS to object to valuations only begins to run when a return is filed. If an executor believes the estate is below the limit and does not file a return, the IRS may challenge the valuation at any time and, if victorious, will assess substantial penalties and interest.

Unless an extension for reasonable cause is granted, the estate tax return must be filed and any tax due must be paid nine months after death. An interest charge at the current rate announced by the IRS is added to the amount overdue, and if there is not reasonable cause for the delay, a further penalty may be charged. The executor may request an extension for filing on or before the due date. The extension for filing is limited to six months, and obtaining an extension for filing does not operate to extend the time for payment of the tax.

An extension to pay the tax, however, may be granted if the assets are part of a "closely held business" of which the artist was a sole proprietor and which constitutes at least 35 percent of his or her adjusted gross estate. In such cases the executor may elect to pay estate taxes over 14 years, after a 5-year deferral period in which interest is paid annually on the unpaid balance.

It would be helpful if the artist took steps to show evidence of business formalities. Printed stationery, business cards, and use of a business name on annual income tax returns are useful evidence of business activity. If the artist sold some artworks directly from the studio or put a sign on the door, the executor may be able to show that it was a proprietorship or a business entitled to tax deferment privileges. Proof of an effort to sell works assists in establishing a profit motive and provides justification for deduction of art-related expenses from annual income tax, further strengthening a claim that it is a "business" within the meaning of the Internal Revenue Code. A record should be kept of sales efforts, participation in competitions and juried shows, and awards or prizes received.

Such an extension may be of great assistance for an estate consisting mainly of works of art and other nonliquid assets.

STRATEGY FOR THE ARTIST WITH A SMALL ESTATE

Even the small estate can benefit from the estate planning concepts we have discussed in this chapter. Assets can safely be left in joint tenancy and passed outside of probate with savings of administrative expenses. Gifts or charitable donations can ensure that no taxes will be due. A gift or bequest between spouses should not add unnecessarily to the surviving spouse's estate or pass more than is likely to be consumed in the surviving spouse's lifetime, as the marital deduction is not available to reduce taxes on the second estate. Above all, do not make a gift to your spouse likely to be returned to you by his or her will unless it will pass free of estate tax. The better disposition of such a gift is to the children.

Use of Trusts

You may want to consider leaving certain assets in trust, giving your spouse income for life and the right, without restriction, to designate by will the ultimate beneficiaries. These assets are not taxed in your estate because of the marital deduction, and should be assets which will be largely consumed during your spouse's lifetime (if the trust permits the unrestricted ability to spend the corpus for your spouse's needs) because the remainder will be fully taxed upon your spouse's death.

Or you can place assets in trust, giving your spouse income for life with the remainder passing at your spouse's death to your children or other beneficiaries you named when you created the trust. These assets will not be taxed in your spouse's estate because they are held in trust and your spouse only had the right to receive income. In addition to saving taxes, the second estate will save probate and administrative costs.

These trusts are most effective for moderate or large estates, but can be employed in the small estate for special situations where you want to provide management of the assets and assure that the corpus will be preserved and passed on to the children or other specified beneficiaries. There are minor expenses in setting up a trust and annual management fees so that the trust is best used for special situations where the tax savings appear worthwhile or where the beneficiary is a minor child or who cannot be depended upon to manage the assets alone.

Benefits

The holder of fewer assets can gain future security by seeking outside employment which offers such benefits as group medical insurance, disability and retirement benefits, and qualified group life insurance. You should inquire about the availability of these benefits before accepting an employment commitment. Qualification for social security benefits requires a number of years' employment and contributions in accordance with specific requirements. Your local Social Security office will provide information explaining the qualifications and benefits, which may be the cornerstone of your old-age security or disability support.

GETTING STARTED

You need not be endowed with Picasso's genius or productivity to amass an estate that takes advantage of the planning ideas discussed here. Tax consequences can be reduced, and, more important, you will be able to provide for the manner in which your property may benefit others and at the same time ensure that your artwork will be preserved. Approach estate planning with the same creative thinking that you express in your artistic pursuits.

PART TWO

PROTECTING

The big break in my life was when I punched the kid next door in the face. He used to constantly push me around. One day I walked across the street and beat the shit out of him, and from that point on I felt, if it doesn't work, hit it.

Robert Longo
Interview, May 1988

6 Keeping Your Artwork Unique

Copyright, Trade Secret, Patent, and Trademark Law

Richard L. Stroup
Robert Wade

RICHARD L. STROUP is a partner with the firm of Finnegan, Henderson, Farabow, Garrett and Dunner in Washington, D.C.

ROBERT WADE is an attorney who served as general counsel for the National Endowment for the Arts from 1972 until 1984. Previously, he served on the staff of the general counsel to the Comptroller General of the United States. From 1966 to 1969 Mr. Wade was in private practice in Washington, D.C. He is also a photographer.

T he members of the art community are continuously creating literary, musical, choreographic, visual, and audiovisual works in their respective fields. During this creative process, artists often develop new methods, materials, articles, and information useful in their profession. As they market and sell their products and services, they may adopt and use certain logos and trademarks to identify their art and services and to distinguish them from the art and services of others. Each of an artist's creative developments and marketing efforts represents a substantial investment of creative energy, time, and effort that deserves protection and compensation.

The copyright, trade secret, patent, and trademark laws provide artists with legal means of protection and compensation for their creations, developments, and trademarks. However, unless artists are aware of these protections and the manner of obtaining, keeping, and using them, the law is of little relative value. It is, therefore, the purpose of this chapter to present a practical overview of the protection available through copyright, trade secret, patent, and trademark law. The chapter will outline the application of these laws to artists and their works, the scope of protection available, the manner of securing the protection, and the use of the protective rights to compensate artists for their work and shield them from unfair practices.

COPYRIGHT

The copyright law often offers the easiest and least expensive way for an artist to protect his or her work. Copyright protection is available for a broad variety of artistic works, and there is no initial cost for receiving copyright protection. Under the new 1976 Copyright Act, which became effective on January 1, 1978, an artist receives a copyright at the moment an original copyrightable work is created in a fixed form. Thus, every working artist has, at least initially, some rights under the copyright law.

The apparent ease in obtaining copyright protection may be deceptive. An artist unaware of the existence and scope of available copyright protection will receive no benefit from the copyright law. It is important that an artist, or his or her representative, be aware of the availability of copyright protection and take the necessary steps to exercise these rights to ensure that they are not lost inadvertently.

Protections Granted by Copyright

The copyright law provides the copyright owner with a broad category of rights. Those rights are statutorily defined as the following exclusive rights:

1. To reproduce the copyrighted work in copies or records or tapes.
2. To prepare derivative works based upon the copyrighted work.
3. To distribute copies or phonorecords of the copyrighted work to the public by sale or other transfer of ownership, or by rental, lease or lending.
4. In the case of literary, musical, dramatic, and choreographic works, pantomimes, motion pictures and other audiovisual works, to perform the copyrighted work publicly.
5. In the case of literary, musical, dramatic, and choreographic works, pantomimes, and pictorial, graphic or sculptural works, including the individual images of a motion picture or other audiovisual work, to display the copyrighted work publicly.

These rights significantly protect an artist and his or her artistic creations. Through copyright, a songwriter, poet or playright has the right to control, license or present (1) the reproduction of his work in books or magazines, (2) the preparation of adaptations of his or her work into other forms, (3) the distribution of the work, its reproductions and adaptations, (4) the performance of his or her work by others, and (5) the display of his or her work in public. Painters, sculptors, potters, printmakers, and photographers have all of the exclusive rights, except the right to perform, since their creations are generally not capable of being performed.

The exclusivity of an author's rights has limits. A copyright only prohibits another from actually *copying* the identical or a substantially similar work. For example, if one artist in New York creates one painting and a second artist in Los Angeles, without seeing or being aware of the New York artist's work, creates an identical painting, the first has no rights against the second. Even if the second painter had access to the work of the first, there is infringement only if the second painting was copied and is "substantially similar" to the first. Finally, there is a certain amount of use, designated "fair use," which is permissible without the authorization of the artist. Examples of fair use might include copying a work for the purposes of criticism, comment, news reporting, teaching, scholarship, or research.

An artist's copyright in her work grants her numerous opportunities to obtain compensation for her creation. For example, a painter can receive royalties for the reproduction and sale of her work by a museum, as well as the reproduction of the work on post cards, greeting cards, and china. A sculptor of a work can license the reproduction and sale of scale models of her work and receive a commission on each sale. The potential is almost limitless. The owner of a copyright can keep all rights to herself, sell the entire copyright, or license only selected rights under special terms.

For work created after 1978, the 1976 Copyright Act affords the artist and his heirs the right to terminate transfers and licenses of copyright made by means other than by will. When this termination right is available, the artist can revoke the earlier transfer and has the option of keeping future rights for himself, renegotiating the terms of the transfer, or transferring the rights to other interested parties. This right is extremely beneficial to artists who originally received little if any compensation for the original transfer and who later became established and highly recognized. The termination may be effected at any time during a 5-year period beginning at the end of 35 years from the date of execution of the grant, or, if the grant covers the right of publication of the work, the period begins at the end of 35 years from the date of publication of the work under the grant or at the end of 40 years from the date of execution of the grant, whichever term ends earlier. The termination is effected by serving an advance notice in writing, signed by the owners or their agents, upon the grantee or the grantee's successor in title.

Finally, the copyright grants a copyright owner a number of remedies which can be asserted against a person who without authorization copies a copyright work. The remedies available against an infringer include temporary or final injunctions against future infringement; impounding and destruction of all copies or phonorecords and of all plates, molds, masters, tapes, films, negatives, and other articles by means of which such copies or records may be reproduced; and damages and profits. It is also possible to receive attorneys' fees.

Copyrightable Works of Art

A broad range of artistic works can be protected by copyright. Copyrightable works of authorship include the following broad statutory categories:

1. Literary works
2. Musical works, including any accompanying works
3. Dramatic works, including any accompanying music
4. Pantomimes and choreographic works
5. Pictorial, graphic, and sculptural works
6. Motion pictures and other audiovisual works
7. Sound recordings

These broad categories apply to works of fine art, such as oil paintings and sculptures, and works of applied art, such as manufactured vases and greeting cards.

Copyright protection is available for the original works of artists who fix their works in any tangible medium of expression. Copyright can provide protection for artistic works expressed in or on physical articles such as books, periodicals, manuscripts, notes, cards, sketchbooks, records, films, tapes, magnetic disks, canvas, clay, paper, and almost all physical objects on which an artist's expression can be fixed. In addition, copyright law applies to both two-dimensional and three-dimensional works of fine, graphic, and applied art. For example, photographs, prints, paintings, drawings, photoengravings, etchings, lithographs, sculptures, art reproductions, maps, globes, charts, technical drawings, diagrams, and models are all protectable by copyright. Similarly, motion pictures, musical scores and lyrics, pantomimes, and sound and video recordings are protectable.

An artist can protect his or her works of applied art through copyright. Copyright protection is available for artistic works included in or on utilitarian object such as clocks, lamps, textiles, jewelry, china, dolls, jewelry boxes, candlesticks, chandeliers, and a host of other items. The design in a work of applied art, however, is protected by copyright only if the design incorporates a pictorial, graphic, or sculptural feature which can be identified separately from and is capable of existing independently of the utilitarian aspects of the article. Thus, a hand-painted design on a vase would be protectable, whereas a Bauhaus-inspired chair in which form and function are blended would not. If the pictorial, graphic, or sculptural work contained in or on a useful article is copyrighted, the copyright will afford the copyright owner protection against unauthorized reproduction of her work in useful as well as nonuseful articles.

Copyright protection is available not only for original works but also for compilations and derivative works which feature some degree of creativity and originality. A derivative work is a work based upon one or more preexisting works and can be a translation, musical arrangement, dramatization, fictionalization, motion picture version, sound recording, art reproduction, abridgement, condensation, or any other adaptation or transformation of an earlier work. A compilation is a work formed by the collection and assembly of preexisting materials or of data that are selected, coordinated, or arranged so that the whole constitutes an original work of authorship. In the field of art, a derivative work might be a reproduction of a work of art in the same or a different medium of expression. Works falling within the "reproduction" category would include lithographs, photo engravings, and copies of previously existing paintings, sculptures, and similar works. An art book including illustrations of several artworks is an example of a compilation.

While derivative works and compilations that contain some original work are copyrightable, the copyright protection for a derivative work or compilation of preexisting material extends only to the material contributed by the author of the derivative work or compilation. The author does not receive any protection for the pre-existing material. Thus, the infamous bearded and mustachioed Mona Lisa ("L.H.O.O.Q.") by the artist Marcel Duchamp would have been copyrightable, but Duchamp would not have been able later to stop Salvador Dali from making his own copy of the original Mona Lisa painting. It should be noted that if the preexisting work is protected by a valid copyright, the artist creating the derivative work or compilation should obtain permission to copy the preexisting work. If the artist fails to secure the permission, he or she may infringe the copyright in the original work and may be sued.

For a work of art to receive protection under copyright law, it must contain some degree of creativity and originality and be fixed in a tangible medium of expression. Creativity refers to the nature of the work itself, while originality refers to the nature of the artist's contribution to the work. Fixture means that the art is fixed in a material object so that it can be perceived, reproduced, or communicated for a period of more than momentary duration.

The issue of creativity is highly subjective, and the courts have traditionally been very hesitant to make such judgments. As a result, a work need only display a minimal amount of creative authorship to satisfy this requirement. Similarly, the requirement of originality (not to be confused with novelty) is easily satisfied if the work is original to the artist; that is, it is not exactly copied from the work of another. Often, any distinguishable variation created by the artist in an otherwise unoriginal work of art will constitute sufficient originality to support a copyright. For example, the courts have found sufficient originality in reproductions of oil paintings on scarves, engravings made from original paintings of old masters, and an accurate reproduction of Rodin's "Hand of God" sculpture. The general rule of thumb for the artist is "when in doubt copyright the work." Leave it to the copyright office (or perhaps eventually the courts) to make the rare decision to deny a copyright application on the ground that the work lacks creativity or originality.

Certain subject matter is not protectable under copyright. Copyright generally protects the author's particular expression, not his ideas embodied in the expression. The copyright statute specifically provides that copyright protection for an original work of authorship in no case extends to any idea, procedure, process, system, method of operation, concept, principle, or discovery regardless of the form in which it is described, explained, illustrated, or embodied in such work. Also, works that are not fixed in a tangible form of expression are not protectable. For example, an author cannot obtain a copyright for a choreographic work that has not been notated or recorded, or a speech or performance that has not been written or recorded. Titles, names, short phrases, and slogans; familiar symbols or designs; mere variations of typographic ornamentation, lettering, or coloring; and mere listing of ingredients or contents are not protectable. Similarly, works consisting entirely of information that is common property and containing no original authorship are not protectable. For example, standard calendars, height and weight charts, tape measures, schedules of sporting events, and lists or tables taken from public documents or other common sources are not considered to be copyrightable.

While a copyright may be obtained for artistic designs used with objects of applied art, a copyright does not protect the mechanical or utilitarian aspects of the applied art. Therefore, a copyright for a design on a useful article, such as a plate, would provide its owner with the right to stop others from copying his design and placing the copied design on plates, canvas, or any other tangible item. The copyright would not, however, afford its owner any greater or lesser rights with respect to the making, distribution, or display of plates in general. Furthermore, a copyright does not include any right to prevent the making, distribution, or display of photographs used to advertise a useful article with a copyrighted design or to stop commentaries or news reports relating to the distribution or display of the article.

The works of art protected by copyright are usually not protected by the law of patents and trade secrets. In general, a copyright covers an artist's expression, while trade secret and patent law more closely protect information, processes, devices, materials, and applied inventive concepts. In certain instances, however, a person may be able to receive both a copyright and a design patent for a particular work of applied art. Thus, the design on a watch or a lamp base may be protectable under both a copyright and a design patent.

Ownership and Transfer of Copyrights

Copyright protection is easy to obtain and, if an artist properly protects his work, the protection lasts throughout an artist's life and beyond. As soon as an artist creates a copyrightable work in a tangible form of expression, he immediately receives copyrighted protection for that work. A work is created when it is first fixed in a copy in which the work can be read or visually perceived directly or with the aid of a machine or device. Whenever an artist fixes a copyrightable creation in a tangible form, the work is copyrighted. Thus, as soon as an artist commits to paper a book, play, poem, novel, lyric, or musical composition; or records or places a work on tape, record, film, or video tape; or sketches, paints, or sculpts a work of visual art, the work is copyrighted.

Who owns the copyright to a work of art? Generally, the artist, as creator of the copyrightable artwork, is the initial owner of the copyright in the work. When a work is prepared by two or more artists with the intention of merging their contribution into a single work, it is deemed a "joint work." The artists of a joint work are co-owners of the copyright in the work, and each has the independent right to authorize the use of the work. However, each co-owner must share the profits received from such use with the other(s).

When a work brings together several independent contributions into a collective whole (e.g., magazines, anthologies), it is deemed a "collective work" and may be copyrighted as a whole. The owner of the copyright in the collective work as a whole is not necessarily the owner of the copyright in each contribution. Under the new law, absent a written agreement to the contrary, the presumption is that the visual artist, whose work is reproduced in the collective work, retains the copyright. The publisher is only presumed to acquire the privilege of reproducing and distributing the contribution as part of that collective work.

An artist who creates a copyrighted work initially has rights in the material object itself and in the copyright for her work. These rights can be transferred together or separately. For example, the artist can sell the material article and keep the majority of the copyright rights to herself. On the other hand, she can transfer in writing all or some rights to the work.

Under the old copyright law, if a copyright owner unconditionally sold a painting or other work of art, the copyright privileges normally were transferred to the buyer. The law presumed that all rights were intended to be transferred in connection with the sale. Under the 1976 Act, that result is different. The transfer of ownership of any material object, including the copy or record in which the work is first fixed, does not of itself convey any rights to the copyrighted work embodied in the object. The purchaser or owner of a particular copy or record may lawfully sell or otherwise dispose of the work and display the copy publicly to viewers present at the place where the copy is located. Barring a written agreement, however, the copyright owner continues to have the other copyright rights, including the right to reproduce the work, to distribute the work, and to control the public display of additional material objects including the work. Unfortunately, the law does not give an artist the automatic right of access to his work, and without access the artist cannot really make reproductions and thereby exercise his right of reproduction. Therefore when an artist sells the only copy of a work, he should consider obtaining, by contract, the right to gain access to his work periodically to make reproductions.

There are some circumstances in which the creator is not the owner of the copyright. When a work is prepared by an employed artist who under the scope of his or her employment creates the work, the copyright belongs to the employer for whom the work was prepared. Thus, if an artist employed by an advertising agency creates a sketch for an advertisement, the copyright belongs to the agency. On the other hand, if the same artist at his home and on his own time creates a painting which is not made for his employer, the artist owns the copyright. In certain limited circumstances, works for commission may be owned by the person commissioning the work, not the artist. Under the 1976 Copyright Act, however, the artist will retain the copyright for a commissioned work unless the artist specifically transfers the copyright in a written contract signed by both the author and the person commissioning the work.

The copyright rights in a work can be transferred, in whole or in part, by gift, sale, assignment, exclusive or nonexclusive license, or upon death, by will, or intestacy. The majority of these transfers must be in writing, and all such transfers should preferably be placed in writing and then recorded in the records of the Copyright Office. Except for transfers by gift or will, an artist can and usually should receive compensation for these transfers.

Publication and Its Consequences

As long as the artist does not publish his work, it is protected under the federal copyright law, and none of his exclusive rights will be lost. Once an artist does publish the work, however, he can lose some or all of his rights unless he places a copyright notice with the work. Thus, if an artist keeps his works to himself, he has little need to worry about formal requirements such as copyright notice or registration. Normally, however, an artist will desire to sell, distribute, or reproduce his work in order to receive compensation for his artistic creation. The publication of a work is therefore a significant occurrence.

When is a work published? The word "publication" has a special meaning in the copyright law. Under the 1976 Copyright Act, publication is defined as follows:

> Publication is the distribution of copies or phonorecords of a work to the public by sale or other transfer of ownership, or by rental, lease or lending. The offering to distribute copies or phonorecords to a group of persons for purposes of further distribution, public performance, or public display, constitutes publication. A public performance or display of a work does not of itself constitute publication.

Thus, the sale or distribution of copies of a book which includes an artist's story, poem, play, song, or script would constitute a publication. Similarly, the sale or distribution of records, cards, lamps, tapes, posters, and other items containing a copyrighted work would constitute publication. The distribution of a few copies of an artist's work for review by others probably would not constitute a publication. Nonetheless, whenever an artist distributes copies of her work, it would be prudent for her to assume that publication occurs and therefore place a copyright notice on the work.

The definition of "publication" provided by the 1976 Copyright Act is significantly beneficial to artists, when compared to the old law. Before 1978, the single publication of a work without notice resulted in a complete loss in copyright. The law was strictly applied to the point that an artist by merely exhibiting her work without a copyright notice could and often did lose all of her copyright protection. Under the 1976 Act, the mere public display of work may not, in itself, constitute publication. Similarly, the public performance of a work is normally not a publication, regardless of how many people are exposed to the work. However, if the displayed copies or phonorecords are offered to a group of consumers, wholesalers, broadcasters, or motion picture theaters, for the purpose of further distribution, public performance, or public display of the work, the work is published.

The display or exhibition of a work for purposes of sale could be viewed as an "offering to distribute copies" and as such might constitute publication. Artists seeking to distribute works for public display run the risk of losing some or all of their rights by exhibiting the work without proper copyright notice. Prudence would seem to dictate that artists include a copyright notice on their works whenever exhibition is intended for purposes other than mere display. Therefore, a painting or photograph exhibited in a museum or gallery should include a copyright notice.

COPYRIGHT NOTICE, REGISTRATION, AND DURATION

Whenever a work protected under a copyright is published in the United States or elsewhere by the authority of the copyright owner, the notice of copyright should be placed on all publicly distributed copies. The 1976 Copyright Act provides that the notice appearing on copies shall consist of the following three elements:

(1) the symbol © (the letter C in a circle), or the word "Copyright," or the abbreviation "Copr."; and

(2) the year of first publication of the work; in the case of compilations or derivative works incorporating previously published material, the year date

of first publication of the compilation or derivative work is sufficient. The year date may be omitted where a pictorial, graphic, or sculptural work, with accompanying text material, if any, is reproduced in or on greeting cards, post cards, stationery, jewelry, dolls, toys, or any useful articles; and

(3) the name of the owner of copyright in the work, or an abbreviation by which the name can be recognized, or a generally known alternative designation of the owner.

The law requires that the notice be affixed to copies in such a manner and location as to give reasonable notice of the claim of copyright.

The 1976 Copyright Act requires only that the copyright notice be positioned to give reasonable notice of the claim of copyright. If the notice is on the title or first page of a book, article, play, script, or music sheet or in a viewable portion of a work of visual art, the notice would be proper. For pictorial works, a notice may be placed on the face or margin of the work or on the reverse side of the work, as long as it may be seen upon examination. Placement of a notice on the reverse side of a painting would be permissible, as long as the notice is visible upon inspection. Arguably, the placement of a notice next to the work on display would be sufficient, but if an artist decides to follow such a procedure, he would have to make certain that the notice was always placed next to the work. For framed artwork, the placement of the notice on a frame permanently affixed to the work would seem to fulfill the notice requirement. However, if a frame is readily removable, a notice on the frame may not fulfill the requirement. For sculpture, the notice can and probably should be placed on the base or pedestal which is permanently affixed to the sculpture. In general, an artist should make a good-faith effort to place the appropriate notice on or with his work in a manner which reasonably notifies the public and does not unduly detract from the artist's creation.

The notice provisions of the 1976 Copyright Act permit the copyright owner to choose from a number of alternative notices. In general, the proper notice for copyrighted works (other than records or tapes) first published in 1988 would be this:

© 1988. Artist

Since many fine artists sign and date their works, the only additional action necessary to secure an artist's copyright is the inclusion of the symbol ©. This notice is proper for use with all artistic works and also complies with the notice requirement for significant international protection. If an artist has a recognized abbreviation or other designation, she can substitute the abbreviation or designation for her name. The abbreviation or designation must, however, be recognized. Therefore, if there is any question concerning the degree of recognition, the copyright owner should use her name, not a designation.

For a few special categories, an artist does not have to include the year of publication in the notice. The copyright notice for designs and other copyrighted work placed on useful articles, such as post cards, lamps, and textiles, can be this:

© Artist.

That notice, however, will not meet the notice requirements for international copyright protection and, more important, will not meet U.S. requirements for most artistic works. Therefore, an artist should use this special notice only when he is sure that it is appropriate.

The omission of a copyright notice can ultimately lead to the complete loss of an artist's rights in her work. Under the previous copyright law, the failure to include a notice automatically placed the work in the public domain, and all copyright rights were lost. Under the new law, that result has been made less harsh. Omission of a copyright notice from publicly distributed copies does not invalidate the copyright if

> (1) the notice has been omitted from no more than a relatively small number of copies or phonorecords distributed to the public; or
>
> (2) registration for the work has been made before or is made within five years after the publication without notice, and a reasonable effort is made to add notice to all copies or phonorecords that are distributed to the public in the United States after the omission has been discovered; or
>
> (3) the notice has been omitted in violation of an express requirement in writing that, as a condition of the copyright owner's authorization of the public distribution of copies or phonorecords, they bear the prescribed notice.

Thus, by taking reasonable efforts to correct an omission of a notice on a work, an artist can save most, if not all, of her copyright.

If a person innocently infringes the copyright in reliance upon an authorized copy or phonorecord from which the copyright notice has been omitted, he would incur no liability before receiving actual notice that the work was protected by copyright. However, the copyright owner would in the future probably be able to enforce his copyright against that person and others. In contrast, a prolonged failure to include copyright notice will place the work in the public domain and all copyright rights will be lost.

Within three months after the date of first publication of a work with a copyright notice, the owner of the copyright is obligated to deposit in the Library of Congress two complete copies of the best edition. Certain exemptions may be made by the Register of Copyrights, but at present an artist is generally obligated to deposit copies of his work in the Library of Congress. For a work of fine art like a single painting, photographs can be submitted. The Library of Congress can in its discretion levy a fine if a deposit is not made after an author receives and fails to comply with a written demand from the Register of Copyrights.

Although registration in the Copyright Office is not required, registration does provide the author with some additional rights. The law provides for the registration of both unpublished and published works. In most circumstances, the most opportune time to file a registration is when the work is published. Registration establishes a public record of the copyright claim. Furthermore, a copyright owner cannot sue another for infringement until the owner either obtains a registration or applies for registration. In addition, if the registration is made within five years of the first publication date, registration will establish prima facie evidence of the validity of the copyright and the facts stated in the certificate. A registration also may entitle the copyright owner to an award of statutory damages and attorneys' fees. Without a registration, those remedies are not available. Finally, registration makes the recordation of assignments and other documents easier.

The registration of a copyright is a relatively simple process. Generally, the procedure consists of filling in a proper copyright form, including with the completed form one copy of an unpublished work or two copies of the best edition of the published work, and submitting the form and copies with a statutory filing fee of $10. The forms can be obtained free of charge from the United States Copyright Office. That office also has an excellent information office which will by telephone answer questions regarding copyright protection.

The requirements for the submission of copies vary, depending on the work. If multiple copies of the work, such as a book, are available, copies of the book should be submitted. In the case of many artworks, the Copyright Office often will accept visual substitutes to fulfill the copy requirement. For example, to register an oil painting, the artist could submit a photograph or 35mm transparency of the work, rather than the original. In similar circumstances, the submitted identifying material could include photographic prints, transparencies, photostats, drawings, or similar two-dimensional reproductions or renderings of a work, in a form visually perceivable without the aid of a machine or device. The copies should identify the actual size of the work and the position of the notice.

A copyright, whether registered or not, provides an artist with a significant term of protection. Ordinarily the term of a copyright is the author's life plus an additional 50 years after the author's death. In the case of a joint work prepared by two or more authors, the term lasts for 50 years after the last surviving author's death. The duration of the copyright for a work of unknown authorship or a work for hire normally will be 75 years from publication or 100 years from creation, whichever is shorter. All these terms apply for copyrightable works first created after January 1, 1978. For works created before 1978, the rules are different. Under the old law, unpublished works were protected under state law for as long as the work was not published. Works which were unpublished before 1978 are now protected under the 1976 Copyright Act, and generally the duration of the copyright in these works is computed by either (1) the life plus 50 year rule or (2) the 75 years from creation, 100 years from publication rule, whichever rule provides the shorter protection. However, all works unpublished before 1978 are guaranteed at least 25 years of protection beyond 1978. For works that before 1978 were either published with proper notice or registered, the 1909 Copyright Act afforded protection for a period of 28 years from the date of publication or registration. Under the 1909 Act an additional 28-year renewal period could be added by filing at the Copyright Office a timely claim for renewal. Under the new act, the renewal term has been extended from 28 years to 47 years, giving those works a potential life of 75 years. However, a timely renewal must be filed in the United States Copyright Office before the original 28-year term ends. If a renewal is not filed, the copyright expires at the end of 28 years. For works created after 1978, no renewals are required.

TRADE SECRETS

Many artistic innovations can be protected under trade secret law. For example, an artist who discovers a new secret process, such as a new method of painting, etching, or sculpting, may be able to protect it by keeping it secret. Customer lists also can be protected as trade secrets. Every state in the United States has some type of trade secret law. That law is important to artists because it is often the easiest and least expensive way to protect many of their discoveries. This type of protection, however, has limits.

Under the law of trade secrets, certain information can be protected from unauthorized use. To be protectable, the information must be (1) secret, (2) substantial in nature, and (3) valuable. Information that may be protectable includes customer lists, methods of doing business, methods and techniques of making or protecting artwork, material lists, material formulas, artistic techniques, and other information of particular value that is gathered and unknown to others.

Because of the secrecy requirement, many discoveries will simply not be protectable under this law. Artistic techniques that are visually perceptible, like pottery shapes and color combinations, could easily be copied by others. This copying technique is known as "reverse engineering," and the law fully permits this, unless the product is patented.

In short, an artist can protect his developments under trade secret law only if he can somehow keep it secret. For example, if an artist invents a particular process to fire pottery and keeps that process secret, a competitor could not simply look at the finished pottery to determine how it was fired. The della Robbia family of Renaissance Italy produced ceramics by a unique glazing and firing process which competitors never discovered.

The requirement of secrecy and confidentiality may initially offend an artist's sensibilities. Shared thoughts, techniques, and developments strengthen the artistic community and lead to increased creation in all fields of art. Artists aware of the benefits of trade secret law surely will not suddenly try to keep every little development to themselves. Such a procedure would only injure the artistic community without benefiting the individual artist. However, someone may on occasion discover or create something truly innovative, valuable, and worthy of protection. When he does, he should be aware of trade secret protection and consider its use.

Why should an artist try to keep a siginificant development secret? Simply, to keep others from misusing her idea and competing unfairly. As long as information is kept secret and confidential, the artist can stop use of the information by people who learned of it improperly. For example, the owner could stop someone who stole a secret and attempted to use it. Similarly, if an owner disclosed her trade secret to someone who promised to keep it confidential, the owner could legally stop that person from disclosing her secret. Furthermore, if the information remains secret, she can then contract to sell the information for profit.

Trade secret protection can last for minutes or for decades. The law will protect an artist's discovery as long as it is kept secret and is not known or legally discovered by others. If an artist voluntarily discloses his finding to his friends, his fellow artists may profit from the sharing, but the trade secret rights are lost; everyone may then use his process freely. On the other hand, if an artist keeps his discovery confidential, his rights may last for years. Sometimes, however, even if he does keep the information confidential, his rights may be lost. If another person through his own efforts and without knowledge of the original artist's work develops the same information, the first artist's trade secret protection ends. Suppose, for example, someone discovers that a particular chemical in a photographic bath gives his photographs a special quality. He then keeps his discovery a secret. If another photographer, without knowledge of the first discovery, himself learns that the same chemical gives him the same result, the first cannot stop the second from using the chemical or from disclosing his discovery. If the second photographer does tell others, the entire trade secret of the first is lost. Everyone will be free to use the photographic bath.

If you develop a significant trade secret, what must you do to keep that information protectable? How much will it cost? The simple answer to the first question is that you must take all reasonable steps to keep your valuable information secret. The answer to the second is that protecting trade secrets does not cost much more than your time and efforts. In that regard, the law of trade secrets is particularly beneficial because it is relatively inexpensive to qualify for protection.

There are a number of procedures to follow. First, any documents that disclose or contain the significant trade secret information should be kept in a safe place, and preferably should be under lock and key. It would be best to place a notice or stamp on any confidential documents. The notice might say

> Confidential Information of (Artist's Name), Not to Be Copied, Disclosed, or Used for Any Purpose Without the Express Written Permission of (Artist's Name).

Confidential documents should also be placed in an envelope marked with the same notice or stamp. If you use the trade secret information in your studio, you should take all reasonable steps to control access to the studio so that others cannot steal or otherwise wrongfully learn of the information.

Other steps can be taken to ensure better that trade secret rights are not unnecessarily lost. Commercial industries often place confidential notices or signs in any work areas where trade secret information is used. Similarly, industries often require that their employees agree to keep all trade secret information confidential and not disclose it to others. Along the same lines, industries often require that even guests agree in writing not to disclose any confidential information they may learn during a visit.

If you do decide to protect certain significant trade secrets, there probably will be times when you will want to disclose your secrets to other people, such as friends or a potential buyer, perhaps. Whenever you do so, you should ask that person to sign a written agreement of confidentiality. That agreement should be signed before, not after, the disclosure. It might read as follows:

> The undersigned (name or person of corporation) in consideration for the disclosure, review, and observation of the trade secrets and confidential know-how of (artist's name) promises to hold in confidence and not to reproduce, divulge, or use any and all trade secrets and unpublished know-how observed by or given to him by (artist's name), or his agents or representatives, concerning (general discussion of your trade secret) without the written consent of (artist's name).
>
> Name: _____
> Title: _____
>
> _____
>   signature
> Date: _____

It is important that you take as many of these steps as are reasonable. If you do not, the courts simply will not be able to protect you.

If you design or develop something particularly useful to others, you may soon get offers for the disclosure of your secret. Under those circumstances, you can enter into a written contract which specifies the particular payment and use of your trade secret information. Often, parties are willing either to pay a percentage of the proceeds of sales of products they make using another's trade secret information or pay an initial down payment and continuing royalties. A person might even pay a lump sum for all rights.

A variety of contract terms are possible. If you enter into a contract with another person, it should be in writing. It is also important not to disclose the secret information until the agreement is signed. It would be wise to have a lawyer help in negotiating and drafting such agreements.

PATENTS

New designs, processes, tools, products, machines, or substances may be able to be patented. A patent holder has the exclusive right to make, use, and sell his invention throughout the United States for the life of the patent. He can also sell his patent or license others.

There are two different types of patents: design patents and utility patents. A *design patent* is available for any new, original, and unobvious ornamental design for an article of manufacture. Design patents might be appropriate to protect ornamental designs for clothing, jewelry, furniture, hollowware, glassware, china and other articles of manufacture. *Utility patents* are available for any new, useful and unobvious process, machine, manufacture, or composition of matter or any new, useful, and unobvious improvement in those areas. Utility patents might be appropriate to protect new tools and machines used in creating works of art, new art materials such as acrylic resins, paints or glazes, and new methods or techniques for creating or manufacturing artwork.

Design patents protect only the appearance of an article, not its structure or function. In some circumstances, both a design patent and a utility patent can be obtained for a particular patentable product which includes a patentable utilitarian feature and a patentable ornamental design.

Patents can be extremely valuable to an artist. Patent law, unlike trade secret law, gives the patentee the exclusive right to make, use, and sell his invention, regardless of whether the invention can be kept secret. Patent law can also often give broader protection than trade secret law. For example, if an artist obtains a patent on a particular airbrush, he can use his patent to prevent anyone from copying the invention. Depending upon the novelty of his invention, he might be able to stop people from making, using or selling airbrushes that are similar, but not identical, to his. He can also license selected persons to make, use, or sell his invention and require them to pay him for those rights.

Patents offer a definite period of protection. A design patent can have a life of 3.5 years, 7 years, or 14 years, depending upon the application fees initially paid to the Patent and Trademark Office. Utility patents have a life of 17 years.

Neither design nor utility patents can be renewed. When the patent expires, any person has the right to make, use, or sell the previously patented invention.

The degree of patent protection is defined by the claims of the patent. If an invention represents a major technical advance, the scope of protection can be extremely broad. A claim in the patent for the very first paintbrush might recite:

> A paintbrush comprising a handle and flexible, absorbent material at the end of the handle for holding paint and transferring it to a surface to be painted.

Such a broad claim would give the inventor the exclusive right to make, use, and sell almost every paintbrush. On the other hand, if an artist today invented an improved paintbrush having a particular form and made from a special material, he might be able to obtain a patent for the improved brush, but the claims would have to be more specific or narrow.

Before an artist can obtain a patent, he must invent a new design or invention. However, not every new design or invention is patentable. For a new design or invention to be patentable, the law requires that it be "unobvious" over the "prior art." The terms "unobvious" and "prior art" have special meanings in the law. Generally, "prior art" refers to the knowledge and information known or available to others before the inventor made his invention. That includes all printed publications anywhere in the world and any public use or sale of similar designs or inventions in this country. Previously issued patents, magazine and newspaper articles, public speeches, and the sale and use of products in the market are all prior art.

To be patentable, an invention cannot be exactly like those already known. Even if there are one or more differences between an invention and similar previous products, a patent may still be refused if the differences would have been obvious at the time the invention was made. An invention must be sufficiently different in ways that would not be obvious to a person of ordinary skill in the area of invention. For example, the substitution of one known material for another, or changes in size and shape, are ordinarily not patentable.

Design and utility patents are examined and issued by the U.S. Patent and Trademark Office. Its address is

U.S. Patent and Trademark Office
Crystal Plaza
2021 Jefferson Davis Highway
Arlington, Virginia 22202

The U.S. Patent and Trademark Office has an information office to provide general information on patent protection. The Patent and Trademark Office also publishes a number of booklets and pamphlets concerning patent and trademark law, which can be obtained free or for minimum fees, usually under five dollars.

To obtain a patent, the artist must file a formal application in the Patent and Trademark Office. Once filed, the application is classified and given to an examiner who specializes in the area of the invention. The examiner determines whether the application complies with all legal requirements and compares the invention with whatever prior art patents and publications he finds.

If you invent a new design or invention that might be patentable, it is important to act quickly. In the United States, an inventor cannot receive a patent for his invention unless he files an application in the United States Patent and Trademark Office within one year from the date he first publicly discloses, uses, or sells his invention. In some foreign countries it is impossible to obtain patent protection unless the inventor files an application before any public use occurs in this or a foreign country.

Design and utility patent applications are complex legal documents, and it is almost impossible for a layperson to prepare a patent application. Thus, you should probably consult an attorney or agent who is registered to practice before the U.S. Patent and Trademark Office. Attorneys and agents are usually willing briefly to discuss patent protection free of charge—but ask first. Also, a volunteer lawyer's association might be able to provide some assistance to artists interested in patent protection.

Because of the complexity of the application process, patents can be expensive. Design patents normally are less expensive than utility patents, and the prices for either design or utility patents vary depending upon the complexity of the invention and the attorneys' fees. Because of these costs, patent protection is most appropriate when an invention has commercial applications, such as large-scale manufacture or use.

The protection available from a patent can be well worth the expense. Many banks will make loans using patents as collateral. More important, if an artist has an extremely valuable invention, the exclusive right to make, use and sell it can be worth a great deal. If an invention is of use to the artistic or general manufacturing field, it probably has commercial value. Often, licensing a patent is the only way to make the largest return, particularly if the demand is great. For example, a woodcraftsman in Virginia designed and patented a process to make a wood chair. He was able to license his utility patent to a furniture manufacturer who agreed to pay him a percentage of the sales price of each chair sold. (See illustration on page 94.)

Finally, if an invention is sufficiently important, patent protection throughout most of the world can be obtained. Such patent protection, however, is extremely expensive and would make sense only if the invention were valuable in selected foreign countries.

United States Patent [19]   [11]   **4,210,182**

Danko   [45]   **Jul. 1, 1980**

[54] **METHOD OF MAKING A CHAIR**

[76] Inventor: **Peter J. Danko**, 408 Gibbon St.,
                  Alexandria, Va. 22314

[21] Appl. No.:   **693,837**

[22] Filed: **Jun. 8, 1976**

[51] Int. Cl.² B27D 1/08; A47C 5/00
[52] U.S. Cl. **144/317**; 29/416;
        144/309 B; 144/315 A; 144/322; 156/196;
        156/267; 297/418; 297/447; 297/419; 297/446
[58] Field of Search 156/196, 267;
        144/309 B, 313, 314 R, 315 R, 315 A, 316, 321,
        322, 317; 297/418, 446, 447, 419, 421; 29/416

[56]   **References Cited**

              U.S. PATENT DOCUMENTS

1,385,387   7/1921   Morandi .... 144/316 X
2,642,118   6/1953   Lamb .... 297/447 X

2,649,147	8/1953	Sanford	297/447 X
2,670,787	3/1954	Vandas et al.	297/447 X
2,818,107	12/1957	Thaden	297/418

Primary Examiner—Robert Louis Spruill
Assistant Examiner—W. D. Bray
Attorney, Agent, or Firm—Jacob Shuster

[57]   **ABSTRACT**

A stack of flat rectangular blanks are deformed in a single bending operation during which adhesive coatings between the blanks is activated to produce a laminated wood chair. Preceding the bending operation, the blanks are cut to remove a front end section and to form internal tongues struck out during the bending operation into rear leg elements. The removed front end section forms a rigid core for a seat cushion fitted onto the seat panel portion of the chair.

7 Claims, 10 Drawing Figures

TRADEMARKS AND SERVICE MARKS

When an artist places his or her artwork or services in the marketplace, it may be advisable to use trademarks, service marks, or logos to identify them to the public. These marks can help market artwork or services, and the law provides for their protection.

A trademark is any word, name, slogan, logo, or device (or combination) that a person uses to identify his goods and services and distinguish them from others. A mark identifies its owner as the source of the artwork and advertises the value and uniform quality of his or her work and goodwill. A service mark is similar to a trademark but is used in the offering or advertisement of services.

Examples of trademarks in the art world include arbitrary and distinctive signatures or logos on paintings and sculpture, stampings of a name or logo on pottery and pewter, a printmaker's chop mark, labels used to identify an artist or gallery, marks on packaging or display information, and labeling placed on boxes.

Examples of service marks are arbitrary and distinctive words or logos used with appraisal services, galleries, artist's consulting services, interior decorating firms, and architecture firms. These marks might be placed on stationery, envelopes, business cards, advertisements, and signs.

Trademarks and service marks are protectable under both state and federal law. In the United States a person receives protection for a mark only when he actually begins to use the mark. The geographical area of protection available under the law depends upon where the mark is actually used and whether a federal registration has been obtained.

Since an artist cannot receive protection for every mark he might wish to use, the selection of a mark is important. Some words or logos are not protectable as marks. Others may infringe upon marks already existing.

It is important to select a mark that is not confusingly similar to marks already used by others who deal in similar products or services. If one person doing business in a geographical area is using a particular mark for his gallery, a second gallery owner should not select a confusingly similar mark. If he does, the first gallery owner may sue the second to stop confusion. If he wins, the second user may have to destroy all products, signs, and labels that include the mark and may have to pay damages.

There are procedures for discovering if a mark is already in use. Telephone directories and trade directories are a source. If the mark is to be used nationwide, or if big investments are to be made in printing and advertising, it is wise to ask a trademark attorney or specialist to conduct a thorough search.

Certain words, phrases, and logos are not protectable as trademarks. No one can obtain trademark protection for a mark that is immoral, deceptive, or scandalous or consists of a governmental flag or coat of arms. Also, the law will not protect a mark that is used in its generic or "dictionary" sense. If a person calls his art gallery "The Art Gallery," for example, he probably would not get any protection. The law considers it unfair for any one person to have exclusive rights to the generic use of a word or phrase. Similarly, it is unlikely that an artist would be allowed rights to the frequently used mark "wearable art" for clothing which is also art.

Certain marks are protectable only if the owner can establish that through prolonged and continuous use and advertisement, the mark has become distinctive and recognized by the public as representing his goods or services. Within this category are marks that are merely descriptive or deceptively misdescriptive of goods or services, marks that are primarily geographically descriptive or misdescriptive of the origin of the goods or services, or marks that are primarily surnames. Therefore, descriptive, geographical, and surname marks like BEAUTIFUL, PARIS, and JONES promise little, if any, immediate protection.

The marks providing the strongest protection are those which are distinctive and arbitrary in meaning. For example, if an artist sells his paintings under a trademark like the word SOURCE, there is no generic, descriptive, or geographic link between the mark and his work. Through use and acceptance the mark will strongly identify the artist's goods or services, and the law will give him broad protection. Well-known arbitrary marks in the commercial fields include the marks EXXON®, KODAK®, and IBM®. These marks are distinctive and had little meaning when first used. Today, they are probably worth millions of dollars in sales.

One of the most common trademarks in the art field is a person's surname or signature. Under trademark law, the amount of protection given to such surnames and signatures varies depending upon the circumstances. If an artist's name is Smith and he signs his name in block letters, he will probably receive little, if any, protection. Any other artist by the name of Smith would be able to use his name and sign it in block letters. Furthermore, the Trademark Office probably would not register the mark. If an artist signs his name with a particular signature or script, he possibly could stop others from making a copy of his signature on similar artwork. Still, the protection for a surname is not great unless the name becomes well known as a trademark through widespread use. An artist should therefore consider using both his signature and a separate word or logo as a mark.

Once an artist selects a trademark or service mark, it is important to use it properly. The law requires that a trademark or service mark be used in conjunction with his goods or services, respectively. That means that the trademark must be placed on or with the artwork or services. A trademark can be drawn or stamped on the actual artwork, used as a label, or placed on display next to the art. If an artist ships his artwork, he can use boxes having the marks on the outside. For a trademark, the use of an artist's mark merely with advertisement of his artwork will not fulfill the use requirement. For a service mark, an artist can meet the use requirement by placing the mark on his stationery, in advertisements, on signs, on envelopes, on shopping bags, or on business cards.

It is a good idea to place a warning or "notice" next to a trademark or service mark. Such notices serve to let the public know that the mark is protected under the law. If an artist has not obtained a federal registration, he can use the "TM" notice with his trademarks (VISION™) and the "SM" notice with his service mark (GRAFIX^SM). If the mark is federally registered, he can use the "®" notice (COCA-COLA®). It is illegal to use the "®" notice unless the mark is actually registered in the U.S. Patent and Trademark Office.

Under state law, protection for trademarks or logos begins with use of the mark and initially extends over the geographical area of actual use. That protection enables the first user to prevent others from using the name or a confusingly similar mark with similar goods in the first use's geographical area. Protection of the mark continues as long as it is actually used.

It is also possible to register trademarks in most states, and a mark can be federally registered in the U.S. Patent and Trademark Office. A separate state registration only protects the mark in all or a portion of the state. Federal registration grants essentially exclusive rights to a mark throughout the country, even if it is not presently used in certain parts of the United States. There are exceptions to this rule, so it would be a good idea to talk with a trademark attorney or specialist who should be able to file and obtain a registered trademark for a relatively modest fee. A federal registration has an initial life of 20 years and can be renewed as long as the mark is in use.

Once an artist adopts and uses a mark, it is important to protect the mark from confusing use by others. If there is some confusion with other marks, and the artist allows the situation to continue, his own mark loses its strength, and in time the courts will not enforce the mark against others.

The cost of obtaining legal protection for an artist's marks is small. To receive protection under state law, an artist only has to select a protectable mark and actually use and enforce it properly. For a simple federal registration, the current cost would probably be between $500 and $1,000 if no real problems were involved. The process for obtaining registrations for marks in most foreign countries is expensive and should be used only when foreign sales would support it.

The effort necessary to adopt, use and protect a mark justifies the cost. Marks are strong marketing tools. As an artist's artwork and services become better known to the public, his mark becomes an important asset. He may also use his mark to stop others from attempting to copy him. If necessary he can sue for damages. Finally, if a mark becomes well known, he can license others to use his mark with products and services which he authorizes. If he is considering such licensing or franchising opportunities, he should seek an attorney's advice.

CONCLUSION

The copyright, trade secret, patent, and trademark laws offer artists a wide scope of protection for their creations, creative developments, and marketing efforts. Through copyright, artists can protect their literary, visual, audio, and audiovisual works from unauthorized copying by others. Trade secret law enables an artist to protect her trade secrets and stop the unauthorized use of her secret information by others. Through patents, an artist can secure the exclusive right to make, use, and sell her inventions throughout the United States, regardless of whether or not the inventions can be kept secret. Finally, trademark law enables an artist to market exclusively her rights and services under her selected trademarks and service marks and to stop others from using identical or confusingly similar marks. In short, the copyright, trade secret, patent, and trademark laws collectively enable an artist to protect the vast majority of her works and creations from unauthorized use. Because of these legal protections, an artist can practice her art to the exclusion of others or can contractually transfer her rights and receive compensation from authorized users.

The cost to obtain the protections available under these laws is not prohibitive. When an artist creates a copyrightable work, he immediately has a copyright in that work, at no cost. By simply placing a copyright notice on the work when it is published, the artist will ensure that the majority of his rights under the copyright law will not be lost. With respect to protecting his trade secrets, an artist only has to expend the time and effort necessary to keep his developments secret. Any disclosure of the trade secrets must be made in confidence. Whenever an artist uses his trademarks or service marks with his goods and services, state trademark laws protect the artist's marks from unauthorized use, at least in the geographical area of actual use. Thus, without paying any immediate out-of-pocket expenses, an artist can receive substantial protection under the copyright, trade secret, and trademark laws.

To receive the maximum protection available under the copyright, trade secret, patent and trademark laws, an artist may need to apply for federal registrations or patents. For example, an artist can receive patent protection only after the U.S. Patent, and Trademark Office issues a patent based upon a formal patent application filed by the artist or his representative. Similarly, an artist can receive additional copyright and trademark protection by registering his copyrightable works in the Copyright Office and his marks in the U.S. Patent and Trademark Office. Registration of a copyrightable work provides the artist with certain rights not otherwise available, and an artist cannot enforce his copyright in a court of law until he has at least filed a copyright application. The federal registration of an artist's trademark or service mark grants him essentially exclusive rights to his mark throughout the United States, rather than in the more limited geographical area of actual use. Furthermore, a federal registration of a mark provides the artist with certain rights not provided by state law. In view of the added protections provided by copyright and trademark registrations and by patents, an artist should always consider these procedures when he creates or develops a new work, invention, or mark. By being aware of the protections available by federal registration and their costs, the artist can then selectively protect his most important creations, developments, and marks. Often, the additional protections are well worth the expense necessary to file applications and obtain a patent or a copyright or trademark registration.

In conclusion, there is no real excuse for not protecting an artist's creations and marks through copyright, trade secret, patent, and trademark law. Many of these legal rights are available free, and an artist can secure the available additional rights on a selective basis. The protections provided by these laws can be well worth the expense. Through the use of these laws an artist can prevent the unauthorized use of her works and creations and can sue to stop others from stealing her creations and otherwise unfairly competing with her. Perhaps more importantly, the rights provided by these laws can be sold or licensed by the artist to others for direct compensation. Thus, as an artist succeeds in her creative talents and reputation, she can by law receive adequate compensation through her legal rights.

7 | Insuring Artwork and the Artist

Huntington T. Block

HUNTINGTON T. BLOCK is the sole proprietor of Huntington Block Insurance in Washington, D.C., specializing in fine arts insurance and insurance for businesses and professionals.

There is perhaps no more independent a businessperson than an artist. You may not think of yourself as a businessperson, but you are. You make something which you hope to sell. You lease or own working space, you sometimes hire assistants, you own and use the tools and raw materials of your craft, and you deal with the public. If you stop to think about it, these are the sorts of things that any business does, and in this litigious society in which we live you have the same legal responsibilities and potential liabilities as anyone else.

You also have assets to protect, but none is more important than yourself. This is supposed to be a chapter on insurance, but I hope it will be a chapter which will just as emphatically remind you of risks you can avoid just as it will address itself to insurance you can buy. Nothing is more devastating to an independent businessperson than sickness. Productivity stops, and presumably income stops as well. We all get sick at one time or another, but a lot of sickness is the result of carelessness, and to an independent artist an unnecessary illness is an inexcusable waste of time—and time is money. Take care of yourself!

GROUP INSURANCE

Hospital and medical insurance is available on an individual basis, but it's expensive. It's best to shop around for a group you can belong to. For example, if your spouse is working in a large organization, chances are you can be included as part of a "family" coverage in the organization's group policy. Perhaps you can find an artists' group which has negotiated a good program you can join.

When you enter a hospital and medical program, beware of something that sounds too cheap—chances are the benefits are cheap too. You want a hospital plan that guarantees a semiprivate room in a local hospital; you want a doctor benefit that reimburses your physician in accordance with the fees he normally charges; you need to be assured of adequate expenses like drugs, operating room fees, and so on; and you want dental coverage if it can be included at a reasonable premium.

LOSS OF INCOME INSURANCE

Just as troubling as the expense of getting well is the loss of income while you are sick, particularly if you are faced with a long illness. Rent and taxes go on regardless of whether you're sick or well. You can usually arrange loss of income insurance at a reasonable premium if you are willing to accept a fairly long waiting period before benefits commence. For example, if you make a philosophic decision that you need loss of income insurance only for a catastrophic illness, you might be willing to accept a six-month waiting period before benefits start being paid. Such a program is relatively inexpensive, especially if it can be purchased as part of a group policy. Your benefit, usually payable on a monthly basis, will represent a percentage of your normal income—enough to keep the wolf away from the door, but certainly not enough to encourage you to stay on your back any longer than you must.

LIFE INSURANCE

Artists have never been great believers in life insurance, but there are some important uses for life insurance that deserve mention. If you have dependents, the need for some form of life insurance is self-evident. You may want to buy sufficient life insurance to guarantee that your mortgage will be paid off in case you die, so your family will have a place to live free and clear. You may have to buy life insurance to help guarantee a loan. These days a good deal of the life insurance that is sold is pure term life insurance, that is, just death benefit life insurance, no cash value, no loan option, hardly any frills. Term is the cheapest form of life insurance available, and most money men will advise you to buy term insurance, and look to real estate or the stock market for your investment income. However, if you own an ordinary life insurance policy which has accumulated a cash value, don't overlook the possibility of borrowing against that policy at very favorable interest rates.

RETIREMENT INSURANCE

No one really likes to think about retirement, especially an artist whose productive years may never stop. Picasso certainly didn't need any retirement income. However, the IRS recognizes that many independent businesspeople do retire, and they have established the Keogh Plan which encourages an independent to set up his or her own retirement plan, and enables annual contributions of tax-free income into that plan. Any artist who has not taken advantage of the Keogh Plan is missing a great opportunity to save.

There are many ways to put money aside for retirement. You can buy an annuity which will guarantee a certain fixed income beginning at age 65 or 70, or however you decide to set it up. You can make a contribution to a group pension plan if you can find one to join, or you can set up your own pension plan with an annual tax free contribution under the aforementioned Keogh Plan. It's hard enough to grow old, but it's twice as hard if you haven't also planned in advance how to keep the wolf away from your door.

INSURING YOUR STUDIO

So much for your life and health. Let's give some thought to your environment. Your studio is the center of your professional life. You may own it or lease it, but whatever you do, you have stocked it with brushes, easels, tools, and equipment of all kinds. Chances are, also, that one of the heaviest concentrations of your own work is held in your studio. Collectors and would-be dealers come to see your work. Occasionally you might share your studio with another artist or artists. The point is that whether you share a space or work alone, people tend to come and go in any artist's studio.

What can happen? Obviously a fire can be devastating, so can serious water damage from burst pipes, and so can a major theft or act of vandalism. On the liability side, someone can claim to have been injured on your premises, and sue you for negligence. All these perils can be insured against with what is generally referred to as a commercial multiperil policy. It is a package of insurance which, on the property side, will cover your building if you own it, all of your contents including your business-related personal property, and your liability as a building owner or as a tenant, whatever the case may be.

If you own your building, or the building that houses your studio, you should ask for a policy that provides "all-risk" perils and that guarantees replacement cost if a part or all of your building is damaged or destroyed. When arriving at a figure to use to insure your business personal property, remember all of the studio furniture and equipment, your leasehold improvements, if any, all materials and supplies, any commercial camera equipment or audio equipment you use in your work, and your art library, including catalogs, periodicals, and so on. You should again insist upon "all risk" perils, and you should understand that if you don't insure to value, you could be penalized in any loss adjustment. Your inventory of your own artwork, and that of other artists, can best be treated under another form of policy which will be described later in the chapter. The commercial multiperil policy can be extended to provide for reimbursement of extra expenses as a result of a fire or other insured peril which temporarily forces you to locate elsewhere while your own space is being repaired.

A second section of the policy deals with all of the liability exposures that arise out of the premises itself, and all of your other operations as an artist, including installations, art in public places for which you are responsible, your activities away from your studio, and so on. Coverage can be extended to include your potential liability arising out of the activities of independent contractors, your liability as a result of an alleged act of libel, slander, or invasion of privacy, and your possible liability arising out of serving alcohol at a business-related party or reception. If you are working in a medium that could cause eventual physical harm, such as a large steel sculpture, the policy can be extended to cover product liability. If you lease your studio space, you can even cover your liability for fire damage to the owner's walls, floors, and ceilings if it can be proved the fire was started as a result of your negligence.

Other forms of liability insurance are just as important. Automobile and truck insurance is mandatory in most states, and mandatory or not, absolutely essential to carry. Don't forget motorcycles, mopeds, and tractors. If you have employees, workers' compensation is a statutory requirement. So is disability benefits in some states. In fact, if you are incorporated, you are your own employee, so you can buy workers' compensation insurance for yourself. It is valuable coverage, because it reimburses an employee for medical expenses and loss of income arising out of a work-related accident or sickness.

CATASTROPHE LIABILITY INSURANCE

Furthermore, there is what can best be described as catastrophe liability insurance, or umbrella liability insurance. Smart plaintiff's attorneys often sue for a good deal more than they expect to get, and $1 million suits are fairly commonplace these days. Insurance people generally recommend substantial liability coverage, and the best way to buy it is through an umbrella policy which provides $1 million or $2 million additional liability protection on top of all of your basic liability policies.

HOMEOWNER'S INSURANCE

If you work at home, your insurance needs are tied into the homeowner's or tenant's policy you buy to protect your home or apartment. However, many working artists don't realize that most such policies designed for the home specifically exclude business personal property and liabilities arising out of business pursuits. It behooves you, therefore, to ask your agent or insurance company representative to endorse your policy to recognize you are a professional artist with a studio in your home. The cost is not great, and the extra peace of mind is substantial.

INSURING YOUR INVENTORY

Finally, there is the question of your own work, your own art inventory, and that includes work in process, work in storage, work on consignment and so on. Insurance of this inventory calls for a carefully constructed fine arts policy, one that responds to a broad range of perils and one that establishes insured value in a form easily understandable to artist and insurance adjuster alike.

Such a policy is generally referred to as a fine arts policy, and heretofore underwriters have been somewhat reluctant to offer this broad insurance coverage to a working artist. Happily that attitude is changing, and the market is opening up, influenced by the persistence of various artists' organizations.

Perhaps inhibitions exist because of the stereotype of the poor, starving artist working in a four-story walk-up, classified by insurance people as a fire trap. There is nothing more devastating to an artist than the loss of months, sometimes years, of work in a major fire or as the result of a burst pipe. The fact is that artists are just as concerned about so-called fire traps as are the underwriters, and while there are undoubtedly some shining exceptions, the majority of people who paint and sculpt are as careful about safety and security as is any other responsible businessperson.

Another problem has been the difficulty of establishing value, particularly for an artist whose work has as yet not attracted an active market. In fact, it is not unreasonable for insurance people to require evidence of some sort of sales record before agreeing to insure studio inventory at a particular level of value. However, if valuations can be established, according to size, medium, or whatever, it should be possible to insure not only completed works held in the studio, but also work in process at whatever percentage of completion exists at the time a loss occurs. Since the artist generally consigns his work to a dealer at a percentage of selling price, say, 60 percent of selling price, the consigned value is usually the amount the artist and the insurance company agree upon for insurance purposes. The purpose of insurance is to make you whole, but no more than whole. Insurance wouldn't and shouldn't be arranged to reimburse you for more than you might expect to receive if a loss had not taken place.

CONSIGNING YOUR WORK: WHO IS RESPONSIBLE?

Artists must be careful to review the insurance responsibility when they consign their work to a dealer or a cooperative gallery. Generally the insurance responsibility lies with the dealer or the gallery, but that's not always so. If the dealer or gallery is carrying the insurance, which will be the case in most instances, the consignment agreement should be in writing, because the first document an insurance adjuster asks for after a commercial art gallery fire is the consignment agreement with the gallery's several artists.

Furthermore, when an artist submits some of his work to a juried show or to a museum show, he should determine who will be responsible for the insurance—and whether it begins when the art leaves the studio, and continues until the art returns, or if it covers only while the art is on the premises where the show is being held. Remember also that if you are sent a loan agreement form by a museum or other borrower, the figure you put opposite each object you agree to lend is usually an "agreed value," and that is exactly what you receive in the event your object is lost or destroyed, no more, no less.

If a loss does occur, you will be dealing with an insurance adjuster. He is a representative of the insurance company charged with bringing your claim to a reasonable and satisfactory settlement. He isn't the enemy, and he generally tries to be fair. But he does need you to supply certain documentation to support the claim you are making. For example, if your loss involves works of art, he'll want to see the aforementioned consignment agreements so he can establish value in accordance with the terms of your policy. If the loss involves business or household personal property, he'll want to see bills of sale if they're available, and he'll want to know how long you've owned a desk, or a table, or whatever, to determine how much depreciation to allow. If someone has been injured on your premises, he will need to know from you all the circumstances of the injury, because he has to establish whether or not there has been any negligence on your part.

Where do you go to get the best insurance buy and the best insurance service? It's usually wise to try to find a person or a firm where there is an interest in and understanding of the needs of an artist. Such people exist. All you have to do is ask around among your fellow artists, and find out which ones seem most satisfied with their insurance relationship, and who's dealing with people who seem to grasp the special insurance needs of the artist. There are even insurance people who are part-time artists!

The whole business of evaluating the risks you face is not without its rewards. You certainly don't have to buy an insurance policy in every instance. Good common sense can prevent most accidents from happening in the first place. If a studio space opens up at an attractive rental, but in a rundown building, don't be pennywise and pound foolish. Wait for a space in a well-maintained building where your neighbors have the same concerns for safety and security as do you. Remember you can be the most careful person in the world, but you can't do much about your neighbor, and the fire that his carelessness starts will most certainly spread to yours.

Think about the things that can happen to you, and think about the things you can prevent. Be particularly concerned about a catastrophe, like a major fire, a long illness, or a six-figure liability suit against you. Then begin to construct your insurance program, perhaps with the counsel of an insurance broker who knows and understands art and the artist.

SAFETY AND SECURITY

Two spectacular art thefts in the winter of 1987–88 have alerted the art community to the value of proper security. Late in 1987 felons entered the apartment of the late Raphael Soyer and stole a substantial amount of his work, and then in February 1988, thieves dropped through an unsecured skylight in New York's Colnaghi Gallery and perpetrated one of the most spectacular art thefts of the decade. In both instances law enforcement officers have pointed to poor or inadequate security as the cause of loss. With newspaper headlines and magazine covers trumpeting the runaway prices brought on by the art boom, even the casual thief no longer "walks by the Renoir to get to the television set" as he once was prone to do. Not everyone needs an elaborate security system, but consider what you have and what you can afford to lose, and design your security system accordingly. For some it might be no more than burglarproof locks on the doors and windows, but for others it should be no less than a UL-approved central station fire and burglar alarm system.

Furthermore, with water damage still such a major problem, be careful how you store your inventory. Remember that cellars flood, and be sure to wrap your objects and see to it that they are stored on platforms several inches above what may someday be the flooded floor.

The best advice is simply to reemphasize that safety and security are important, and to tell you that there is no greater a truism than that which reminds us that "an ounce of prevention is worth a pound of cure."

8 | Safeguarding Your Health

Health Hazards for Artists

Michael McCann, Ph.D., C.I.H.,

Monona Rossol, M.S., M.F.A.

DR. MICHAEL McCANN has a Ph.D. in chemistry and is a certified industrial hygienist. He is founder and executive director of the Center for Safety in the Arts (formerly Center for Occupational Hazards). He is author of *Artist Beware* and *Health Hazards Manual for Artists,* and is a frequent lecturer and consultant on art hazards.

MONONA ROSSOL is a potter, art teacher, and chemist who in 1977 helped found the Center for Occupational Hazards. She lectures and writes extensively on health hazards in arts and crafts.

For years, artists and everyone else assumed that art materials were innocuous—an attitude reinforced by the inadequate labeling of art materials. Today we know that this is not true—many art materials are hazardous. As a result, many artists have been getting ill from overexposure to these materials due to a lack of knowledge of the hazards and a lack of suitable precautions.

ARTISTS AND CHEMICALS

Artists are exposed to lead in artists' paints, ceramic glazes, enamels, lead fumes from soldering, welding, and casting of lead-containing alloys such as bronze, and from working with stained glass. Artists are exposed to asbestos when sculpting asbestos-containing stones such as soapstone and serpentine, when working with asbestos-containing talcs in clays, glazes, industrial talcum powders and French chalk, asbestos-coated welding and brazing rods, old asbestos gloves and welding curtains, and many other asbestos-insulated items.

Other chemicals to which artists are exposed include many hazardous solvents such as benzene, carbontetrachloride, and n-hexane. Artists also work with dyes which are either highly toxic or cancer-causing, toxic heavy metals in pigments and ceramic colorants, silica (which can cause silicosis) in clays, glazes, stone dusts and jewelry buffing compounds, and more.

Artists often have a greater exposure to toxic chemicals than do industrial workers for several reasons: (1) lack of knowledge as to the composition of art materials and their hazards, (2) lack of suitable precautions, (3) working long hours (e.g. when preparing for an exhibit), and (4) using art materials in the home and other nonindustrial settings. In addition, working in the home might expose other family members.

Unlike many industrial workers, artists usually have no union to fight for safe and healthful conditions or to promote educational programs to alert workers to workplace hazards. Instead, artists often work in isolation and independently, making their own decisions about what materials to use and how to use them.

As a result we are seeing artists contracting the same types of occupational diseases that have plagued industrial workers. Artists and craftsmen are contracting work-related illnesses such as silicosis, chronic bronchitis, liver and kidney damage, crippling nervous system disorders, dermatitis, and heavy metal poisoning. Occupationally induced cancers are also showing up. A recent National Cancer Institute mortality study of artists (primarily painters) showed dramatic elevations (above the normal population) in brain, kidney, and bladder cancer and leukemia in male artists, and in breast, rectal, and lung cancer in women artists.

Statistics such as these are cold and meaningless when compared to the individual stories of occupational illness and death among artists. Here are three examples: The first is the story of a California mural painter who contracted mercury poisoning from her acrylic paints—probably from her habit of eating while working. Her physical suffering is complicated by the mental and emotional effects of mercury poisoning. These mental symptoms have been known since the 1800s, when felt hat workers used mercury vapor to block hats. From this came the phrase "mad as a hatter," which Lewis Carroll drew on when he included the Mad Hatter character in his *Alice in Wonderland.*

The second story is that of weaver Dennis Friend, who died of inhalation anthrax (a bacterial disease which used to be called "wool sorters' disease") from working with contaminated wool. Mr. Friend left a widow and a six-week-old baby. His widow, also a weaver, has been actively alerting others to the dangers of anthrax and has personal knowledge of a number of other cases of skin anthrax among American weavers.

The third case is that of Erica Barton, a college artist, who has been disabled by exposure to a solvent in spray adhesives. This solvent, n-hexane, is commonly present in rubber cement and its thinner, aerosol spray cans, contact adhesives, some lacquer thinners, and low-boiling naphthas. The disease it can cause is similar in many respects to multiple sclerosis.

Mrs. Barton's symptoms began as a numbness in the hands and feet and progressed to difficulty in walking, exhaustion, loss of interest, vision problems, paralysis, and other symptoms affecting the peripheral nervous system. Two years later the peripheral nervous system symptoms have mostly disappeared, but she has permanent central nervous system damage including vision problems, muscle weakness, and difficulty in controlling fine motions. Her doctor does not expect that she will ever recover completely and return to being an artist.

There are many other dramatic examples of occupational illnesses among artists, but there are even greater numbers of artists who are suffering undiagnosed, chronic illnesses which they do not know are work related. For example, there are artists somewhere right now who are suffering from repeated respiratory infections, which are actually due to inhalation of irritating dusts or solvents.

Such infections might even be manifestations of early silicosis. There are others, constantly fatigued, who are actually suffering from low-level lead intoxication, chronic carbon monoxide inhalation, or who may be in the early stages of occupationally induced blood diseases such as leukemia. These conditions are often attributed by the artists to other causes. Even well-meaning physicians who are not trained in occupational medicine commonly misdiagnose these conditions.

These artists could do a lot to protect themselves from chronic illness and aid physicians in making diagnoses if they knew what toxic chemicals were present in their art materials and what symptoms they can produce. Artists must educate themselves about the effects of toxic materials and the proper precautions necessary to work safely with these chemicals.

HOW MATERIALS AFFECT YOU

The symptoms produced by toxic chemicals will vary with the amount of a material to which you are exposed. In general, the effects of toxic materials on the body can be divided into two categories of illness—acute and chronic.

Acute and Chronic Effects

An *acute* effect results from exposure to a toxic material in a single dose large enough to produce harmful effects within a relatively short period of time. It is usually not difficult to diagnose an acute illness because cause and effect are easily connected. For example, narcosis (headache, loss of coordination, nausea, and dizziness) is a common acute effect of intense exposure to solvents such as lacquer thinner or turpentine.

A *chronic* effect is harder to diagnose. Chronic effects are produced by repeated exposure to low doses of toxic materials, usually over a long period of time. Symptoms may vary from individual to individual. For example, exposure to the same lacquer thinner at lower doses over a period of months or of years on a regular basis might produce individualized chronic effects like dermatitis (if skin contact were involved), psychological problems (apathy, irritability, depression, etc.), liver damage, and nervous system damage. Another example of a chronic or long-term effect is cancer, which in some cases can take up to 40 years to develop. Examples of materials used by artists that may cause various types of cancer are benzene, asbestos, benzidine-based dyes, lead chromate used as a ceramic colorant and a pigment in some paints and inks, and uranium compounds (used in some photographic toners and glazes).

Are You at Risk?

You should ask yourself a number of questions to determine the extent of your risk from exposure to toxic materials.

1. *How much do you use?* Keep track of the amounts of material you use. A pint of solvent, for example, presents a smaller hazard than a quart.

2. *Under what conditions are you exposed?* How close is your contact with the material? For example, do you get it on your hands or breathe its vapors? A pint of solvent, for instance, is less hazardous if it is used with good ventilation than if you use it in a small unvented room.

3. *How often are you exposed?* The body will tolerate exposure once a month better than daily exposure.

4. *How long are you exposed?* A few minutes' exposure to a chemical presents a smaller risk than exposure for many hours. The government standards for permissible exposure levels are based on an 8-hour day. This allows the body 16 hours to detoxify and excrete materials. If you work more than 8 hours (a common occurrence among artists), you experience a substantially higher degree of hazard. The worst exposure occurs when you also work with the same materials at home when you free lance in addition to your regular job. Lingering fumes and dusts in your home can mean that you are exposed for 24 hours a day.

5. *How toxic is each material you use?* Some materials are more toxic than others. The higher the toxicity, the less of a material it takes to cause harm. Among the most toxic compounds are those that are not easily eliminated from the body and tend to accumulate (such as lead). Learn which chemicals you use are the most dangerous.

6. *What is your "total body burden"?* The total body burden of a particular substance is the amount of that substance in your body from all sources. For example, if you are an average city dweller, you already have a total body burden of lead from pollution (air, water, food, smoking) that is higher than experts would like it to be. If you add more from workplace exposure to lead-containing materials like paints, your total body burden of lead may be a source of real concern.

7. *Are you exposed to many different chemicals?* If you are exposed to several chemicals all of which can cause injury to the same organ, then the total damage to that organ is the sum of the contributions from each chemical. For example, if you are exposed to several solvents all of which damage the liver and you also consume alcohol, the total liver damage is

the result of the toxic action of each of the solvents plus the alcohol. In addition, some chemicals will act together synergistically to produce an effect much greater than expected. The well-known interaction of barbiturates with alcohol is an example of synergism. Another example is smoking and inhalation of toxic dusts such as asbestos. People exposed to asbestos increase their chances of developing lung cancer by 5 times. If the exposed people are also smokers, they increase their chances of developing lung cancer 92 times. This is a classic example of synergism. We are only beginning to identify many more examples of this effect among various chemicals.

8. *Are you a member of a high-risk group?* Government standards that specify the amounts of various substances to which workers can be exposed safely are based on the tolerances of *healthy adults.* High-risk groups which may not be able to tolerate these levels include children, the elderly, those with preexisting illnesses, those taking medication, people with allergies or sensitivities, pregnant women, smokers, and drinkers.

How Toxic Materials Enter the Body

Toxic materials must enter the body in order to cause damage. Three ways this can occur are through skin contact, through inhalation, and through the mouth and digestive system.

- *Skin contact.* The skin's barrier of dead cells and waxy layers can be penetrated by chemicals such as caustics, acids, solvents, peroxides, and bleaches. Once past the skin's defenses, these chemicals can damage the skin or tissues deep beneath the skin, and some may enter the bloodstream. In addition, once the skin is damaged either by chemicals or by cuts and abrasions, many other chemicals which normally would not be hazardous now are able to damage the skin or enter the bloodstream. Some chemicals penetrate the skin's barrier directly and enter the bloodstream without your knowing it. Among these are phenol, benzene, toluene, xylene, and methyl alcohol.

- *Inhalation.* When inhaled, some chemical vapors and fumes can damage or attack lung tissue immediately. Among these are welding fumes, resin vapors, and fumes from heating some plastics. Other chemicals such as some dusts and mists may take longer to act and can cause chronic irritation or illness. In general, the smaller the dust or mist particle, the greater the damage it can cause. Examples of chronic lung diseases are chronic bronchitis and emphysema. In addition, many substances can pass through lung tissue into the bloodstream where they can reach other organs. Examples are liver damage resulting from the inhalation of solvent vapors and nerve damage resulting from inhalation of lead-containing spray paints.

- *Ingestion.* Most ingestion of toxic materials is caused by hand-to-mouth contact with soiled hands, for example, when eating, smoking, biting nails, or licking fingers to turn pages. "Pointing" paint brushes with your lips can also result in ingestion of pigments. Inhaled dusts or mists also can be ingested when they are trapped in lung mucous, coughed up, and then swallowed.

Occupational Diseases

Once in the body, each different chemical produces its own particular effects or disease. Correct diagnosis of occupational illness often requires the unique skills of doctors who specialize in occupational medicine or toxicology. Here are only a few of the many diseases that artists might develop and a few of the chemicals that might cause them:

- *Allergies to sensitizers.* Sensitizers are chemicals that can produce allergic responses such as asthma or allergic dermatitis in significant percentages of those exposed. Known sensitizers include epoxy resins and glues, formaldehyde, polyurethane resins (diisocyanates), cold water dyes, turpentine, some wood dusts, chromium, and nickel.
- *Metal fume fever.* A temporary flulike disease usually caused by inhalation of zinc and copper fumes from welding or soldering (not to be confused with the same early symptoms of cadmium poisoning, which can be fatal, caused by inhaling fumes from cadmium-containing metals or solders).
- *Primary dermatitis.* From acids, alkalis, solvents, and all chemicals that can irritate or remove oils from the skin.
- *Skin cancer:* From ultraviolet light, carbon black pigments, and arsenic compounds.
- *Lung fibrosis.* From silica (silicosis), asbestos (asbestosis), beryllium, and some woods.
- *Pulmonary edema (chemical pneumonia).* From nitrogen dioxide (from etching baths), cadmium fumes, chlorine, and ozone.
- *Lung cancer.* From asbestos, smoking, and inhalation of chromium and nickel-containing fumes, dusts, or pigments.

- *Hepatitis.* From chlorinated hydrocarbons, toluene, and many other solvents, styrene (used in polyester resin casting), and phenol compounds.
- *Liver cancer.* From chlorinated hydrocarbons such as vinyl chloride, methylene chloride, perchlorothyene, and so on.
- *Bladder cancer.* From benzidine-type dyes no longer used.
- *Heart damage.* From carbon monoxide, methylene chloride, methyl chloroform, cobalt, and barium compounds.
- *Nervous system damage.* From mercury, lead, manganese, arsenic, n-hexane, methyl butyl ketone, and all solvents to varying degrees. Both acute and chronic effects are possible, depending on the solvent.
- *Kidney damage.* From chlorinated hydrocarbons, mercury, lead, cadmium, turpentine.

WHAT CAN YOU DO ABOUT IT?

Use Label Information

Do not buy unlabeled materials. Read labels carefully, although many products (especially art materials) are incompletely labeled. For additional information, write to the manufacturer's address on the label and ask for a Material Safety Data Sheet. Manufacturers are not required by law to give you a copy of this form unless you are an employee, but most reputable manufacturers will. These forms include information on hazardous ingredients, fire and explosion data, health hazard data, special protective equipment and ventilation to be used with the material, and more. The quality of this information will vary greatly depending on the care with which the company prepares these forms, but they are a good addition to label information.

Use Safer Substitutes

1. *Use the least toxic material for each job.* Many products are more hazardous than they need to be. Compare labels on similar products to see which contains the least toxic ingredients. An example would be to substitute acetone, whenever possible, for commercial lacquer thinners, which are usually a mixture of more toxic solvents.
2. *Switch to the water-based or latex products whenever possible.* Solvents are among the most hazardous chemicals used in art. Try to replace solvent-containing products such as oil-based paints and enam-

els when possible. Watch for the appearance of new and improved water-based paints and inks as the marketplace responds to the restrictions placed on the sale of photoreactive (smog-causing) solvents by ecologically minded state legislatures. For example, several water-based silkscreen systems have recently been introduced to the art market.

3. *Choose products that don't create dusts and mists.* Try to buy products that are in solution rather than in powdered form, and avoid aerosol cans and spray products whenever possible to avoid inhalation of toxic chemicals.

4. *Avoid products containing carcinogens.* Contrary to popular opinion, there are relatively few carcinogens among the vast number of chemicals used in art. Keep abreast of information about cancer-causing chemicals and replace products that contain them. Remember, although there is no safe level of exposure to carcinogens, the lower the exposure the lower the risk.

Ventilate

Ventilation is the most important defense against toxic materials. Open windows and doors, air conditioners, or fans that simply circulate the air in the room are not good ventilation. In most cases, installation of proper ventilation requires professional advice. There are two basic types of ventilation: general or dilution and local exhaust.

1. *General or dilution ventilation* dilutes airborne toxic chemicals with fresh air, producing a lower, safer concentration through the combined action of exhaust fans and make-up air inlets which replace exhausted air. For example, fresh air enters a room at one end through an opening or a blower. This fresh air mixes with the contaminated air in the room, while an exhaust fan located at the other end of the room removes the mixed air to the outside.

 General ventilation systems produce air currents, making them unsuitable for any dust-generating art operations, since such currents make it impossible to avoid inhaling the dust. These systems are also incapable of controlling large amounts of toxic vapors or highly toxic materials. They are suitable for operations where small amounts of materials are produced, such as in acrylic or oil painting studios.

2. *Local exhaust ventilation* captures the toxic materials at their sources before they can contaminate the general air in the room, and removes the captured material to the outside air by means of hoods, ducts, and fans. Local exhaust systems are preferred to general ventilation systems,

because they capture contaminants more efficiently, remove contaminants before they get into the general air, and are more energy efficient. (They require smaller fans and move less air to the outside, thereby lowering heating and cooling costs.)

Examples of local exhaust systems include spray booths which use a fan to pull spray mist away from the operator; canopy hoods over ceramic kilns to collect rising hot gases and fumes and remove them; and slot vents behind photochemical baths, acid etching baths, and cleaning operations to pull airborne materials away from the operator and to the outside air.

RULES FOR GOOD VENTILATION

1. Use local exhaust ventilation rather than general dilution ventilation whenever possible.
2. Have all systems designed, installed, and maintained by qualified professionals.
3. Provide adequate make-up air to replace exhausted air.
4. Arrange tables and work areas so that fresh air is drawn through the workers' breathing zones before being contaminated.
5. Enclose the source of contamination with the hood or collector so that toxic materials cannot escape.
6. Make sure that once air is exhausted it is not drawn back into the room or into some other area in which it is not welcome.

Personal Protective Equipment

Art processes employ a great number of toxic materials and produce dangerous by-products such as heat, ultraviolet light (in welding, for example), and noise. The best solution is to keep on hand a variety of multipurpose protective devices.

- *Gloves.* A variety of different kinds and sizes of gloves to withstand heat, abrasion, or chemicals may be needed. To resist heat, woven fiberglass (not asbestos) gloves should be used. Chemical-resistant gloves, such as nitrile and neoprene gloves, should be chosen because of the large number of chemicals they can resist. Cotton work gloves can be used to resist abrasion.

- *Face and eye protection.* Impact-resistant goggles and face shields should be available in the shop. For welding use both face and eye protection that meet Occupational Safety and Health Administration (OSHA) standards. (See section on OSHA.)

* *Hearing protection.* In general, hearing protection should be used if shop noise is at or above the level at which you must continually raise your voice to be heard by someone two feet away. One-size-fits-all earplugs are inexpensive in bulk and should be adequate for most shop circumstances.

* *Respiratory protection.* Ventilation, and not respiratory protection, should be the primary method employed for protection from airborne toxic substances. The OSHA regulations make it clear that respiratory protection devices are to be used only when ventilation is not feasible (not likely in most art situations), while ventilation is being installed, or for emergency situations. In addition, some people should never use respirators. Because all respirators increase breathing strain to some degree, *respirators should not be worn by most people who have heart or respiratory difficulties.* Consult your physician.

   When purchasing masks, respirators, or filters, *buy only equipment that is "NIOSH-approved."*

   Air-purifying respirators may be either disposable or reusable ones with replaceable filters or cartridges. Try them on before purchasing them to be sure they fit and are comfortable. Filters and cartridges provide protection only against certain types and levels of contaminants. For example, for protection from solvent vapors you would need an organic vapor cartridge, while a toxic dust filter would be needed for protection from dyes or pigment powders. Sometimes a combination of filter and cartridge may be necessary. Choosing the right filters and respirators requires some thought and study.

   Air-supplied respirators provide a source of outside air. The two most common types of air-supplied respirators are airline and self-contained breathing apparatus (SCUBA). The airline type has a hose which supplies clean air from an outside source. The self-contained type is similar to scuba-diving equipment, with air tanks usually carried on the back of the user. Air-supplied respirators require extensive training in their use, and are not normally recommended for artists.

Personal Hygiene Rules

1. Do not eat, smoke, or drink in the studio to prevent ingestion of small amounts of toxic materials. Smoking also can be a fire hazard, can increase the effects of hazardous materials on the lungs, and even can convert some materials into more hazardous forms. For example,

methylene chloride used as a plastics and paint solvent can be converted into poisonous phosgene (war gas) by lit cigarettes.

2. Wear special work clothes and remove them after work. Wash them frequently and separately from other clothing. Don't wear scarves, ties, or loose clothing. Tie back long hair.

3. Wash hands carefully in soap and water after work, before eating, and during work breaks. Never use solvents to clean hands. If soap and water are insufficient, use waterless hand cleaners and follow with soap and water. For clean-up after painting, use baby oil, and then soap and water.

4. Wear gloves to protect hands against solvents, acids, and alkalis. Barrier creams may be used for light or occasional hand contact with irritating chemicals.

Storage and Handling of Materials

1. Label all containers clearly, noting both contents and hazards.

2. Use nonbreakable containers such as metal or plastic. Do not store large containers on high shelves where they are difficult to retrieve and might fall and break.

3. Do not store chemicals that may react with each other, such as acids and ammonia.

4. To prevent escape of dust or vapors, keep all containers closed except when using them.

5. In case of accidental skin contact with toxic chemicals, wash affected areas with lots of water. In case of eye contact, rinse eyes for at least 15 minutes and seek medical help.

6. Do not sweep floors or brush dust off shelves. Use a wet mop or industrial vacuum cleaner with a filter system.

7. Dispose of waste or unwanted chemicals safely. For large amounts of regularly produced wastes, engage a waste disposal service. Do not pour solvents down the sink. Pour nonpolluting aqueous liquids down the sink *one at a time* and with lots of water to avoid reactions between chemicals. If you don't know how to dispose of a material, contact the manufacturer.

8. Clean up spills immediately so solvents won't evaporate and dust won't become airborne. Clean up small spills of flammable liquids with paper towels, place this waste in an approved, self-closing waste can, and empty the can daily. Large spills require more extensive procedures.

9. Store quantities of solvents greater than one quart in approved, self-closing safety cans.

10. Do not store flammable or combustible materials near exits or entrances. Keep sources of sparks, flames, UV light and heat, as well as lighted cigarettes away from flammable or combustible solids or liquids.

11. Keep an ABC-type extinguisher handy and get training in how to use it.

Occupational Safety and Health Administration

The purpose of the Occupational Safety and Health Act of 1970 is to "assure safe and healthful working conditions for working men and women" by establishing and enforcing safety and health standards. All employees (not students) are protected except those in public agencies and their political subdivisions in certain states which have chosen not to come under the OSHA-approved state plans. This means that employees in state or municipal public schools in over half the states are not protected by OSHA. If you are a public employee, check to see if you come under OSHA's jurisdiction.

If you are protected by OSHA you have certain rights, one of which is to complain if you think your workplace is unsafe. In major cities, local OSHA offices are listed in the telephone book either under the Labor Department of the U.S. government or under the states' Labor Departments in those states with a state plan.

The Center for Safety in the Arts*

The Center for Safety in the Arts (CSA) is a national clearinghouse for research and information on health hazards in the arts, including the visual arts and crafts, theater, and museum conservation. COH has a number of programs.

1. *Art Hazards Information Center.* The Information Center researches, prepares, and collects written materials for dissemination to artists. It distributes about 75 different books, pamphlets, articles, and data sheets on art hazards. For example, there are publications to help you select the proper respirator or other personal protective equipment for your particular work, or to acquaint you with the hazards of your particular medium.

   CSA will also answer your letter or telephone inquiries about health-related matters directly. Enclose a self-addressed stamped envelope for a reply or a copy of their publications list.

---

* The Center for Safety in the Arts is located at 5 Beekman Street, New York, N.Y. 10038. Telephone 212/227-6220.

2. *Art Hazards News.* CSA publishes a four-page newsletter ten times a year. It covers such topics as new hazards, precautions, government regulations, lawsuits, a calendar of events, and so on. Subscriptions cost $15 per year. Send a self-addressed stamped envelope for a sample copy.

3. *Lecture Program.* CSA provides speakers on art hazards and precautions for lectures and workshops.

4. *Consultation Program.* Dr. Michael McCann, a certified industrial hygienist, conducts walkthrough surveys of art schools and art facilities and provides a written report on observed hazards and recommendations for their correction. Write to inquire about fees and other particulars.

SELECTED BIBLIOGRAPHY

A. M. Best Company. (1982). *Best's Safety Directory,* 2 volumes, Oldwick, NJ. Updated regularly.

American Mutual Assurance Alliance. (1980). *Handbook of Organic Industrial Solvents,* 5th ed., Chicago.

Clark, Nancy, Thomas Cutter and Jean-Ann McGrane. (1984). *Ventilation,* Center for Safety in the Arts, New York.*

Committee on Industrial Ventilation. (1986). *Industrial Ventilation: A Manual of Practice,* 19th ed., American Conference of Governmental Industrial Hygienists, East Lansing, MI. Updated regularly.[†]

Gosseline, Robert, Roger Smith, and Harold Hodge. (1984). *Clinical Toxicology of Commercial Products,* 5th ed., Williams and Wilkins, Baltimore MD.

International Labor Office. (1983). *Encyclopedia of Occupational Safety and Health,* 3rd ed., 2 volumes, Geneva, Switzerland.

McCann, Michael. (1979). *Artist Beware: The Hazards and Precautions in Working with Art and Craft Materials,* Watson-Guptill, New York.[†]

McCann, Michael. (1985). *Health Hazards Manual for Artists,* 3rd ed., Nick Lyons Books, New York.[†]

Society for Occupational Safety and Health. *Health Hazards in the Arts and Crafts, Proceedings of the SOEH Conference on Health Hazards in the Arts and Crafts,* McCann, Michael, and Gail Barazani, eds. (1980). Washington, DC.

McGrane, Jean-Ann. (1987). *Reproductive Hazards in the Arts and Crafts,* Center for Safety in the Arts, New York, 14 pages.[†]

---

[*] The Center for Safety in the Arts is located at 5 Beekman Street, New York, N.Y. 10038. Telephone 212/227-6220.

[†] Available from the Center for Safety in the Arts. For a complete listing of publications and information about the *Art Hazards News,* available from CSA please send a stamped, self-addressed envelope to the Art Hazards Information Center, 5 Beekman Street, New York, NY. 10038. Telephone: (212) 227-6220.

Moses, Cherie, James Purdham, Dwight Bowbay and Roland Hosein. (1978). *Health and Safety in Printmaking: A Manual for Printmakers,* Occupational Hygiene Branch, Alberta Labor, Edmonton, Alberta, Canada.

Patty, Frank, ed. (1982). *Industrial Hygiene and Toxicology,* 3rd ed., Vol. 2, three parts, Interscience Publishers, New York.

Quinn, Margaret, Sharon Smith, Laura Stock, and Jeff Young, Eds. (1980). *What You Should Know About Health and Safety in the Jewelry Industry,* Jewelry Workers Health and Safety Research Group. Providence, RI.[†]

Rossol, Monona. (1980–82). *Ceramics and Health,* compilation of articles from *Ceramic Scope.*[†]

Sax, N. Irving. (1979). *Dangerous Properties of Industrial Materials,* 5th ed., Van Nostrand Reinhold, New York. Updated regularly.

Shaw, Susan. (1983). *Overexposure: Health Hazards in Photography,* Friends of Photography, Los Angeles, CA.

Stellman, Jeanne, and Susan Daum. (1973). *Work Is Dangerous to Your Health,* Vintage, New York.

9 Financial Resources for Artists
The Visual Arts Program at the Arts Endowment

Jim Melchert

Michael Faubion

JIM MELCHERT, director of the Visual Arts Program at the National Endowment for the Arts from 1977 until 1981, is Professor of Art at the University of California, Berkeley.

MICHAEL FAUBION has worked at the Arts Endowment since 1977 and has been assistant director of the Visual Arts Program since 1983.

The Visual Artists Fellowships category of the Visual Arts Program at the National Endowment for the Arts provides individual grants for visual artists of exceptional talent and demonstrated ability of any aesthetic persuasion. The artists to whom we award these fellowships include painters, sculptors, printmakers, and artists specializing in the crafts, in photography, in drawing or artists' books and artists working in performance, video, conceptual modes, and new genres.

We do not fund students pursuing their degrees or individuals who have received a major fellowship from Visual Arts Program within the last two cycles. Beyond these eligibility requirements, however, the opportunity to be considered for a grant is open to any American professional artist.

Currently, the fellowships category operates on a two-year funding cycle, with half of the six mediums or genres offered each year. Applications are received and reviewed according to the materials with which visual artists work. The areas are painting, works on paper (includes drawing and printmaking), new genres (includes video, performance, and conceptual work), crafts, sculpture, and photography. Artists must select only one of these areas to apply to. Applications are reviewed by panels of artists working in that medium.

The amount of a fellowship is $20,000 or $5,000. Generally, artists who have been working professionally for at least 10 years will be considered for a $20,000 grant; those working less than 10 years for $5,000. During the program's 20-year history, about 3,500 grants have been awarded. In the 1987–88 funding cycle, we received a total of 10,690 applications. In 1982, we received 10,162 applications, in 1979 7,275, in 1977, 5,865, and in 1975 4,510. Statistically, it has turned out that the average age of those who apply is 35 or 36 years. Out of all the applications we receive, generally only about 5 percent receive funding.

We return all slides and videotapes and make every effort to handle all materials with care. The Endowment, however, cannot be responsible for any damage or loss. We do not return catalogs or reviews and do not accept any original works of art.

As well as offering fellowships at the national level, the Visual Arts Program initiated a regional fellowship program in 1983. Designed to provide additional support for the country's most talented visual artists, the program is patterned after the national fellowships application and review process. Grants of $5,000 are offered in areas not open for application at the national level that year and are available to artists who have never received a national fellowship. The program is administered by regional arts organizations and is funded and monitored by the Endowment. Currently, regional fellowships are available in all areas of the country except New England. Competition is as intense at the national level (twice as many applications are received); however, approximately 100 additional artists per year are receiving support through this complementary category to the national Visual Artists Fellowships.

The specifics of the national application process, as well as information on the regional program, are spelled out in our guideline booklet, which is available on request from the Visual Arts Program, National Endowment for the Arts, (202)682-5440.

THE VISUAL ARTS PROGRAM

Many artists are aware of the Visual Arts Program, but often the information they have is thirdhand and inaccurate. Usually rumors have to do with strategies that you can use to increase your chances of getting a fellowship from the Visual Arts Program. It is sometimes tempting to think that factors other than the merit of your work are what will do the trick. For example, we hear that some artists believe it is better to use your parents' mailing address in Indiana than your own in New York, or the other way around. Actually it is not of much consequence where you are from. (If you look at statistics from previous years, you will find that about the same percentage of applications are funded from all the various regions of the country.) There is another rumor that regards that review as a lottery. It suggests that if you keep applying year after year you will eventually be successful. In reality, if your work is not growing and strengthening there is not likely to be a fellowship in your future no matter how persistently you reapply. Still another aspect of the lottery notion is that decisions will be made without a serious look at the slides you send in. It would be a mistake to believe that. The slides are the most important part of your application.

THE REVIEW PROCESS

Consider how your application is reviewed. As soon as it arrives at the Endowment, it is logged in and checked for completeness. It is given a number and placed in a separate file folder together with supplementary material that you may want to include. It is not a bad idea to send in catalogs of recent solo exhibitions you have had. Reviews of your work by critics, on the other hand, are not useful. When your slides come up for review, particularly after several viewings, the panel will begin referring to your file folder for more information about your career and your circumstances. The most telling part of your presentation, however, will be the ten slides you submit. (Or in the case of artists working in video, conceptual, or performance areas, video tapes.) The images are projected on a wall, five at a time, and shown in chronological order from left to right. It often helps to include a few details among the ten. Generally speaking, the panelists get a better idea of what you do if you select work from a period of a few years. That is preferable to showing only the things that were included in your most recent exhibition. You have to decide what best represents your work and the direction it is taking.

The panel that will be looking at the material will be made up of six people usually five artists and one curator. They sit together and watch the slides, and they rank each presentation according to how strong they feel the work is. When the score is tallied, applications that received high ranking are brought back to be shown again. At that point, discussion begins to get lively, especially if the panelists differ in their perception of what they are seeing. With each round of viewing, some applications are dropped and others are brought back for more viewing and further discussion.

THE IMPORTANCE OF SLIDES

It should be clear now how important the slides are in this process. You would be surprised at how many artists send in transparencies that are badly shot. Often the exposure will be so badly off that you cannot tell what is on the screen. Sometimes there will so much glare on the surface of a painting that you cannot see the paints. Also, all too frequently, the slide will show the painting propped against a porch railing and a bicycle, and it gets lost in the clutter of the background.

Artists who have not yet learned to photograph their work would do well to find out how, if they plan to continue using slides to represent what they do. If you find that you cannot take good pictures, find someone who can and who would be willing to do it for you.

While Visual Artists Fellowships do not require a statement describing what you plan to do, there are other types of grants that artists can apply for from other agencies where a proposal is requested. (Many state and city arts councils now offer fellowship and project support for individual artists, as well as opportunities for public art commissions.) In that case, that applicant should be aware that simple, concise writing will be greatly appreciated. If the proposal meanders for paragraphs without getting to the point, no panelist will take an interest in it. It is a good idea to use the opening two sentences to lay out precisely what the project is about. After that you can go into details without worrying that the reader will get lost.

In case of grants that require a project description, make sure that what you are applying for is actually something you yourself want very much to do. Some people are clever at thinking up attractive proposals, but few of them have the kind of experience that is needed to do the project well. It is better not to waste your time gambling for grants or the time that panelists have to put into reading and evaluating them.

THE REVIEW PANEL

Who are the people who sit on panels and make decisions that affect artists? For the most part, they are artists who are known for having a particularly keen eye and who in the normal course of events see a great deal of artwork. Frequently they are artists who have received Endowment fellowships themselves. They are selected by the staff, based on input from previous panelists and a wide variety of other sources. That person and the program director compare names from many lists, aiming for a group who will be knowledgeable and compatible as well as reasonably representative of gender, geography, age, ethnic and aesthetic styles.

Panel recommendations must be approved by the chairman of the Endowment and by the National Council on the Arts. Aside from having had substantial experience in the field, panelists are also chosen for their openness to a broad spectrum of aesthetic approaches. In addition to that, considering how many hours and days go into the deliberations, it is essential that the panel have considerable stamina and a sense of humor. Frequently we look for panelists among curators of museums as well as artists, or directors of artists' organizations who work closely with practicing professionals and who understand their lives and their work.

The composition of the grants panels changes continually. With a rotation system, it is possible to bring many points of view to the evaluation. The way that a panel views work one year may be somewhat different the next. The rotation system also allows many more people to take part in the responsibility of making decisions that affect the development of art in this country. Visual Arts Fellowships panels rotate completely each funding cycle.

Receiving a fellowship makes a number of things possible for an artist. It basically means that an artist can drop everything and concentrate on artmaking for a year. It means being able to work without interruption and with as few distractions as a person can manage. It also means getting hold of materials and whatever else may be needed. To put it another way, the fellowship provides a chance for an artist to devote his or her time to doing major work at a point when that person is ready to take it on.

WHEN TO APPLY

It has been the policy of the Visual Arts Program to let the artist decide when he or she is ready to submit an application. Too often an artist applies before being anywhere nearly ready for the heavy competition that exists in such a review. Most applications are, in fact, submitted prematurely, when the work largely reflects the thinking and stylistic approach of another more experienced artist. All too frequently, applicants will try to compete even though their efforts fail to go beyond the obvious. In the past, the panels have not responded favorably to work that simply restates what is already known or lacks fresh, original insight.

Artists who are considering submitting their material for a fellowship review are advised to take timing into account and apply only when they feel they are ready.

Artists who are associated with an arts organization may want to consider other categories of funding that are described in the program guidelines. There are opportunities for communities to get assistance in commissioning works of art for public places. Assistance is also available for organizations that provide artists with facilities for producing new art or for exhibiting work. There is also a category whereby arts organizations can get matching funding for their publications, for seminars, residencies, or visiting artists' programs.

Other sources of funding that you may find helpful are local and state arts commissions. They too will have information and guidelines that you can get by calling them directly or by writing.

10 Financial Resources for Artists
Art in Public Places

Patricia Fuller

PATRICIA FULLER is a former administrator of the Art in Public Places grant category in the Visual Arts Program at the National Endowment for the Arts. While at the Endowment she also advised other federal agencies in their Art-in-Architecture programs. Prior to that she was coordinator of the City of Seattle's Art in Public Places Program and served as executive director of the Dade County, Florida, Art in Public Places Program. She is currently an independent consultant on public art.

During the past 20 years, interest and activity in public art have grown dramatically across the country. At the national level, the National Endowment for the Art's Art in Public Places grant category and the General Services Administration's Art-in-Architecture Program have heightened the visibility of art in public places and have broadened support and stimulus for increased activity at the state and local levels. Across the country, public art programs have been instituted at state, county, and local levels in increasing numbers.

PROGRAMS THAT SUPPORT
PUBLIC ART

The concept of "percent-for-art," which ensures the set-aside of a percentage of construction costs for artwork in public construction projects, has gained broad acceptance, and often public agencies set aside funds for art in major building projects as a matter of policy—even where legislation does not require it. Commissions for art in public places continue to be initiated and supported through the efforts of private organizations and citizens' groups as well.

The result has been a broadening range of opportunities for artists to work in public settings—at sites ranging from major downtown revitalization projects; to parks, transit facilities, and public buildings; to public school, college, and university campuses. As experience has been gained, an even greater range of media has been opened up for exploration. Light, sound, and a variety of nontraditional materials have been used by artists in public settings as contemporary extensions of public art.

This proliferation of activity at many levels and through various agencies has led to some confusion both in gaining information about, and in distinguishing among, the various programs. What follows is a brief guide to the major areas and types of support for art in public places, and some thoughts on some of the more important points to consider in undertaking public commissions.

ART IN PUBLIC PLACES

The Arts Endowment's Art in Public Places grant category, located in the Visual Arts Program, was initiated in 1967. Grants are made to public and private not-for-profit organizations so that they can sponsor commissions to artists in their communities. Eligible grantees include state and local governments or their agencies (such as arts commissions, housing and redevelopment authorities, and so on, or private not-for-profit agencies (such as ad hoc citizens' committees, universities, and colleges). Grants are given to match dollars that are raised, or that are set aside through percent-for-art, to support the commission of new works by living American artists. Applicants are responsible for securing the site and in most cases the artist(s) prior to requesting matching funds, although the agency increasingly encourages involvement of the artist in planning and design, and supports this activity through special planning grants. Collaboration of design professionals and visual artists in the planning and design of new public facilities has also been supported through special joint initiatives with the Design Arts Program. Applications are reviewed by a national panel of experts from the field for decisions on funding. The projects are carried out locally, each grantee being responsible for all the aspects of implementation once the grant is awarded.

For further information, see the Visual Arts Program's guidelines for the current fiscal year, available from the National Endowment for the Arts, 1100 Pennsylvania Avenue, N.W., Washington, D.C. 20506.

ART-IN-ARCHITECTURE

The General Services Administration's Art-in-Architecture Program was begun in 1963 by administrative directive, and it has continued without legislation, subject to periodic suspension, to the present. The GSA policy calls for setting aside .5 percent of the construction budget for each new federal building built by the agency. (Not all federal buildings are under GSA jurisdiction: post offices generally are not; whole federal office buildings and courthouses generally are.) The architect is encouraged to plan for works of art in the design, and when GSA is ready to bring an artist in (usually when the building is well into construction), the Arts Endowment is requested to convene a panel to nominate artists available for selection. The Visual Arts Program has the responsibility of appointing an ad hoc panel of experts in contemporary art—such as artists, critics, educators and curators. The architect sits as the fourth member of the panel. The group meets at the site and nominates between three and five artists, who are chosen on the basis of their past work and ability to deal with the site within the given budget. The GSA administrator then makes the final selection, and a member of the agency's Art-in-Architecture program staff invites the artist to visit the site—at the artist's expense. If the artist accepts the commission a contract is negotiated; otherwise the second-ranked artist is offered the job, and so on, until a contract is signed. The artist is then responsible for all costs—travel, expenses, materials, fabrication, and installation of the work, although site preparation costs are usually excluded.

GSA commissions are negotiated and administered by its Art-in-Architecture program staff based in Washington, D.C. The program maintains a registry of slides and biographical material of artists interested in being considered for these commissions. The registry is reviewed by the program staff prior to each on-site panel meeting, and slides of work by artists who might be appropriate are presented to the panel for consideration.

Further information on this program is available from the Director, Art-in-Architecture, General Services Administration, Washington, D.C. 20405.

VETERANS ADMINISTRATION
ART-IN-ARCHITECTURE PROGRAM

In 1979 the Veterans Administration, which constructs and operates medical facilities across the country, instituted a similar Art-in-Architecture program. Again, .5 percent of the construction budget—up to a maximum of $50,000—is set aside, and similar procedures for the selection of artists and commissions are followed. A registry of artists is also maintained at the Veterans Administration.

For further information, contact the director, Art-in-Architecture Program, Veterans Administration, 811 Vermont Avenue, N.W., Washington, D.C. 20402.

OTHER FEDERAL AGENCIES

Other federal agencies which do not generally undertake public works construction projects, but fund them at the local and state level, such as the Department of Transportation and the Department of Housing and Urban Development, have from time to time encouraged the inclusion of artwork as a local option. The Department of Transportation has published a guide to assist in planning for public art in such projects as transit facilities, airports, and highways: "Aesthetics in Transportation." It is available from the Superintendent of Documents, U.S. Government Printing Office, Washington, D.C. 20402.

Generally, plans for including artwork must be part of the initial application and budget submitted to the federal funding agency by the local community to be eligible for the application of federal funds received. Therefore it is the responsibility of local arts groups and interested citizens to become involved in the planning of such projects and to ensure that artwork is included in the funding request, or that at least expenditure of funds received for artwork is not precluded.

PERCENT-FOR-ART PROGRAMS

Percent-for-art legislation has created more than 100 ongoing programs at state and local levels to commission art for public places. The actual percentage of construction funds set aside and the procedures that are followed vary widely among jurisdictions. Access to information about these programs and current commissions has been difficult to obtain, although better dissemination of information to make more artists aware of such programs and commissions seems to be the trend. Many of these programs maintain registries of interested artists and advertise commissions regionally in arts publications. Some limit eligibility to artists within the jurisdiction or the surrounding region.

Current information about public art programs can be requested through the National Assembly of State Arts Agencies (NASAA), 1010 Vermont Ave., N.W., Washington, D.C. 20005. (NASAA provides information for programs at the state level.)

For programs at the local level, information is available through the National Assembly of Local Arts Agencies (NALAA), 1420 K St., N.W., Washington, D.C. 20005. After receiving the information, you can then write to the individual programs and ask to be put on their mailing lists.

A listing of over 200 public art programs nationally is included in the publication *Going Public: A Field Guide to Developments in Art in Public Places.* Published in cooperation with the NEA Visual Arts Program, it is available from Arts Extension Service, Division of Continuing Education, University of Massachusetts, Amherst, Mass. 01003.

PUBLIC COMMISSIONS

Public commissions offer the opportunity to work on a scale, and with materials, that might otherwise be impossible. They also give artists the chance to explore new possibilities for sites, as well as for the relationship of their work to the matrix of the built environment. Commissions also bring the process of creating a work into a public context, and the public process inherently entails considerations and restraints that are not encountered in a studio, museum, or gallery or in situations involving private and corporate patronage.

The procedures for selecting artists vary considerably among different programs, but three basic methods are in general use: (1) open competition, (2) limited or invitational competition, and (3) direct selection. Many publicly legislated programs use open competition, and some use open competitions exclusively. Usually a prospectus announces the competition and describes the site, the amount of the commission, and the parameters of the project. The announcement also invites proposals from artists. (If specifications for proposals are not given, it is important to check what restrictions may apply to size and materials, and whether models are expected.)

Open competitions are generally used on the assumption that they will reach the broadest possible range of artists and therefore offer the widest choice to those who make the decisions. Many artists, however, have pointed out the drawbacks to this process. Only artists living near the site of the proposed project can actually visit and become familiar with its limitations and possibilities as the basis for a considered and feasible proposal. There is also no compensation for the time and materials an artist invests in the proposal. There have also been problems when proposals have been returned damaged, and in many cases proposals have not been returned at all! (It's a good idea to make sure your submissions are insured.) For these reasons, many artists are unwilling to make the considerable investment on speculation which is required by the open competition process.

The limited or invitational competition presents fewer drawbacks. Normally, between three and five artists are initially selected to prepare proposals for the commission. Many sponsors advertise and invite the submission of slides to be considered by the selection panel at the initial screening step. This system provides the same access to artists without requiring the speculative investment in time and materials which an open competition does. Each invited artist is normally paid an honorarium—plus expenses—to cover the costs of visiting the site and developing a proposal. It may also be possible for the invited artist to renegotiate the requirements named in the proposal by requesting, for instance, the elimination of maquettes and the presentation of only drawings. Hidden costs can often make what seems like a generous fee less than adequate. It is important to make clear at the outset whether developing the proposal will require such things as an engineering analysis of the site. In many cases necessary information, such as architectural plans and engineering drawings, already exists. In that case, it is the responsibility of the sponsor to supply such information for the artist's use. Otherwise, the proposal development fee should be adequate to meet those costs. Even if documentation of engineering and cost feasibility is not required, it is a very good idea to have those analyses made to ensure that the work, if commissioned, can be executed within the budget. In the long run, it can be well worth the extra expense. Ideally, the sponsor should pay these costs through a design development contract following approval of a preliminary proposal, if the initial fee was not calculated to cover them.

Direct selection is the third method of choosing artists that is commonly used. Normally, the selection committee meets at the site and considers a number of artists, finally agreeing on the one whom they feel is best suited for the particular project. As with the invitational competition, sponsors may first invite the submission of slides by artists for the consideration of the panel, or they may draw on available slide registries, or rely solely on panelist nominations. The chosen artist is then invited to the site, and it is reasonable to require that travel be at the sponsor's expense. If the artist accepts, a contract should then be negotiated for the commission.

NEGOTIATING CONTRACTS

Once the artist agrees to accept the commission, a written contract should be negotiated between the artist and the sponsor before work on a proposal is begun. The function of a contract should be to make clear and equitable the responsibilities and expectations of each party. Good contracts lessen the possibility of misunderstanding and disputes which could jeopardize completion of the project or lead to costly legal proceedings. In all cases, the advice of a lawyer is recommended in the design of an equitable and workable agreement. Presented here are some major points to consider in contracting for a public art commission.

Budget

Usually the artist's commission must cover the cost of materials, fabrication, transportation, installation, and the artist's fees and expenses. The sponsor is usually responsible for preparation of the site (foundation, landscaping, water supply, etc.), and in some cases the sponsor may provide or arrange for donation of materials, fabrication or labor, and equipment for installation. These responsibilities should be clarified at the outset and set down in the agreement, so that the artist can prepare a reliable estimate of all costs during the proposal process.

Proposal

A preliminary proposal is generally required as the first step, if it was not already used as the basis for selection. Usually a portion of the commission amount is allocated as the proposal fee and is paid on submission of the proposal by the artist. As with the invitational competition, it should be adequate to cover costs of travel to the site and the materials and time invested.

The process for review and the agency or individual(s) responsible for approval of the proposal should also be designated to avoid later confusion and delay. A time limit may also be determined for this process, as well as the steps to be taken in the event of rejection. The artist may want to reserve the right to submit an alternative proposal.

Normally, the artist will want to retain ownership of the proposal drawings and/or maquette, as well as copyright to them. The sponsor then receives photographic or other reproductions.

The proposal should include a budget, which realistically estimates all anticipated costs, including the artist's time and expenses.

Timetable

All parties should agree upon a timetable and set up a procedure for extending the deadlines if problems should arise. Construction schedules should be consulted if the commission site is under construction. Difficulties in obtaining materials and labor, and construction delays, are typical problems, and should be taken into consideration. The contract should make it easy to amend this timetable by mutual agreement, as it is often in the best interests of the project to do so.

Schedule of Payments

Normally payments to the artist are made sequentially, and often a substantial advance is required to purchase materials, or cover other upfront costs and time. The final payment is usually made on completion of the installation. Intermediary payments should be linked to stages of completion, not to dates.

Dealers' Fees

The National Council on the Arts (the presidentially appointed advisory committee to the National Endowment for the Arts) has approved the policy that a dealer's fee should not exceed 10 percent of the artist's fee for commissions funded in part through the Endowment's Art in Public Places grants. This is widely used as a guideline in the field, although agreements between artists and dealers vary widely. Most often, if commissions are covered in such agreements, they are handled differently from gallery sales. In fact, many artists act independently in the area of public commissions or have other agents handle their public commissions. It is important to agree on the dealer's role at the outset, particularly if it has not been previously established.

Other matters between artist and sponsor that should be clarified at the outset and that may become part of the agreement include

- *Access to information and cooperation,* if the commission is part of a site under design or construction. Coordination with architects, engineers, contractors, and others becomes critical in planning and executing the work. It is the sponsor's responsibility to facilitate this coordination and to make pertinent plans and documents available to the artist. Access to the site while under construction should be facilitated by the sponsor as well.

- *Care and maintenance of the work.* This is also the long-term responsibility of the sponsor, and procedures should be established at the outset. The artist may in turn be required to address problems of maintenance in the design of the work and provide detailed specifications for proper care of the work.

The contract itself cannot cover all aspects of a project, and there are certain broad responsibilities that are difficult to define but equally crucial to the success of public commissions. Public information and relations with the community at large must be effectively handled to avoid any misunderstandings or controversy that might jeopardize or delay the project. Like fundraising, this is the responsibility of the sponsoring group. A project for which an effective strategy for fundraising and public information has not been adequately planned is a risky undertaking. While the artist should not be placed in the position of soliciting funds or defending the project, participating in a dialogue with the public is important to inform and develop support in the community. Sponsoring agencies may plan activities, such as symposia or lectures or public meetings which involve the artist, or they may ask the artist to exhibit work. Expectations as to the nature of these activities should also be discussed early on, and the artist and sponsor should be in agreement. The assumption is not that public discussion is negative or should be avoided; quite the opposite—this dialogue is an important aspect of art in public places. It is clear that destructive controversy can be avoided by those sponsors and artists who work together to inform the community about the planned piece of artwork, and who invite discussion of it.

The definitive information currently available to artists on contracts for public art is the New York City Bar Association's booklet "Commissioning a Work of Public Art: An Annotated Model Agreement." This is an annotated model contract, designed to cover a conventional situation in which an artist is commissioned to design, execute, and install a work at an existing site. It is a model of clarity, and the annotations provide good rationale for the provisions, which can be of value in the negotiating process. Insurance and liability, indemnity, ownership of documents and models, copyright, artists' rights, and the integrity of the work are all covered, and the issues are explained in the annotations. While it is not specifically designed to cover a design consultation, design team, or collaborative process, most of its basic provisions can be adapted. The publication is available from the American Council for the Arts, 570 Seventh Avenue, New York, N.Y. 10018.

11 Financial Resources for Artists
Grantsmanship

Fred Eversley
Joanne Gigliotti

FRED EVERSLEY, of Venice, California, has been a self-supporting sculptor for 20 years. His first major one-man show took place at the Whitney Museum in New York in 1970. From 1977 to 1980 he was artist-in-residence at the Smithsonian Institution. Among other projects, he produced a 40-foot sculpture installed in front of Miami International Airport in 1980 and was one of three California sculptors (including Freda Koblick of San Francisco and Bruce Beasley of Oakland) to produce the first major commissions at the San Francisco International Airport.

JOANNE GIGLIOTTI is senior program coordinator of the Studio Arts Department at the Resident Associate Program of the Smithsonian Institution. She was founder and director of The Fine Arts Connection, an agency devoted to the promotion of the visual arts, and has worked with the Pennsylvania Council of the Arts.

INTRODUCTION

Many artists today may still dream the dream of long ago—to be funded in order to live, create, and produce their art. They may still believe that a true artist is sought after, found, and awarded the opportunity to create.

Sculptor Fred Eversley's career began in this manner. He received a grant from the National Endowment for the Arts for which he had not applied. Today, however, Eversley believes that artists must not only seek out their own funding, but also must be adept at marketing their own art to the art world, and to the general public. While this approach may not be right for all artists, it reflects a growing need for artists today to understand better how the art world works—and how they can make it work for them. Grants are but one source of funding available to today's artists; to be knowledgeable in this arena is to be aware of how the art world works.

WHAT IS A GRANT?

A grant is a gift of money (not to be returned) given by a foundation to an individual or a nonprofit organization [one that qualifies under IRS Tax Code Section 501(c)3] for a specific purpose. According to the National Endowment for the Arts, "The purpose of a grant is to support the artist of exceptional talent and demonstrated ability and to provide the public with the opportunity to experience the best of American contemporary artwork."

Foundations and corporations (through their "foundation" or "PR" division) are usually looking for a project that affects a wide audience; an educational component is implied or specific. The grantors' goal is often to nurture creativity while promoting public awareness of the corporation or foundation itself.

For example, an individual artist who wants money to take a year to paint in the desert, who can't guarantee a final product, and who wants to keep the results when the project is completed will have a hard time obtaining a grant. However, a project with tangible, measurable results and visibility will have an easier chance to be funded—for example, a performing arts production of a play aired on national television funded by a grant by Mobil or a large traveling museum exhibition funded by Phillip Morris which is seen by a large number of people in many cities.

WHO SHOULD APPLY?

Know yourself. The axiom may be overused, but in arts grantsmanship, it's important. Not all artists are suited to applying for grants.

For example, what kind of art do you do? Is your artwork the kind that would be placed in a corporation's offices? Could it be in homes, hotels, or bank lobbies? Could you find a broad market for your art? Or, is your work so personal, controversial, or statement oriented that such commercial venues are not an option for you? If you have a talent for which the world will not now pay, you should not try to fit into the business world. The rejection is real—and perhaps insurmountable, even with persistence. You may be a perfect candidate for a grant, and your time, when not creating art, may be best spent developing grant—writing skills. As an artist, you may be what Benny Andrews, a past director of the Visual Arts Program at the National Endowment for the Arts, calls a "poet."

What is your temperament? Are you an extrovert who would enjoy promoting your own work? Or, are you an introvert who would rather have either an agent do it for you or quietly write a support request than face the business side of the art world? What is your financial situation? Do you have skills to earn a high wage on a regular basis? Could you borrow seed money from your family (to accomplish certain beginning steps—for example, producing slides or printed materials for your own promotion)? In other words, do you really need a grant to sustain your work as an artist? Depending upon your temperament and the kind of artist you are, a grant may be seed money, or may be your sole source of sustenance.

HOW TO APPROACH A FOUNDATION

Make sure your proposal and purpose are within the scope of the foundation's funding interests. Approaching the appropriate foundation and using the right format and wording as well as persistence in this endeavor are crucial. The Foundation Center (see the following resource list) may help you target some foundations. Research can also be done at the Foundation Center itself. Call on some of the foundations to request application guidelines. They will also send you the most recent annual contribution report. Are the projects they fund similar to yours? Corporate sponsors may be interested in funding a project or adding to their collections—usually the latter. You may even know personally, and may have overlooked, someone who could be helpful to you.

Last, a request for a meeting or a telephone conversation with a foundation officer, though sometimes difficult to obtain, is the best. They may agree to review your request and make suggestions.

After you have decided that the effort is worthwhile, you should clearly state what your goals and objectives are: For what purpose you will use the money? Will it be used for supplies and equipment? Or, will it be used to finish an almost completed project? A thoughtfully written description (clear, concise, and brief) of your proposed use of time, money, and so on is one of your most important assets.

ADDITIONAL RESOURCES
AND PUBLICATIONS

The Support Centers of America: New York, Washington, D.C., San Francisco, Chicago, and others

Foundation grants to individuals

The Foundation Directory Published by the Foundation Center 79 5th Avenue, Dept. EC New York, N.Y. 10003

International Directory of Corporate Art Collections Published by Art News and International Art Alliance, Inc.

Money for Artists, A Guide to Grants and Awards to Individual Artists Published by the American Council for the Arts

FUNDING SOURCES

John Simon Guggenheim Memorial Foundation Park Avenue New York, N.Y. 10016 Prestigious grant; fall deadline

Council for International Exchange of Scholars (Fulbright) 11 Dupont Circle Washington, D.C. 20036–1257

Pollock-Krasner Foundation, Inc. P.O. Box 4957 New York, N.Y. 10185 Grants to individuals for paintings, drawings, and sculpture

National Endowment for the Arts 1100 Pennsylvania Avenue Washington, D.C. $5,000–$20,000 grants The NEA also gives money to state art agencies, which in turn funds their state needs.

The Foundation Center 79 Fifth Avenue New York, N.Y. 10003 Offices in various other areas

The MacArthur Foundation Chicago, Ill, Very prestigious; by nomination only

12 | Joining Together
Artists' Unions

Olive Mosier

OLIVE MOSIER is executive director of National Artists Equity.

On May 29, 1947, the first meeting of Artists' Equity Association was held. The minutes from this meeting record that

> the variety of aesthetic thinking, the forming of cliques, who in turn fought each other, the lack of unity, and organization for the economic welfare of artists, were all good reasons for establishing Equity. . . . Equity was formed by groups who get together to function for the artists' benefit, to relieve the artists' insecurity in the economic world. The artists' compensation should be on par with his contribution. Many careers have not survivéd because of time wasted fighting unfair conditions. Equity intends to protect the artists' rights. By forming this group, the need for individual fighting will be alleviated. There will be more copyright protection, substantial welfare funds, laws revised for the special position of the artist, a decent code of ethics, and no aesthetic discrimination. Equity will be . . . devoted to better and more just compensation, officers will be provisional, and a ruling clique will be an impossibility.

This quotation comes from the minutes of a meeting of the first ongoing organization created by professional visual artists to grapple with the fundamental economic and professional problems which had been plaguing the artist in America. Local, national, and international groups have been and continue to be formed nationwide to address the unique concerns of visual artists. But of those organizations still in existence, Artists' Equity—now called National Artists Equity (NAE)—was the first and remains the country's only aesthetically and politically nonpartisan national organization dedicated to representing all American visual artists, whether or not they are members of NAE. This democratic approach has its roots in the state of the arts in America at the time of NAE's formation. Artists in most disciplines, from acting to writing to music to the visual arts, found themselves in a political atmosphere during the 1930s and 1940s where anything from a certain art form to a particular artist or group of artists could be labeled as "communist." Combined with this was the perception that labor-oriented issues were often linked with communism and "left-wing" ideas. Many artists' groups were newly formed or forming during this period—the Dramatists' Guild in 1912, Actors' Equity Association formed in 1913, the Screen Writers Guild in 1933, the American Federation of Musicians in 1896, to name a few—had been formed in the tradition of the trade union movement. Each of these groups coalesced as representatives of workers who needed a way in which to negotiate with their employers fair economic and professional treatment. Artists in these professions most often had no permanent employer but went where there were opportunities. Collective action on a national scale helped to prevent artists who were competing for jobs from negotiating as individuals for less remuneration in order to win employment. However, to many Americans, such protection had socialist overtones.

Visual artists, therefore, were not alone in facing these issues, the accumulated effect of which helped to spur the creation of artists' unions. One such event occurred in 1946, when the U.S. State Department's Office of International Information and Cultural Affairs purchased for the government 79 paintings by contemporary American artists to comprise an exhibit entitled "Advancing American Art." The exhibit, organized in response to requests from American missions abroad, was to illustrate the newest development of American art and was first shown at New York's Metropolitan Museum of Art. It was then divided into two exhibits, one to open in Paris and the other to tour through South and Central America. At the conclusion, the paintings were to be hung permanently in American government buildings abroad. Among those artists represented were Adolph Gottlieb, Ben Shahn, Robert Gwathmey, and Yasuo Kuniyoshi.

Controversy, however, surrounded the touring exhibit from the outset. Several groups protested the cultural value of any exhibition which was "so strongly marked with the radicalism of the new trends of European art. This is not indigenous to our soil. . . . There had been widespread rumors that the (State) Department was honeycombed with leftists. Whatever merit there is in this belief, certainly, this selection was not made by any rightists." This protest and others similar to it (e.g., "those paintings in the collection that try to tell a story at all give the impression that America is a drab and ugly place, filled with drab and ugly people. They are definitely leftish painting. . . ." And a photo caption in *Journal American,* "This is by Byron Browne and is called 'Still Life in Red, Yellow and Green.' We hope we have it right side up, or does it matter?") reached Capitol Hill and resulted in the tour's premature end. The work was warehoused in New York until, in 1948, the paintings were sold under the auspices of the War Assets Administration by closed competitive bid, with most going to universities and colleges. Subsequent debates in Congress reflect that the recalled art exhibit was used as a way in which to indicate the degree of leftist influence in the State Department.

The incidents surrounding the State Department art exhibit were not isolated, however. For example, in 1949, an art show organized for St. Alban's Naval Hospital in Queens, New York, was accused by a member of Congress of being "subversive." The *Congressional Record* of the 81st Congress contains a speech by Michigan Representative George A. Dondero entitled "Modern Art

Shackled to Communism." Dondero attacks not only the artists and artwork included in the hospital's show but a variety of art forms and noted artists as well:

> Cubism aims to destroy by designed disorder. Futurism aims to destroy by the machine myth. Expressionism aims to destroy by aping the primitive and insane. Klee, one of its three founders, went to the insane asylums for his inspiration. Abstractionism aims to destroy by the creation of brainstorms. Surrealism aims to destroy by the denial of reason.

Dondero goes on to name Picasso, Braque, Leger, Duchamp, Chagall, Miro, Dali, Kuniyoshi, *The New York Times, Artnews,* Cambridge's Fogg Art Museum, Chicago's Art Institute, and many others as part of the art world's communist conspiracy.

During this same period, murals painted by Anton Refregier for the Rincon Annex Post Office in San Francisco depicting incidents in California history, although approved by a jury appointed the National Fine Arts Commission, came under attack for supposedly containing subversive and anti-American messages. Several organizations tried to have the murals repainted.

These examples illustrate the conditions under which visual artists were laboring at a time when Americans were just beginning to recognize their own cultural heritage and not continually looking to Europe for art and artists. In 1908, a New York exhibition funded by and featuring the work of several artists of the "Ash Can School" had been one of the first to present work successfully which broke away from the European academic tradition. Not only were the crowds receptive, but the work sold well. This set in motion a push first by artists and then by people and institutions of the private and public sectors to improve artists' possibilities to earn their livelihood through sales of their art. For artists, these efforts most often took the form of artists' cooperatives and artist-owned galleries. The advantages of such endeavors included the artists' ability to pool resources, coordinate promotion and publicity efforts, and control sales commission costs as well as create increased occasions to exhibit and thus sell their artwork.

The public sector initiative did not take place until 1933, but may not have begun even then had artists not been visibly creating their own opportunities. A variety of government bureaus, such as the Treasury Relief Art Program, the Public Works of Art Program, and Farm Security Administration, employed artists in national projects as a way of demonstrating government support of the arts during the Depression. One of the first efforts was the institution of a mural and sculpture program, run by the U.S. Treasury Department, which used 1 percent of public building expenditures to embellish federal and publicly owned buildings throughout the country.

Most notable of the federal programs were those of the Works Progress Administration/Federal Arts Project (WPA/FAP). WPA/FAP programs were designed specifically to offer financial relief to artists by employing them in some capacity in which their creative talents could be used for the public good. Painters, for instance, were commissioned to supply pictures for small-town museums. The visual artists' movement toward trade unionism began during this era, with issues such as wages, job security, and working conditions being negotiated through collective bargaining with the federal government as the artists' employer. Such an organization was the Artists' Union, which was instrumental in assisting artists achieve eligibility for participating in WPA/FAP projects and in overseeing the running of the programs. Yet, by 1936, as the government began eliminating its art employment programs, the Artists' Unions and similar organizations lost their impetus and folded over the next five years.

The American visual artist of the 1940s and 1950s, therefore, continued to have difficulty in getting his work exhibited and sold. There were too few galleries to accommodate the number of artists producing. Also, not all dealers were willing to sell contemporary work, and those who did often could do so only at very low prices. A survey conducted in 1945 by *Artnews* magazine found that only one living American artist, Rafael Soyer, was able to earn enough money from the sale of his art not to need an additional job for income.

It was, therefore, in this era of mixed signals—government support and government repression, public pride and public outrage—that Artists' Equity was organized in 1947. And some of the conditions which prompted NAE's formation are still being confronted by professional visual artists today. An artist living and working in America can expect to be unemployed more often and for longer periods of time than any other similarly educated professional. This means that artists most often must work at another job to supplement their art income, a job that in turn severely limits the amount of time which can be spent creating art. As a result, artists earn less in a lifetime from their art than any other professional workers earn from their careers. Additionally, American artists work in a country where they lack appropriate protective legislation. For instance, at this writing only 6 states have moral rights laws, 20 states have consignment laws, and 1 state has a resale royalty law. The effectiveness of these laws differs from state to state. So, for example, an artist residing in Oregon, where the consignment law is a fairly comprehensive one, may find considerably less legislative protection when he or she sends work to a gallery in Texas or no legislative protection when work is sent to New Hampshire. It is because of these conditions that many artists' unions have long worked for national legislation in the various areas of the business of art.

First, however, it is necessary to understand the definition of "visual artists' unions." For visual artists, a union is defined as an organization formed to address the professional, economic, and social concerns particular to their lives. A visual artists' union differs from the aforementioned unions such as Actors' Equity in that it seeks to protect artists in the variety of circumstances under which they labor as opposed to overseeing employer/employee relations. For instance, an artist commissioned to produce a work is facing conditions different from these of an artist who has independently produced a piece and wishes to sell it through exhibiting at a gallery. Visual artists' unions do not seek to set wages, although some do give artists guidelines, but instead work to assure the fair treatment of artists in all areas of the profession. This is achieved through legislative and public policy initiatives and through educating artists as to their rights and responsibilities as independent businesspeople. While an artists' union may sponsor exhibitions, it was not formed for that purpose or for any kind of marketing or promotion. A visual artists' union is an artist-run organization whose constituency is exclusively or primarily individual visual artists.

Most artists' unions are organized as 501(c) (3) nonprofit charitable institutions, which sometimes limits their amount of hands-on legislative involvement (NAE is a 501(c) (6) professional membership organization which has no such restriction).

The range of these organizations is as varied as visual artists themselves: the National Conference of Artists (NCA) was founded in 1959 and works for Afro-American artists in the United States; the Women's Caucus for Art (WCA) was founded in 1972 and is dedicated to winning parity for women working in the visual arts profession; the International Sculpture Center (ISC) was formed in 1960 and seeks to address the specific needs of sculptors; the Chicago Artists' Coalition (CAC) was founded in 1974 to unify artists in order to improve conditions for Chicago-area artists; the Graphic Artists Guild was formed in 1967 by graphic artists trying to improve industry standards, professional ethics, and pricing terms; the Boston Visual Artists Union (BVAU) was founded in 1970 by artists who wanted to increase contact and improve conditions for that city's artists; NOVA (New Organization for the Visual Arts) is located in Cleveland, Ohio, and works in the areas of communications, services, and education for emerging and established artists in Northeast Ohio; and the American Society of Magazine Photographers (ASMP) was created in 1944 to further the interests of established photographers and serve as a clearinghouse of photographic information. These are a few examples of the various interests for which visual artists see a need for collective action. Visual artists also have established unions around the needs of craftspeople, Hispanics, Native Americans and the deaf.

Visual artists' unions work in areas ranging from national legislation to public policy, to help the individual artist. For example, the Women's Caucus for Art, headquartered in Philadelphia, has been key in its information gathering in areas of education and sex discrimination in the visual arts. It works nationally to promote women's studies and research/creativity in the visual arts both inside and outside the confines of traditional educational institutions. WCA also facilitates communications among women artists; promotes the nonsexist, nonracist inclusive approach to the formulation and understanding of the visual arts; and seeks to have the contributions of women artists recognized. WCA counts among its major accomplishments a presence of tenured feminist faculty in academic institutions, an increase in the number and breadth of courses, texts, and programs which feature women artists, and greater numbers of women artists able to work successfully. WCA also produces several publications, and in 1988 opened archives at Rutgers University in New Jersey to establish and make available WCA and members' material for scholarly investigation.

In its work for the artists in the Greater Chicago area, the Chicago Artists' Coalition has devised programs which reach beyond the city and into Illinois and the Midwest. CAC presents lectures on the business of being an artist; maintains a slide registry and a job referral service; publishes a number of resource books, including a guide to exhibition spaces in Chicago and Illinois; and provides comprehensive information on issues such as taxes, artists' rights, agreements and contracts, copyrights, live/work space, and grants and fellowships. CAC cites its overall success as lying in targeting and concentrating on the needs of concerns of visual artists and addressing them in a supportive and timely manner.

The International Sculpture Center, based in Washington, D.C., has members in approximately 60 countries, although most live in the United States. ISC produces the only international publication devoted to the interests of contemporary sculptors, including technical, cultural, legal, and aesthetic issues and opportunities, events, commissions, and exhibitions. ISC also maintains a computerized slide registry and provides exhibition services (coordinating, managing, curating, installing, and touring) to museums, collectors, and others for all types of exhibitions. Other ISC programs include conferences, workshops, symposia, and so on, which directly address current issues and ideas in contemporary sculpture. ISC counts its computerized slide registry, established in 1987, as one of its most important programs as it brings artists together with those who buy artwork. In the search for new work, emerging artists are frequently overlooked, and manual slide registries can easily become out of date, regionally focused, and inaccessible. ISC believes that its computerized slide registry addresses the inadequacies of manual registries and will provide greater opportunities for a wider range of artists.

Deaf Artists of America (DAA), located in Rochester, New York, was founded in 1985 to help bring support and recognition to America's deaf and hard-of-hearing artists since its organizers found that many artists' groups do not make their programs accessible to the hearing-impaired. DAA has built a reference library with information on nearly 300 deaf artists, sponsors a biennial conference for hearing-impaired artists, and provides technical assistance to hearing-impaired artists. It is in the process of forming a slide library, an artists' registry, an employment referral service, a speakers' bureau, and other programs suited to the needs of deaf artists. DAA also hopes eventually to establish a National Gallery of the Deaf that would showcase the contributions and talents of America's deaf artists.

The Boston Visual Artists Union, which grew out of meetings held by artists who were dissatisfied with the opportunities available to them in Boston, is structured to address those concerns through a number of standing committees. These include studio space, legislation, exhibitions, ethical practices, education, materials, slide registry, and job referrals. A committee may be formed at any time by any member for the examination of any issue considered significant.

National Artists Equity also has worked in policy areas. Based in Washington, D.C., it has local chapters across the country, and is governed by an all-artist volunteer board of directors. NAE seeks to strengthen the professional knowledge and business effectiveness of artists by providing a forum for discussion and information. It also provides services which improve the circumstances of its members by either decreasing costs or increasing income. For example, by providing group health, life, and fine art insurance, art magazine and book discounts, and a debt collection service, NAE decreases some expenses for its members. But NAE's primary mission is to be an advocate for artists by working for legislation and public policy that protect artists and their work. While NAE has focused state and local levels to secure certain legislative initiatives (e.g., public art programs, consignment, moral rights, and resale royalty), its board of directors believes that adequate protection for artists can best be achieved through national channels. Although finding congressional representatives willing to work actively on behalf of the relatively small constituency of visual artists is often difficult, NAE was instrumental in creating a certain momentum during the mid-1980s to address issues such as national protection to artists in the areas of copyright, moral rights, resale royalties, and labeling artists' supplies for safe use.

Most artists' unions provide their members with group health and life insurance programs, health maintenance organizations, and, often, insurance coverage for artwork. Many, along with offering discounts for art magazines and/or books, regularly publish a newsletter or periodical containing information pertinent to their constituency's professional lives. And the Foundation for the Community of Artists in New York has established the first national credit union for artists. In those instances when a visual artists' union sponsors an exhibition, it does so without regard to stylistic preference, extent of experience, or degree of sales success.

Protection through collective action remains the common denominator of the visual artists' unions. As previously illustrated, protection can be achieved through legislative efforts, through public policy initiatives, through specially designed services, and through educational programs. While protection is often thought of in terms of legislation and public policy, the services and educational programs offered by visual artists' unions are no less important. Services such as group health insurance provide lower-cost insurance to artists who often, as self-employed businesspeople, would have no other group outlet for insurance; yet, obtaining health insurance as an individual is extremely costly. Many artists would doubtlessly go without health insurance coverage were it not offered by visual artists' unions. And disability insurance programs are just now beginning to be made available (with Women's Caucus for Art and National Artists' Equity being among the first to do so). Fine art insurance protects an artist from the loss of or damage to his or her work while it is in the studio, in transit, or on exhibition (particularly important since exhibition spaces often are not insured). And visual artists' unions have long recognized the need for artists to have liability insurance and have worked to create them, although at this writing none have been successful due to industrywide cutbacks in liability insurance coverage. Informational publications and seminars also offer artists protection. They give artists the tools necessary to carry on successfully as professionals and not be exploited. Artists learn about employment and exhibiting opportunities as well as the need for contracts, legal resources, and fair practices. These programs are also the way in which many artists learn of the legislation and public policy protection that has been enacted or is pending.

The successful visual artists' unions are those that are continually reevaluating their mission and updating their policies and programs as the business of art and the protection needed by visual artists change. Their ability to read the changes and the needs comes from the fact that artists who are working in the field are responsible for governing the organizations. No one not involved in the day-to-day struggle to live as an artist in America could possibly stay attuned to the professional climate and respond to the profession's needs.

The definition of equity, as in artists' equity, is the assurance of a free and reasonable conformity to accepted standards of right, law, and justice without prejudice, favoritism, or fraud. Not all visual artists' unions have the word equity in their names, but achieving equity, which is really just another word for protection, is the goal they all seek.

PART THREE

MARKETING

It's impossible to communicate what one can do as a businessman in art. I don't think you can separate art and business in that way. By being a sculptor I run a shop that has to have a certain kind of business logic— people, payroll, materials, budget—but other than that, I'm against advice that per- verts the thinking that there is business and there is art. There isn't.

Robert Graham

13 || Career and the Artist

Henry Geldzahler

HENRY GELDZAHLER is the former Commissioner of Cultural Affairs of the City of New York. Prior to his appointment, Mr. Geldzahler served as curator of the Department of 20th Century Art at the Metropolitan Museum and Director of Visual Arts at the National Endowment for the Arts.

Picasso, as he so often did, said it best: an artist must be two people—one who knows how to paint, one who knows when to stop. We all know the old antiabstraction anecdote about the chimpanzee who, given paper and colors, does a creditable "painting," which is subsequently entered in the local art show and wins a prize. What is less well known is that, left alone, the chimp will continue to apply color to the paper until he gets restless, then will roll the paper into a ball and eat it. What of those chimpanzee paintings the popular press loves so often? Ah, they were snatched away from the chimp by a curator at the moment he or she thought they were most ripe and ready. Who then is the artist?

Picasso was one man who knew when to paint and when to stop. The chimp knows how to paint; the curator when to stop. Picasso is alone; the other two form a team, the nucleus of what in European and Latin American art of the 1960s and 1970s was called an *equipe* or *equipo*.

The artist must often feel like a chump, dependent on the whims, commercial sense, altruism, and general apathy of others—dealers, curators, deans. The system works, of course, but not well and not for everybody.

The question broached by this publication is this: Can a handbook on artists and career be useful? The answer is *yes,* when it comes to such technical matters as taxes, materials, apprenticeship programs, and legal rights. *No,* if the question is how can I make better art. The answer still lies in the private sector, in fact, with the artist. No semigovernmental tract can possibly help.

THE REAL QUESTION

All technical questions such as what laws govern the establishment of a cooperative gallery and when artists can be held liable can be addressed by specialists. Even such quasi-personal matters as how best to present my work, whether to make appointments with dealers through their secretaries, and with which ones is it better to drop in, unannounced, before rather than after lunch, can be answered. But in my opinion all such considerations are rococo frippery compared to the bare and basic query: How good is my *art* (not my career), how

158

original, to what extent is it consonant with my intention, what is my ambition for it, and does it have (this must be asked as diligently of abstraction) redeeming social value, does society have any need of it or use for it? These are the questions that hurt.

THE INFLUENCE OF THE ARTIST

The influence of the artist on American life and style goes far beyond his work as seen in the art gallery and museum. In the past hundred years the artist, particularly the visual artist, has been the pioneer in many things other than the world of depicted forms; most obviously he has led the real estate developer by pointing out to the wealthy that poverty and disuse can make a stretch of coast or a deteriorating neighborhood romantic and desirable. We need only list St. Germain des Pres, the Hamptons, Provincetown, London's Chelsea, Sausalito, Cuernavaca, St. Migel Allende, and in New York the West Village and, most recently and dramatically, SoHo and Tribeca.

In each case a hardy group of artists saw beauty and practicality in buildings and prospects invisible to others. In the case of SoHo, from the early 1960s, artists lived and worked out of abandoned spaces in loft buildings increasingly emptied of their light manufacturers. Some few had enough vision or cash to buy their buildings, or as sophistication grew, their co-op. With the growth of social and peer pressure to live and work in this geographically restricted area, prices rose, and landlords began to encourage artists to rent and renovate. Art galleries, boutiques, and restaurants came next. By the early 1970s, prams, often with fathers at the helm, became common in this so recently light manufacturing district. The career of the artist merged insensibly with that of the minor real estate entrepreneur.

Something similar and, after the fact, equally predictable, happened in the blocks that surround the Lincoln Center complex, a project that was completed by the middle of the 1960s. Once again cultural activity became the lodestone for real estate development. Apartment houses, restaurant rows, and gentrification followed in much the same way as, a decade later, the Marais, a seventeenth-century neighborhood in Paris around Beauborg, began to be rehabilitated and renovated.

For the artist, even one who interests himself only in what goes on in his own studio, alertness to the ways in which his neighborhood, or one he is contemplating moving to, is likely to change can save him the anguish of sudden surprise and displacement. The signs are apparent and easily noticed; count the fancy delis, and if there is more than one, buy your loft or start looking elsewhere. You don't want to fix up yet another place for a landlord or for the next owner.

On mature reflection I withdraw my earlier scowling attitude toward the subject of artist and career. While it is true that I feel altogether too much energy is wasted these days on the careerist and therefore is unavailable to the artist, there clearly are areas in which guidance of the kind available through experts, handbooks, and panels can be helpful.

I have however observed that it is not the cunning careerist who wins in the end. It is the careful nurturer who tills his garden daily and grows the most natural, organic, and unforced flowers—the most beautiful ones and those most aesthetically "necessary" and satisfying. A successful career is, most often, the result of countless decisions made along the way, decisions that always intuitively support the art and, without ignoring life-style, give it the weight it deserves. Success is a reward. Making honest art is the goal. In the short run, career strategies can appear successful. In the long run, only the art remains as witness to a life.

14 Entering the Mainstream

Julian Schnabel

JULIAN SCHNABEL was born in New York in 1951. His artwork has been exhibited throughout the world and is in the permanent collections of the Metropolitan Museum of Art (New York), the Museum of Modern Art (New York), the Whitney Museum of Art (New York), the Museum of Contemporary Art (Los Angeles), and the Tate Gallery (London), among others. Schnabel has been featured in numerous books and catalogs, as well as on the CBS Cable Special "The Great American Art Game," produced by Lee Caplin.

1973: NEW YORK CITY*

In the summer of 1973, I moved back to New York City from Brownsville, Texas. I was twenty-one and had been accepted in the Whitney Museum's Independent Study Program; to get in, I sandwiched my slides between two pieces of bread, stuck them in a paper bag, and mailed it to New York. Dumb trick, but I wanted to be sure they'd look at my slides. I would have come anyway, but I thought this would give me an introduction to a community of other young artists. In New York, my plan was to eat pizza and paint pictures.

During the year I spent in the Whitney program, I was a sunglasses salesman, a cabdriver, and just missed getting a job as a sign painter for the Greyhound bus company. My father had to lend me $500. Still, I was painting while continuing my real education, which regularly began at one in the morning at a bar on Eighteenth Street and Park Avenue South.

Max's Kansas City was the kind of place that doesn't exist anymore. It was a giant, in the tradition of artist's bars like Le Chat Noir, Le Moulin Rouge, The Pont-Royal, and the Cedar Tavern. If a person flew to New York, got in a taxi, and their one word of English was "Max's," they'd be taken to a place where sculptors, rock musicians, movie stars, poets, composers, strippers, groupies, drug dealers, laser artists, lion tamers, acrobats (and their wives, with Yorkshire terriers in their purses), and artists of every aesthetic and sexual persuasion, including painters, even great painters, came to witness each other. Even if they didn't speak, they all came to Max's just to check, just to make sure that life was still going on and to let people know they were still alive.

I met Bob Williamson at Max's. He was the first friend I made in New York. I remember him arriving at his usual time, one in the morning, and I was always glad to see him. I loved talking with him because I felt we were doing something constructive; we weren't just sitting around getting drunk, we were locating a

* The following is excerpted from "C.V.J." by Julian Schnabel, published by Random House, New York, 1987, by permission of the publisher.

162

distance, getting a bead on things. Come to think of it, maybe all people drinking in a bar early in the morning think they are doing that.

There is one useful lesson that Bob taught me. He believed if you declare something so, it is. Don't lose your sense of yourself or forget the reasons why you started.

ABOUT BEING A STUDENT

I made a painting called "Red Cross Painting for Norman Fisher" that had on it a nurse's hat made of plaster. David Diao and another painter, Gary Stephan, came over to my studio and looked at it. Because it seemed extra to them, they both thought I should cut out the nurse's hat. I took their advice and ruined the painting.

Thinking about the nurse's hat now, I realize what I learned: never listen to anybody when it comes to being responsible for your own paintings. It's a mistake for young artists to want to please older ones. They're going to make you take out of your paintings the very things that most characterize them as yours. You might think that someone is really smarter than you are, or wiser, or more experienced, and they may be. But you can't listen to them because nobody knows better than you what you need to do. Most older artists are going to try to get you to conform to the standards that you are out to destroy anyway.

1974, AND I'M NOT HAVING MY FIRST EXHIBITION

Every young artist who comes to New York wants to have a show right away. Suppress this desire. Understand there's no reason to have a show if there's nothing to show. You might feel like you're a great artist. Maybe you are. You might be capable of doing something or saying something, but maybe you haven't done it or said it yet. Young artists are impatient for approval of other people. Approval for what? I think it is better to just continue working, letting everything that is stimulating about New York affect you. Maybe this sounds easy for me to say. It is, but it's a fight that you will always have to fight, because after the galleries like your work, it's even more difficult to keep your autonomy.

TEXAS: SUMMER 1975

Returning home to the provinces is marked by some as an admission of failure. People like to put a tag on you and keep you filed neatly within their own preconceptions of your abilities. The artists in Houston were not particularly friendly. Maybe they perceived my return as a defeat, a contagious disease that they didn't want to catch. There seemed to be a resentment and an antagonism toward New York, based on a fear of failing there; but at the same time, artists would like to have a show in New York or be touched by the excitement of being in the capital of the twentieth century; New York artists are invariably expatriated local artists from everywhere else on the globe.

Living in Houston I felt left out because local art dealers and collectors were always importing art and artists from New York; it was as if they were saying nothing can be any good if it's not exotic.

To those who resent New York because they don't know what it is, come. To those who feel they need to validate their art by showing it here, show it here, but don't be pissed off at those who are doing something that they want to be doing just because you're not. And if you don't want to come, you don't have to. An artist should be able to work anywhere. Many do.

FALL 1976: MY FIRST TRIP TO ITALY

One day, eating a chocolate bar at a kiosk, I picked up the only art magazine I could find. It was called *Prospetiva D'Arte.* I looked up the address and went there. The editor's name was Mimmo D'Brescia. I said, "Hi, I'm an American artist. I brought some slides of my work. Maybe you know a person or a gallery that might be interested in this stuff?" Mimmo asked if he could keep the pictures over the weekend. The following Tuesday, I got a call. He had spoken to a friend who was interested in the paintings; he asked me to come back to the office.

It was there I met Ruggero Jannuzzelli, a handsome, bald-headed prince from Naples, who was the first member of his family ever to have a real job. He was a lawyer and a maker of deals. He looked at me; I think the basis of his support of my art simply had to do with my standing in the room. From the slides, he seemed to think that the holes in my paintings resembled a plausible facsimile of modern art, something he was familiar with in Lucio Fontana's work. This was a good sign. I wanted to work. He asked me how much I needed to make ten paintings. I told him I had no studio and no money for materials. He said he would pay for the materials and find me a place to work. I didn't want to make the price too high. I asked for $3,000 for ten paintings that would each be about 7 by 5 feet. I was so happy that I volunteered to give him whatever drawings I made, too. Since Mimmo had told me that Ruggero lived in a castle and rode horses, I asked if part of the deal could include some horseback riding, since my girlfriend was from Texas. I came home that afternoon and told Jean we were going horseback riding. She didn't believe it. But it was true.

We moved to Via Gentilino 9, near Porto Ticinese, a building that Ruggero owned. I worked in the basement. I had an account in an art supply store. The money was paid to me in installments.

SUMMER OF 1977: BACK IN NEW YORK

It's a great excuse and luxury, having a job and blaming it for your inability to do your own work. When you don't have to work, you are left with the horror of facing your own lack of imagination and your own emptiness. A devastating possibility when finally time is your own.

The thing about being an artist is that you either have a belief or a disbelief that is a reprieve from all your daily duties. This freedom is a freedom of spirit. A freedom of thinking. Thinking that you actually have something that you want to do when you are done with your job.

JUNE 1978: MY BIG EUROPEAN SHOW

Be Sure of Your Dream Because it Will Surely Be Realized

What's behind curtain number three? Nothing except your own illusions and an ad in the newspaper announcing your exhibition in a language you can't read, in what might as well be a fictitious gallery with no audience in an unfamiliar place that is exotic just because of its unfamiliarity.

I was so effervescent with naive expectations about my first European exhibition that I didn't mind buying my own air ticket, carrying the paintings on my shoulder from New York to Paris, then by train to Düsseldorf and, finding my dealer out of town, carrying them to Cologne and setting up temporary shop in a good samaritan's living room, paying for the building of new stretchers, renting a truck to bring my paintings to Düsseldorf, sleeping on the cement floor of Gerald Just's austere gallery, and welcoming all the people who didn't show up at my opening. This great opportunity left me completely broke. I found it very satisfying.

There were three paintings that I brought from New York: "The Red Cross Painting for Norman Fisher" (in its yellow state, without the nurse's hat), "I Don't Want to Be King, I Want to Be Pope," "No. 16 or Kathy," as well as one painting, "Painting for Aldo Moro," that I painted in Germany. Not one was sold. There were no reviews.

After this much-heralded success, I continued my tour of Italy to retrace my depression and possibly retouch the paintings I had started in 1977.

I went to the Venice Biennale of 1978. I wasn't in it. I was a nobody just looking, just another tourist. There was a heavy cloud of enthusiasm and national pride hovering above the heads of the Italian artists. They were all wearing white linen suits with Campari stains. There was a sense of theater, a kind of utopian celebration that made a wreath of historical endowment around these participants. Being an unknown, I could see the double standard for known and unknown artists. There was a lot of posturing in Piazza San Marco by curators, art dealers, and small-time art politicos, culture lobbyists who were lobbying a partisan parochial doctrine that out of fear rejected any kind of work that didn't look like, or fit into, the particular time capsule of the generation that was occupying its own glorious moment. Maybe I would have had a different attitude if they were patting me on the back. I don't know.

Today, I see artists who were courted in the last decade become bitter and antagonistic because of their inability to see the bad faith of their fans. They are worried about being left out and out of work. The fear of being replaced is a product of believing in the art world. This belief destroys the natural dialogue between generations. It is healthier for the older artist to be curious even if it's for the selfish reason of finding a young person to talk to. Good conversation is scarce and there are so few people who know how to make art. An older artist can nurture and make something bloom in a younger one. It's more interesting than trying to erase everybody with a glint of talent, so that you imagine you have no competition, that way being a very lonely and miserly way of living in the world. If you are worried about losing your place to somebody who might be more talented than you are, then you have already lost it.

ANOINTED WITH A PUBLIC

Just before my February show in New York, Mary Boone was bringing prospective buyers to my studio, including Doris and Charles Saatchi, collectors from England. They had seen an article about my work in *Domus* magazine in January 1978, and after tracking me down at Holly Solomon's, were directed to Mary Boone. They had seemed very earnest about their selection and were in the throes of putting together what is now one of the largest and most comprehensive collections of contemporary art in the world.

Mary and I were waiting for Charles and his wife, Doris. They were kind of shy; I liked them. The year before, they bought a painting named "Accattone" out of my studio. So, I felt that they had first choice in selecting one of this new group of paintings. But the day before they arrived in New York, Mary brought over a woman named Vivian Horan.

Mary told me she was a collector of impressionists. It turned out she was an art dealer. I didn't know this at the time. (I don't know if Mary did.) Vivian immediately said she wanted the green plate painting named "Divan." It had a couch turned on its side that was inspired by a little drawing of a divan made by Gio Ponti in the fifties. I didn't understand why Mary brought her over the day before the Saatchis were to come. After Vivian left, I asked why she couldn't have come a day later. Mary told me not to worry about it, there were still two other paintings that were equally as good left for them to choose. Maybe the Saatchis had changed their plans, and Mary didn't want to cancel her appointment with Vivian. Who knows?

The Saatchis arrived and they of course wanted the green painting. I got really confused when Mary told them they could have it; I guess she thought she could convince Vivian to take a different painting. It turned out she couldn't. I told Mary I felt that the Saatchis had the first right and that she should insist. I also told her that if the Saatchis didn't get that one, they could pick either of the remaining two, and I would keep the one they didn't want because I wanted to keep one painting. Mary told me she would take care of everything.

She did. She told the Saatchis that I was giving the green painting to my mother, and not to talk to me about it because I was paranoid and people were bothering me. I was supposed to be skittish. (This I found out later.) Then the show of the plate paintings opened at Mary's gallery. They were priced at $6,000. Two weeks after the opening, I got a call from Annina Nosei, at that time a private New York art dealer; she asked me for a transparency of the green plate painting for her friend Vivian. Why was Annina calling me? Why would Vivian need a transparency of a painting that she just bought? The only time people ask for a transparency is when they want to sell something. I questioned Annina. "Can she be selling it already?"

Mary didn't know that Annina was actually Vivian's silent partner in the deal. But Charles Saatchi had found out and traded "Circumnavigating the Sea of Shit," the one he had bought, with Annina and Vivian for the "Divan" painting—paying them an extra $2,000 commission.

All of this happened without the paintings' ever leaving the gallery. A month later, Annina and Vivian in turn lent "Circumnavigating the Sea of Shit" to Robert Miller from the Robert Miller Gallery, who hung it in his dining room for his Christmas party in order to show me his commitment to my work and to invite me to show in his gallery. I declined. He returned the painting to Nosei's gallery, which in turn sold it to Bruno Bischofberger, the Swiss art dealer, for $10,000. Vivian and Annina doubled their money in a month. The paintings were still $6,000 in the gallery.

Some people buy paintings because they are interested in looking at them. Others buy them for speculation. I'm not going to speculate on their reasons but one thing is for sure: It is a foolish mistake to even try to second-guess the public. Make the things for yourself and if by chance someone agrees with you, it's coincidental.

> "Don't Underestimate The OTHER Guy's Greed."
> —Frank Lopez, Scarface

. . . [T]here are artists who design their work completely for immediate, color-coordinated, discursive digestion by the overly intellectualized art audience and any other literary supporter they can rim to get some credence for their shallow artistic formulas. These strategists bank on the notion that people have short memories; it's not important who did it first, it's who did it last. Their paintings are designed in the same way that ads are; somebody who doesn't know anything can walk in and say "Yes, I get that, I think I'll buy those designer jeans today." This kind of painting is designed to make you feel intelligent if you just stand in front of it. You get to fill its blank ambivalence with your own emptiness and self-doubt. There seems to be a lot of space around to be filled.

For the "professional artist," art is a job. The job of catering to the expectations of a presumed art audience. There's no room for real friendship because any human exchange is just seen as a step in a careerist climb. Much time is spent nurturing liaisons with creatures of the art world mechanism. At first, there is no time for friendship. Later, there is no capacity for it. Art is not a profession.

15 Preparing Your Portfolio

Kate Keller

Mali Olatunji

KATE KELLER is the Head Fine Arts photographer at the Museum of Modern Art in New York City, where she has worked since 1973. She earned her degree in photography from Ohio University.

MALI OLATUNJI has been a Fine Arts photographer with the Museum of Modern Art since 1975. Previously he studied photography in New York City for several years.

Much of the way we see art today is through photography in magazines, books, and lecture slides. It is a primary vehicle for showing one's own work to other artists, dealers, grant juries, and editors. Thus, it has become a substitute for the original work. Because of this prominent position photography has taken in presenting one's work, it is necessary for the photographer to go beyond mere documentation. The special qualities of a particular work of art must be presented to their best advantage. To obtain this one must exercise both understanding and control over the photographic medium.

This does not have to be an awesome task, but it is one that does require practice. To help your understanding we will give some background information on equipment and materials, as well as discuss a variety of shooting situations: the how, when, and what to use. It is impossible to cover all aspects of the process in a few pages. Therefore, we have focused on essential information and techniques to use as building blocks from which to expand your own working patterns.

EQUIPMENT

When buying equipment, whether used or new, do not rely solely on the salesman's word. If you are unfamiliar with the model or manufacturer, check with someone who has had practical experience with the equipment. In purchasing used equipment, be sure that there is a satisfaction guarantee. Conduct your own tests to ensure that the equipment is working properly. When dealing with rentals, familiarize yourself thoroughly with the equipment before leaving the store.

Having the best equipment does not guarantee the best results. To a certain extent the capacity of the equipment does affect quality, but the important factor is the person behind the camera. Understanding the limitations and possibilities of the equipment vis-à-vis the work being photographed is essential.

Aside from the basic equipment of camera, lens, meter, tripod, and lights, there are other necessary accessories which are useful in handling a variety of photographic situations:

Level	Used to ensure that the camera is parallel to the surface being photographed.
Timer	Used to time exposures longer than 1 second.
Cable release	Used with long exposures to prevent movement when the shutter is manually released.
Gray card	Used with reflective meters to ensure proper lighting.
Color patch gray scale	Used to determine proper filtration of color film or prints when necessary.
White boards, sheets, newspaper	Used for bouncing light from its source to a work for proper exposure or lighting ratio; also to cover reflecting colored objects.
Black boards, black cloth	Used to cover objects that reflect.
Diffusing materials	Used to create soft light from a harsh light situation.

CAMERA

Most slide presentations are designed for a 35mm camera. For that reason and because of general popularity, we will concentrate on its use. If you do not have a camera and intend either to buy or borrow one, the single lens reflex is preferable to a rangefinder or automatic camera. Single lens reflex (SLR) cameras are more adaptable to situations that might be encountered when photographing art, but this does not mean the others cannot be used.

Automatic cameras are primarily intended for candid outdoor photography. The camera automatically correlates the light intensity with film speed to expose the film properly. In a fully automatic camera the photographer knows only if there is adequate light, not specific exposure information. The photographer cannot determine the f/stop or shutter speed that is necessary for consistently good results. There are automatic cameras that have manual overrides. The type offering manual f/stop control is best for obtaining depth of field, which is necessary in photographing three-dimensional works.

Light travels through the lens of a rangefinder camera and directly strikes the film plane. There is no mechanical apparatus that translates this exact image to the photographer. The photographer looks through a separate lens that gives a close visual approximation. Because the subject is viewed and photographed from two positions, there is displacement from the image that is seen and the image recorded. This is referred to as parallax. The closer the camera moves to the subject, the greater the displacement. With practice this problem can be minimized. There is a wide variety of rangefinder cameras with interchangeable lenses and accessories, which gives versatility in handling various situations.

With the single lens reflex cameras you see the subject as the lens sees it at all times. This is accomplished by the placement of a mirror inside the camera body which directs light entering the lens to the viewfinder. You are able to get as close to the subject as your lens permits without having to compensate for parallax. When long exposures are necessary, movement of the mirror can cause vibrations in some cameras. This can be compensated for. After the lens is focused, you can use a device that prevents vibration by locking the mirror during the exposure.

As with the rangefinder camera there is a vast assortment of accessories for SLRs. Lenses and viewing screens offer greater flexibility when photographing art with an SLR.

LENSES

Inherent defects or aberrations in lenses can, in a variety of ways, distort the images they produce. Most lenses made today satisfactorily compensate for these problems. The degree to which they have been corrected is often reflected in price. It is better to have a reasonably good camera body with an excellent lens than the reverse situation.

Generally 35mm cameras come equipped with a 50mm or 55mm or "normal" lens. This lens gives you an angle of view similar to that of the human eye, which is about 50°. It is a satisfactory all-purpose lens.

A 35mm lens on a 35mm camera is considered a "wide angle," with a 70° angle of view. A subject can be photographed at a much closer distance when using a wide-angle lens than when using a normal lens. This would seem the ideal solution when shooting in a small area, except that the edges of the image flare out and become more distorted the closer the subject is to the camera.

A long-focus, 85mm lens for 35mm cameras has an angle of view of about 35°. When looking at a subject at the same distance with both normal lens and long lens, the long lens will see only part of what the normal lens sees. For the long lens to cover what the normal lens sees, the distance between lens and subject must be increased. A long lens is not generally used for photographing art, because of the greater space needed. However, it can be used to reduce the glare from a painting, since its increased distance from the object being photographed will result in fewer rays of reflecting light striking the lens. We recommend a good quality zoom lens. We have found zoom lenses to be convenient, especially when photographing works of various sizes within the confines of a single room. The range of the lens should be determined by the size of your working area.

Macro lenses are made for SLR cameras and are designed and corrected for close-up photography. We use a 55mm macro lens, which gives the versatility of a normal lens plus the ability to photograph at close range without adjustments. It is a very sharp lens which is also designed to photograph flat surfaces. It is an excellent lens for photographing art.

Note of importance: lens shades should always be used on lenses. Their use prevents extraneous light from entering the lens and causing a dulled, light-flared image.

METERS

Light meters assist the photographer in making sure a work of art is lighted correctly as well as giving the information needed to properly expose the film. There are two types of meters: (1) a reflective light meter, which measures the light bouncing (reflected) off the subject, and (2) the incident light meter, which measures the light falling onto the subject. The latter is more useful in photographing art. By its readings one can tell if a two-dimensional work has the even lighting it needs, or in the case of three-dimensional works, the correct lighting ratio.

Incident meters are hand held, which enables you to take a reading near the subject. Care should be taken not to let your own shadow interfere with the reading. Meter readings give proper exposure to a medium gray. In most cases all other tones or values will fall into place. However, if you have a work with dominant dark values, extra exposure is required to retain detail. One-half to one stop is the necessary adjustment. Work that is light in value needs less exposure. The correction here is one-half to one stop less than the given meter reading.

To lessen the risks of improperly exposed film, further exposures should be made in addition to the one indicated by the light meter. This is called "bracketing." To bracket black and white film, take three shots in all: (1) your indicated exposure, (2) one stop more exposure, and (3) one stop less exposure. For example, if the meter reading is f/22 at one-fourth of a second, the additional exposures would be f/22 at one-half of a second and f/22 at one-eighth of a second. Because color film is more critical, the brackets should be one-half stops in both directions.

Meters located inside the camera itself are reflective meters. These meters can be adapted to check and correct the amount of light falling on the work of art.

Readings are taken by placing a Kodak gray card in front of the work and parallel to the lens, then moving it to various positions in front of the work. Consult the owner's manual for particular instructions on how close to the gray card one must be to get an accurate meter reading.

TRIPODS

When the shutter speed is below one-sixtieth of a second, a hand-held camera can blur the image. This effect, caused by both mirror (SLR cameras) and body movement, can be lessened somewhat by holding one's breath during the exposure. However, this measure is not a satisfactory one for producing the quality needed when photographing art. Therefore, a tripod is a necessary piece of equipment.

A tripod needs to be sturdy; usually, the heavier the tripod, the more stability it will have. Look for a tripod which can be adjusted to allow movement of the camera in any direction. This allows parallel alignment with the work of art.

LIGHTS

The advantage of indoor over outdoor lighting is the ability to control the direction and distance of the light source and to maintain a near-constant color temperature.

Changes of height, distance, and angle from the subject are easily made when lamps are mounted on movable light stands; while lamps can also be clamped onto ladders, chairs, boards, and so on, their mobility is somewhat limited.

The choice of photo lamps depends on the type of film. The choice is not critical when using black and white film, but is with color. Photo bulbs are available with color temperatures of 3200°K (Kelvin) and 3400°K. Most indoor color film is compatible with 3200°K. The exception is Kodachrome A, which requires 3400°K. The relatively short time some bulbs can maintain constant color temperature makes it important to keep a record of how long each bulb has burned. Use bulbs of similar age together. Once these bulbs have gone past their recommended life for color they can be used for black and white photography, where color temperature is not crucial to the image quality.

There are three basic bulb designs: (1) the standard bulb, which looks like an ordinary house bulb with a long neck; (2) bulbs with built-in reflectors; and (3) the narrow tube quartz light. Regular photo lamps do require aluminum reflector bulbs to reflect their light. Reflector bulbs have a metallic coating which acts as a reflector, making the aluminum bowls unnecessary. However, reflector bulbs can fit into bowls for additional control of the beam. Quartz bulbs require special electrical fixtures.

There are advantages and disadvantages to each bulb. The quartz bulb is the most expensive, with its price being three to five times as high as that of the other two types. The standard and reflective bulbs range in price from $3.00 to $6.00. However, the life of a quartz light is 100 hours compared to four to six hours for the other lamps. The quartz light is very mobile because of the light-weight construction of the fixture head. Quartz lights do require stands. While the quality of this light source is rather harsh, it can be compensated for by bouncing the light or using a diffusion screen. There is a wide range of prices on quartz equipment. It is possible to buy complete set-ups containing several lights and stands at very reasonable sums.

When buying reflectors for standard bulbs, remember that the diameter of the bowl should be the same for each bulb. It will standardize the light beams, making it easier to attain even light. Clamps can be used for securing the lamps either to light stands or to their substitutes. This is an economical set-up, since 10" reflector bowls and sockets with clamps are about $5.00. The quality of light from these lamps is softer than from the quartz.

Standard bulbs are available in different wattages depending on electrical capacity. Most bulbs used are 500 watt, although there are also lower-wattage bulbs. In the following list, figures in the "bulb life" column indicate the hours we feel we can safely use the bulb without color change. They are slightly lower than the manufacturers' recommendations.

NAME OF BULB	DESCRIPTION	WATT	COLOR TEMPERATURE	BULB LIFE
EAL	Reflective bulb	500	3200°K	5 hr
FCX	Quartz	650	3200°K	100 hr
ECA	Frosted inside	250	3200°K	15 hr
EVB	NO. 2 frosted	500	3400°K	4 hr

FILM

The choice between black and white or color film should be based on aesthetic as well as practical factors. A three-dimensional work that is primarily concerned with form can lose its impact if the element of color is brought into play. In much the same way, the shades of gray in a black and white photograph cannot relate the visual intentions of a work whose color values are its distinguishing characteristics.

Final costs are a practical consideration in choosing between the use of a color negative or a transparency film. Although the initial expense in the use of transparencies may be greater, the printing process is eliminated. With the use of negatives that cost less, finding a good reliable printer who has reasonable rates can be a problem. Most commercial labs do not have the necessary experience to deal with the special considerations of reproducing art work. There are exceptions; try to establish a good rapport with your lab.

BLACK AND WHITE FILM

Film emulsions are made with light-sensitive silver halide crystals. The size of the crystal determines the characteristics of the particular film. An emulsion with small uniform crystals produces a film with low sensitivity to light, fine grain when developed, and the power to record fine detail with maximum sharpness. In comparison, larger crystals produce a film that is faster in its response to light with grain that is noticeably larger and that loses acuteness in the recording of fine detail.

SPEED	GRAIN	CONTRAST	DETAIL/SHARPNESS
Slow film	Very fine	High	Maximum
Fast film	Large	Low	Good

I.S.O. is the term used for film speed. The higher the number, the more sensitive the film. Films with an I.S.O. of 8 to 50 are considered low; 64 to 200 medium; 320 to 1600 fast.

The subject of the photograph and the conditions under which you are working determine the speed of the film. Works of art require careful rendering. Therefore, a slow, fine-grain film is usually used. When the need to stop motion is a factor, a faster film must be considered. A shutter speed of 1/125 of a second is the threshold at which motion is stopped. Often fine-grain emulsions are too slow even under high illumination. A high-contrast range, either within a work of art itself or the way in which it is lighted, can be reduced by using a film with a medium or high I.S.O. rating.

All brands of film have about the same degree of quality and constancy. The choice of a manufacturer is a personal one, which can be made only through trial.

MANUFACTURER	TYPE OF FILMS	FILM SPEEDS
AGFA	AGFA-Pan Professional-25	I.S.O. 25
"	AGFA-Pan Professional-100	I.S.O. 100
"	AGFA-Pan Professional-400	I.S.O. 400
ILFORD	Pan-F	I.S.O. 25 (changes with developer)
"	FP 4	I.S.O. 64
"	HP 5	I.S.O. 400
KODAK	Panatomic X	I.S.O. 32
"	T-MAX 100	I.S.O. 100
"	Plus X pan	I.S.O. 125
"	Tri X pan	I.S.O. 400
"	T-MAX 400	I.S.O. 400

Kodak's pamphlet S-23 describes direct positive films and processes for making black and white transparencies. Satisfactory slides can be made with Panatomic X developed in Kodak's Direct Positive Film Developing Kit. Black and white slides can also be made with color film. One thing to remember: since the film will respond to the dominant color of the medium used in the work of art, what the eye sees as black might record as another color on the film. To correct this response, use a correction filter.

COLOR FILM

All films are sensitive to heat and humidity, and should be stored properly before and after exposure and processing. This is particularly true with color film, since improper storage can alter color response. It is necessary to eliminate as many variables as possible when using color materials. By referring to the following list, you will help maintain color constancy and, in the long run, save time and money.

1. Read manufacturers' information sheets; use as guide for initial testing.
2. Buy film in quantity. A "brick" containing 20 rolls of film will cost less than buying 20 individual rolls.
3. Store film in refrigerator with low humidity. This keeps film stable and prevents color shifts.

4. Warm film to room temperature for one hour before using to prevent condensation marks and change in film speed.

5. Test film under the same conditions that will exist where actual photography will occur (lights, camera, medium). Determine correct I.S.O. and color filtration, if needed.

6. Bracket exposure. Once I.S.O. has been established through testing, it is advisable to expose film both one-half stop over and one-half stop under the given light meter reading.

7. Use a reliable lab. Processing should remain constant without any drastic color changes.

8. Check color with original. This should be done under the same color temperature source. In the case of slides, a white board is held under the slide at a short distance away with the same light illuminating both the original and the slide.

9. Correct color with cc filters. After the tests have been compared to the original, and if there is an unsatisfactory color change, cc filters can be used for correction. Kodak's book E-77 explains the theory and use of cc filters.

10. With color negative film, place color near work without interfering with the image. It is used as a guide by the printer.

Remember: color film responds to color with varying degrees of accuracy. This is due to the particular sensitivity of the film in relationship to the medium used in the work and how it is applied. For instance, pinks tend to be paler than other colors present in a slide. Undercoatings not visible to the eye often show up in color film. In some of these cases cc filters can bring the colors into acceptable balance. All colors will not record perfectly at all times, and a compromise is often required. Generally, the compromise will not greatly affect the overall quality of the slide.

The correct film and light source combination is essential when photographing in color. A color slide of an artwork, when illuminated simultaneously with an incandescent light and daylight, will render false color. Color film cannot compensate for mixtures of light as can the human eye. Manufacturers make three-color emulsions, each responsive to a different color temperature (°Kelvin) light source. The sources and temperatures are daylight 5600°K, tungsten 3200°K, and photolamps 3400°K.

If an incorrect film/light source combination is used, the results are usually unsatisfactory. Tungsten film used outdoors will produce a blueish cast over the image. Deep yellow will dominate when daylight film is shot indoors under tungsten light. With the use of color conversion filters, a film that responds correctly to one color temperature can be converted so as to record accurately in another. This is not generally recommended, however, because it means the light must travel through another piece of glass, thereby lessening the overall sharpness of the image. It also means additional exposure is required.

It is possible to photograph works outdoors, but a variety of problems arise. Daylight is a variable source of light, making it difficult to maintain the constancy needed for color work. Its quality depends on the amount of direct light from the sun. Altitude, haze, and time of day are all variables and must be considered. Because there is less blue in the sky after sunrise or just before sunset, all colors will be warm. When photographing in open shade on a clear day, the reflected light from the blue sky will cast blue on the image. Objects bounce color when photographing outdoors so the work must be carefully placed. For instance, green foliage will reflect green onto the image. It is much easier to control light in a studio.

It is possible to obtain acceptable slides of gallery installations under existing lighting conditions. Find out the types of bulbs that are used. Consult a Kodak Professional Photoguide to determine color balance of the light, what filter to use, and the required additional exposure. Low light levels generally exist in galleries, and tripods are rarely permitted. To compensate, the I.S.O. of Kodak's Ektachrome film can be increased by one stop without noticeable contrast or color shift. It is important for proper processing that you tell the lab if you have increased the film speed. When shooting in an area with fluorescent lights, the same procedure is necessary. Because heavy filtration is needed, Kodak's suggestions for filtration are guides, but your tests must be made for accurate results.

The same relationship between film speed, sharpness, and grain applies to color as well as to black and white. The choice of manufacturer for color is more dependent on what film the lab is able to process. For this reason Kodak is used when it is important to get results quickly. Ektachrome is primarily used because of the convenience of obtaining results from the lab within the same day. Now that there are a few local labs that have begun to process Kodachrome, check labs in your area. Due to the special processing, which is usually done by Kodak, it will take several days for the film to be processed and returned. Again, the choice of film should be made by testing and by your particular requirements. The following is a list of some possibilities:

MANUFACTURER	FILM TYPE	FILM SPEED	COLOR TEMPERATURE
AGFA	Agfachrome	50	Daylight
"	Agfachrome	100	Daylight
"	Agfachrome	200	Daylight
"	Agfachrome	1000	Daylight
"	Agfacolor	100	Daylight
"	Agfacolor	200	Daylight

(*continued*)

MANUFACTURER	FILM TYPE	FILM SPEED	COLOR TEMPERATURE
KODAK	Kodakchrome 25	25	Daylight
"	Kodakchrome 64	64	Daylight
"	Kodakchrome 40	40	3400°K
"	Ektachrome 64	64	Daylight
"	Ektachrome 64	64	Daylight
"	Ektachrome 100	100	Daylight
"	Ektachrome 200	200	Daylight
"	Ektachrome 400	400	Daylight
"	Ektachrome P800/1600	800 plus	Daylight
"	Ektachrome 50	50	3200°K
"	Ektachrome 160	160	3200°K
"	Vericolor 111-S	160	Daylight
"	Kodacolor VR-G 100	100	Daylight
"	Kodacolor VR G 200	200	Daylight
FUJI	Fujichrome 50D	50	Daylight
"	Fujichrome 64T	64	3200°K
"	Fujichrome 100	100	Daylight
"	Fujichrome 400	400	Daylight

The films listed are by no means all that is available, however; it is a good practice to experiment with several different types until you find one with which you obtain consistently good results.

SETTING UP

Being organized is essential in photography. The following procedures should be kept in mind during the shooting session.

1. The shooting area should be clear of extraneous objects. Start with a minimum amount of equipment—two to four lights, tripod, camera, and light meter. Other equipment should be off to the side for safety reasons.

2. With one or two lamps lighting the work, carefully position the work in the viewfinder of the camera and focus.

3. Determine the lighting possibilities to stress or deemphasize the particular qualities of the work. Experiment.

4. Save time by keeping a record of how a work is photographed. Make a small diagram of the set-up. Note angle and distance of the lights to the

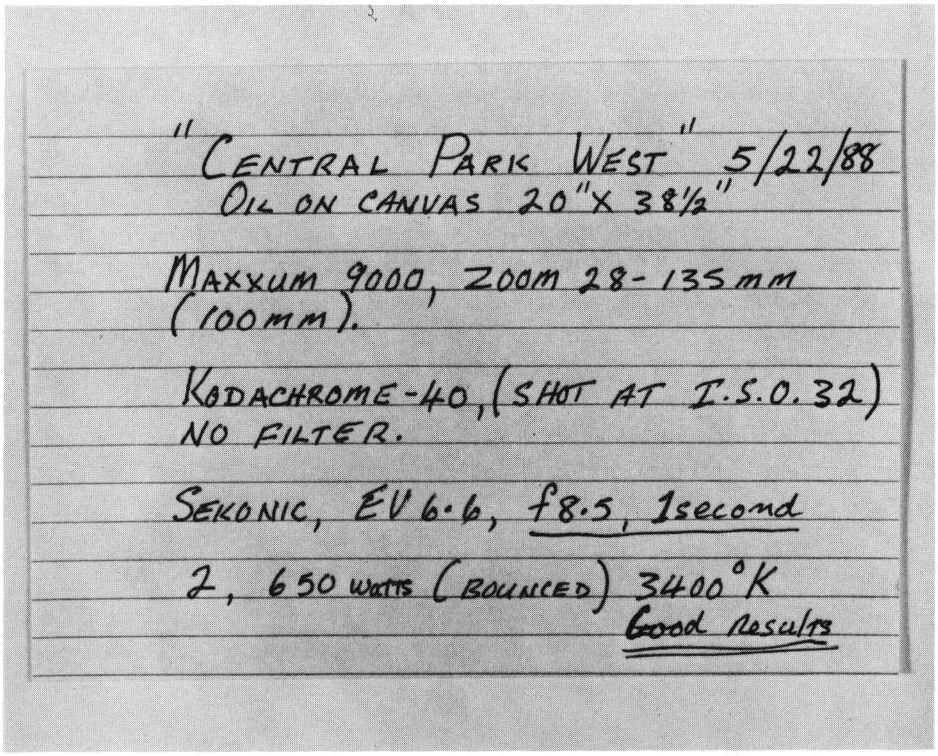

"Central Park West" 5/22/88
Oil on Canvas 20"x 38½"

Maxxum 9000, Zoom 28-135mm
(100mm).

Kodachrome-40, (Shot at I.S.O. 32)
No Filter.

Sekonic, EV 6·6, f8·5, 1second

2, 650 watts (Bounced) 3400°K
Good Results

Illustration 1. Note card with set-up information.

work. List camera, lens, film, meter reading, f/stop, and shutter speed (Illustration 1). If the results are good, this information can be a basis in photographing a similar work at another time. Or if the results are unsatisfactory, the mistake can usually be pinpointed.

LIGHTING

Surfaces, textures, shapes and colors alter their character in response to changes in the quality of light. For this reason and because of the uniqueness of each work, it is important to investigate various lighting possibilities. Most information on how to photograph works of art begins by saying, "Place lights at a 45° angle to the object being photographed." In principle, the surface reflection will be minimal at this angle. We have found this the exception, not the rule. We firmly believe there are no rules when lighting works of art—only guidelines.

TWO-DIMENSIONAL WORKS

There are two requirements for photographing two-dimensional work: (1) the camera should be parallel to the work, and (2) light must fall evenly on the work.

The camera must be horizontally and vertically parallel to the surface of the work. If it is not, the camera image will be distorted and unsharp. A level reading on both the camera and the artwork will help in achieving proper alignment. If the work is tilted, the camera must be at the same angle. The gridded viewing screen available to some SLR cameras can facilitate the necessary parallel alignment of the work with the camera (Illustrations 2, 3, 4, 5).

Even distribution of light is of critical importance. Varying light intensities will cause the film to record false information. This is particularly true with color film. A slight variation in intensity (one-half stop) will cause a noticeable exposure change.

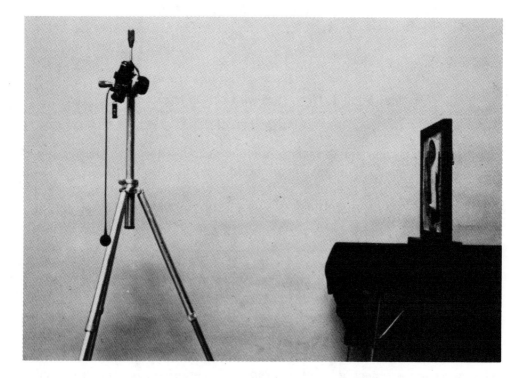

Illustration 2. Camera not parallel to artwork.

Illustration 3. Result of Illustration 2. Note lines converging and lack of sharpness.

A hand-held incident meter placed and read at nine points near the surface of the work is the easiest way to insure even illumination (Illustration 6). Remember not to cast your shadow on the meter (Illustration 7). The procedure mentioned earlier, in discussing reflective meters, can also ensure even lighting of a work. Place the 18 percent gray card near the work at the same nine points (Illustration 8).

Conventional lighting set-up consists of lights placed approximately at a 45° angle to the artwork (Illustration 9). It can be used when the surface of a work is not reflective, and when texture is not an important quality to emphasize. This is

Illustration 4. Camera parallel to work.

direct, harsh light. Although the characteristics of some work (water colors, drawings, etc.) generally lend themselves to this light, those works with delicate values may need softer lighting to delineate tones. Try bounce lighting.

When photographing small works, it is possible to have even illumination with two lights. With larger works, four lights and sometimes more should be used. When trying to light a large area with only two lights, a "hot spot," or overlapping of light, will occur in the center of the image. The greater the distance the lights are from the work, the easier it is to obtain even light.

Illustration 5. Result when camera is parallel to work. Compare with Illustration 3.

When even illumination exists on a work except at the very bottom—a problem with larger works—place a white board or cloth under the work. This will bring up the light level to match the rest of the work. This cannot be used with dark shiny surfaces, because the card will reflect its own shape onto the surface. A black board or cloth is placed under a work when the light level is too high, thus absorbing some of the light that would otherwise bounce onto the surface.

Illustration 6. The nine points where light readings are taken. Note position of hand and body placement for accurate readings.

If you are working in a confined area it may be impossible to get the distance needed for even illumination. One solution is bounce lighting, which can be accomplished in a variety of ways:

1. Lights bouncing on floors, walls, ceilings (Illustrations 10, 11)
2. Light coming from one direction striking a wall or board (Illustration 12)
3. Lights facing each other (Illustration 13)

Lights bouncing around a room will cause environmental reflections and cast unwanted colors. Walls and boards should be neutral or white. Furniture, floors, walls, and even the clothes you wear can affect color. Cover objects that

Illustration 7. An incorrect incident meter reading will be obtained due to the body casting a soft shadow over much of the painting as well as a stronger shadow from the hand. See Illustration 8 for correct method.

might influence the color the film records. If a work is being photographed on or near the floor, place a newspaper under the work, making the floor neutral.

When you want to emphasize a strongly textured surface, use side lighting. Texture is exaggerated to convey the feeling of three dimensionality. The smaller the angle of light to the work, the greater the effect (Illustrations 14, 15).

It is often difficult to maintain even illumination with side lighting; a fill is then used. By using a wall or board near the darker side of the work, light will bounce from the boards back onto the surface of the work. If you use a board, note its angle, because this affects the density of the shadows cast from the primary light source. (Refer to Illustration 12.)

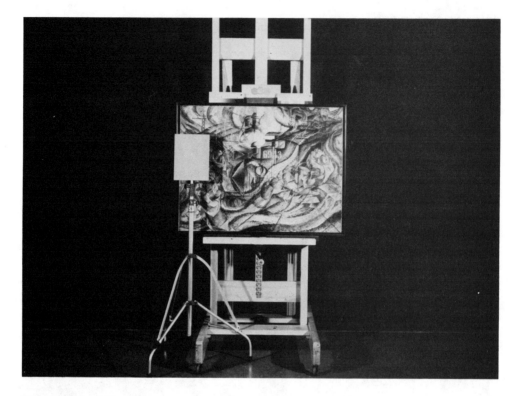

Illustration 8. Convenient way to place gray card when taking a meter reading from a camera. Gray card is clipped onto light stand.

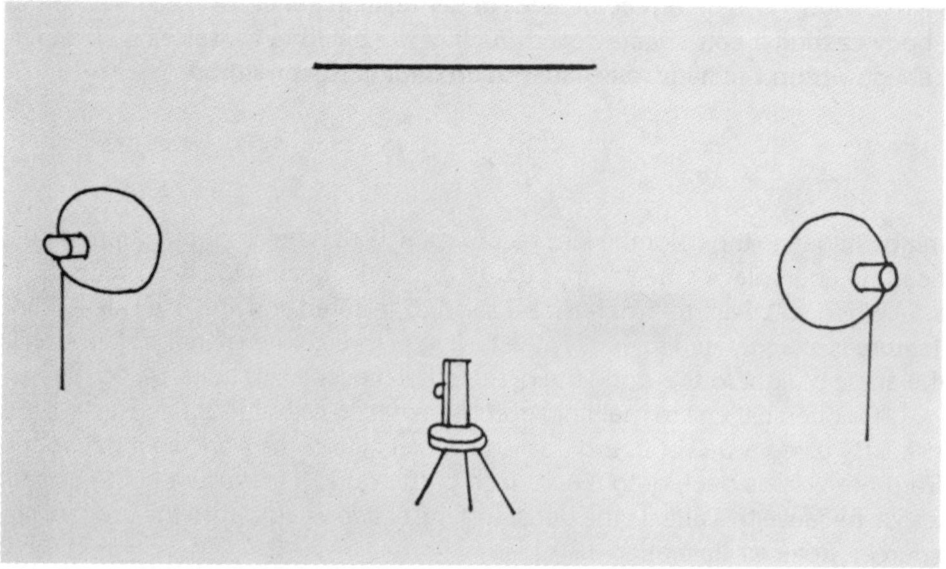

Illustration 9. Diagram of conventional 45° lighting set-up.

Illustration 10. Bounce lighting set-up. Four lights bounced off ceiling and floor. The nine meter reading points are all equal.

There is often a problem with reflection and glare when photographing two-dimensional surfaces. There are three ways to minimize this problem:

1. Bounce lighting
2. Long lens
3. Polarizing filters

Conventional lighting can create glare, which makes definition of the image difficult (Illustrations 16 and 17). Bounced lighting helps to eliminate this problem. (Refer to Illustrations 11 and 13.) It is sometimes helpful when using bounce to place a black cloth over the camera. This cuts down further glare from the light bouncing off the wall opposite the work of art. A black cloth in front of the camera is also used when photographing a work under glass to stop reflection (Illustration 18).

Illustration 11. Result of bounce lighting.

Glare can be minimized to some extent with the use of the long lens. Compare it to the image produced by the normal lens (Illustration 19). Refer to Illustration 17.

Although polarizing filters can eliminate all reflection and glare, they are used as a last-resort measure; filters are needed on both camera lens and light sources; additional exposure of at least two stops is needed; contrast is also increased, which gives a false feeling to the work (Illustration 20). For these reasons we try to avoid using polarizing filters. However, there are materials that

Illustration 12. Set-up of light source coming from one side when bouncing off a white board.

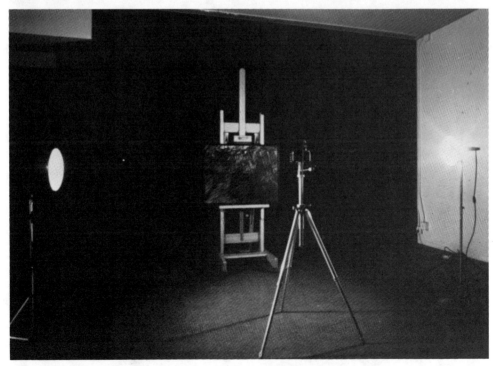

Illustration 13. Set-up of two lights facing each other to obtain even lighting. Used to minimize glare.

Illustration 14. Side lighting for texture.

Illustration 15. Same painting when lighted with lights at 45°. Note flat look.

Illustration 16. Conventional lighting set-up. Normal lens used.

demand their use. For instance, graphite is very difficult to light since reflective problems cause part of the image to fade. Polarization in this case would be preferable.

THREE-DIMENSIONAL WORKS

The functions of lighting ratio, depth of field, and background all help to convey the feeling of three-dimensionality on the two-dimensional photographic surface.

Lighting in a studio is the simulation of daylight. When looking at a photograph we unconsciously compare it with daylight and are aware of a

Illustration 17. Result of conventional lighting set-up shown in Illustration 16. Compare painting with Illustrations 10 and 11, where bounced lighting was used. A normal lens was used.

dominant light source and its direction. If there are two light sources of equal strength casting their shadows on an image, there is a slight feeling of uneasiness. It upsets our viewing patterns, because we know it cannot exist in nature. Therefore, most three-dimensional lighting has one light dominating the subject.

Illustration 18. Set-up when photographing through glass or other reflective surfaces. Lights at 45°.

Under most circumstances the use of one light creates too much contrast for the film to record all detail in both highlight and shadow areas. A second light must be used as a fill. The second light is placed at a greater distance from the subject. A piece of translucent material can also be placed in front of the second lamp to reduce the intensity of the light. A white card or cloth can also be used as a fill when positioned at the darkest side and held in such a way as to bounce the rays from the light source into the darker side of the work (Illustration 21).

The difference between the dark and light sides is called lighting ratio. To find the ratio, meter readings are taken from both the light and dark sides. If the difference is one stop, the ratio is 1:2, with the lighter area getting twice as much light as the darker area. The difference should not exceed two stops (1:4). Ratios above 1:4 will create a dramatic effect, but detail will be lost in the highlight and shadow areas (Illustrations 22, 23, 24).

Illustration 19. Same set-up used as in Illustrations 16 and 17, but here a long lens was used. Note reducing of glare when compared to the normal lens.

The exposure is determined by taking the average of the two readings. If, for example, the meter reads f/16 at 16 seconds in the lighter area and f/16 at 4 seconds in the darker area, the correct exposure of f/16 at 8 seconds will be used.

When the camera is focused on a particular point of a three-dimensional piece, every element of the piece at that distance will be in sharp focus. Part of the background and part of the foreground will also seem to be in focus. The distance from the nearest point to the furthest point in acceptable focus is called "depth of field." Depth of field is controlled by f/stops. The higher the f/stop

Illustration 20. Same painting when photographed with polarizing filter. Note increase in contrast.

number, the greater the depth of field that is obtained. The numbers generally assigned to a 35mm camera are f/1.8, f/2, f/2.8, f/4, f/5.6, f/8, f/11, and f/16. The higher f/stop number has greater depth of field because the size of the aperture decreases as the number increases. Example: f/16 is capable of greater depth of field than f/8.

The depth of field of a lens extends further into the background than into the foreground. To ensure sharpness in the foreground, the point of focus should be measured one-third into the work. Do not use the midpoint (Illustrations 25, 26, 27).

Illustration 21. Set-up when using white card to control lighting ratio.

Normal lenses can be used to photograph three-dimensional works; however, the use of a longer lens can eliminate distortions. Photographing at a high or low angle can also cause unwanted exaggeration, so beware of the angles you choose.

Background is a consideration with both two- and especially three-dimensional work. In both cases keep your background clean. If working with paper or cloth, make sure there are no creases or wrinkles (Illustrations 28, 29). Dark backgrounds bring the work to the foreground but can destroy the three-dimensional feeling by absorbing the shadows of the work. In cases when a light background is preferred but the shadows are unwanted, place the work far away from the wall or background paper and close to the camera. Bounce lighting can also eliminate shadows. The placement of a small spotlight on the background of a work helps to separate the work from its surroundings (Illustrations 30, 31, 32, 33).

Lighting various materials used in sculpture can be challenging because there is usually more than one satisfactory way in which to represent a work. Again, it is best to experiment to see what is possible and then determine which situation has worked best. As an example of the choices to be made we have photographed a translucent vase two ways. First, we emphasize the form by placing white cards on either side and bouncing light off them. The forms of the

Illustration 22. Using a ratio of 1:1.

cards are reflected onto the vase. Further definition of the form is accomplished by placing a small spot on the background. Stronger representation of the internal design is seen in the second example. A light in the background is the primary light source, with bounce light as fill (Illustrations 34, 35, 36, 37).

INSTALLATIONS

There are inherent problems that one must contend with when photographing installation works. According to artist Beverly Semmes, whose work deals primarily with sculpture that is site specific and temporary, "It is a difficult task because the photographs are the only documents of a work's existence." What the photographs must reveal and relate are the complexities of the work such as scale, tone, dimensionality, setting, materials, and so on. To achieve a success-

Illustration 23. Using a ratio of 1:2.

ful result Semmes suggests that one walk through an installation piece photographing from different viewpoints, with different focal length lenses and in some cases different lighting conditions—choosing later the photographs that best communicate the artist's intent (Illustrations 38, 39).

It is better to photograph when the installation is first on view so that you can reshoot if you feel the photographs are not satisfactory.

PRESENTATIONS

Slides are made when viewing is intended for more than one person and enlargement is necessary, as in classroom or art jury situations. They are also used when approaching galleries, because it is expedient to have a number of images neatly fitted together in one pocketed 11 × 9 transparency sleeve, ready

Illustration 24. Using a ratio of 1:4.

to view on a light box. Each viewing situation needs a different slide density. Because of a projector's strong illumination and the enlargement needed, slides for projection should be slightly darker than those that will be viewed on a light box. When using transparencies for publication, printers prefer a denser image to work with, because it is easier to retain detail in highlight areas. However, the density should not be so great as to change the color or character of the artwork.

Prints are also used to show to galleries. Paper and emulsions are fragile, however, and prints should be kept in protective transparent sleeves. Black and white prints are often used for opening invitations and publications because of lower reproduction costs. Generally, prints with a little less than normal contrast but with separation in all tones are the best for reproduction. Whenever possible, check with the printer beforehand and ask for his specifications.

In general, trust your common sense about what looks good and right to you, and simply do the best you can with what you can afford.

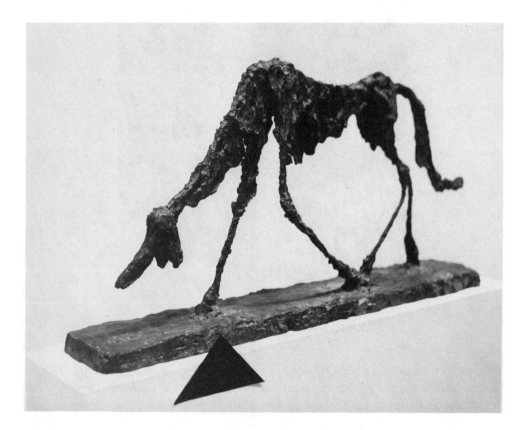

Illustration 25. Depth of field. Lens wide open at f/1.8. Focus is at one-third the depth. Focus falls off noticeably in the front and back.

Illustration 26. Lens set at f/11. Tape measure focus still not sharp toward the far rear or front.

Illustration 27. All areas in focus when f/22 used.

Illustration 28. Painting on light background.

Illustration 29. Same painting on dark background. Individual taste will dictate best background for work.

Illustration 30. Sculpture on dark background loses some three-dimensional feeling but can look dramatic.

Illustration 31. Same lighting set-up with sculpture placed on gray background.

Illustration 32. Same set-up as Illustration 31 but with background light added to create more separation.

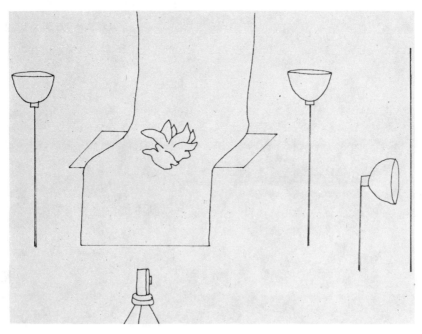

Illustration 33. Diagram of set-up for Illustrations 30 and 31.

Illustration 34. Set-up for photographing translucent piece. Light bounced from two white cards at the side.

Illustration 35. Result from light bounced from two white cards.

Illustration 36. Light bounced from the background through the work.

Illustration 37. Result of light bounced from background.

Illustrations 38 and 39. Specific site installation shot from different viewpoints.

SUGGESTED BIBLIOGRAPHY

Artificial Light Photography, Ansel Adams
Basic Photography, M. J. Langford
Color Photography in Practice, D. A. Spencer
Craft of Photography, David Vestal
Kodak Black and White Transparencies with Panatomic X AD50
Kodak Color and Black and White Films AF1
Kodak Copying M-1
Kodak Existing Light Photography KW-17
Kodak Professional Photoguide
Hand Book for Contemporary Photography, 4th ed., Arnold Gassan
Photography for Artist and Craftsmen, Clause-Peter Schmid

ACKNOWLEDGMENTS

A note of thanks to Robert Kobayashi for his help in preparing the manuscript, and Rosa Zaster for Printing.

The following works of art have been used as illustrations through the courtesy of the Museum of Modern Art and with the help of Richard L. Tooke, supervisor, Rights and Reproductions.

Boccioni, "States of Mind: The Farewells," 1913, oil on canvas. Illustration 8.
Boccioni, "States of Mind: Those Who Go," 1913, oil on canvas. Illustrations 10, 13, 16.
Braque, "Road near l'Eataque," 1908, oil on canvas. Illustration 12.
Laurens, "Bowl of Fruit." Illustrations 2, 3, 4, 5, 15.
Beverly Semmes, "Formal Garden," Yale University Art Gallery, March 1987. Photo: T. Charles Erikson. Illustrations 38, 39.
Lois Comfort Tiffany, Vase, c. 1900, Favrile Glass. Illustrations 34, 35, 36, 37.

The following works have been used through the courtesy of the artists:

Robert Coats, "2nd Fat Line," 1980, oil on canvas. Illustrations 28, 29.
Nancy Fuller, "Nature Study," 1978, plaster. Illustrations 30, 31, 32.
Alberto Giacometti, "Dog," 1951, Bronze. Illustrations 25, 26, 27.
Robert Kobayashi, "Martine," 1980, tin on wood. Illustrations 22, 23, 24.
Pablo Piccaso, "Violin and Grapes," 1912 Oil on Canvas. Illustration 18.
Niles Spencer, "Near Washington Square," Ca. 1928, Oil on Canvas. Illustrations 11, 17, 19, 20.

16 | Selling Art Under Contract

Tennyson Schad

TENNYSON SCHAD is the founder and owner of LIGHT Gallery, a New York gallery dealing in fine photographs. Mr. Schad is also an attorney specializing in intellectual property.

How an artist achieves a relationship with a gallery is the stuff of which seminars are made. The fact that a thousand or so artists would spend the better part of a day in New York recently to hear artists and dealers expound on that issue underscores the depth of the concern on the part of the artistic community. All of us, in search of insights, have spawned an entire industry of seminars and "how-to" books, and we are still left with ourselves to deal with. To be cynical, how does a young woman make it to the top in Washington? How does a young actor achieve fame and fortune in New York City? The analogies are manyfold.

The idealist in us says that success for artists is based upon excellence, new ideas and insights, and in some measure that is true. But it is also true that those artists are few and far between. The pragmatist knows that when everything else is equal other factors come to bear. Society being what it is, there are, of course, other factors. Visibility is a big one, as is being in the right place at the right time and knowing the right people. But I've said nothing new. Dealers receive calls all the time on behalf of the shy and retiring artist. That sort of reticence is perhaps endearing, but it's also self-defeating. While the dealers, to survive, must be on a constant search for new talent, at the same time someone has to be back in the gallery selling your work. In short, you must take the initiative. Don't hunker down in Moose Jaw, Saskatchewan, and wait to be discovered.

If you want to exhibit and sell your work, you must work at your craft, develop a coherent body of work, and take whatever steps are necessary for that work to be exhibited as often as possible, in museums, universities, cooperative galleries, wherever. There is no substitute for exposure. A word of caution, however. Nothing reveals a thin body of work faster than multiple exhibitions.

Dealers are always interested in adding new artists to complement their gallery rosters. Even though you may not be an established artist, you should not hesitate to explore with a gallery the possibility of an exhibition and even representation.

You may be one of that hearty number of successful artists who prefer to represent their own work and to arrange personally their exhibitions at galleries and museums throughout the country. I admire these vagabond artists-entrepreneurs, but it takes a person of considerable stamina and self-possession and one who loves to travel. The style is particularly suitable for photographers, not tied to a studio workplace, who enjoy mixing it up with dealers and museum people and who often can use the travel time to their own advantage as working artists or to satisfy their wanderlust.

Other artists have agents who work through galleries and also sell directly to the art buying public. For some, that arrangement works well, but generally speaking, an agent can't give you the reputation-building exposure of a prominent gallery. With the right gallery, you can relax and concentrate on your work. Moreover, a gallery association is, to many artists, an act of self-affirmation, a metaphor not unlike the Tinman's testimonial or the Scarecrow's diploma.

Before you establish a relationship with a gallery, first decide what kind of relationship you want and with whom.

WHAT TO LOOK FOR IN A GALLERY

Before you sign with a gallery, you should be satisfied that (1) the gallery understands and feels a sense of commitment to your work, (2) your work fits in with that of the other artists represented by the gallery, (3) you feel comfortable working with the dealer or the gallery director, and (4) the gallery will enhance the visibility of your work and your reputation.

Your eagerness to align yourself with a gallery should not blind you to the realization that you may be better off without a gallery than with the wrong gallery or the wrong people.

SHOULD YOU HAVE A CONTRACT?

There are divergent views on the question of whether artists and dealers should execute a written contract defining their relationship.

Much instructive material has been written about artists' dealings with galleries. The source books abound with legal clauses and authorities, but for the most part they appear to be concerned more with form than with substance. While the form contracts are useful checklists, they are not graven in stone and do not touch upon the heart of the artist-dealer arrangement.

Some artists, not wishing to be in the thrall of anyone, shy away from a written commitment. A number of dealers, too, find the contract an unnecessary burden on their autonomy and freedom. One could draw an analogy to a formal marriage contract, which also has its vocal exponents. But allocation between marriage partners as to responsibility for child care, washing the dishes, and watering the houseplants suggests a basic distrust or insecurity and lack of understanding. Many artists and galleries have flourished under long-standing commitments that have been cemented with little more than a handshake. They reason that the relationship will work only as long as both parties are content with the deal. It is that excitement that makes the marriage work. You can't force an artist to produce and you can't compel a dealer to get excited by and to push your work.

Where the ephemeral agreement suits the needs and personalities of the parties, well and good. An artist-friend of mine produces one painting a year, and occasional drawings, and is represented by a single gallery. And he trusts his gallery. They see little need to set their mutual responsibilities in concrete. Nevertheless, such a loose arrangement is not without its perils.

There is little need, it seems to me, for an artist and dealer to execute a written contract when the relationship falls short of actual representation, that is, for a single exhibit or the consignment of a few works for a limited period of time. But that does not mean there should be nothing in writing.

WHAT TO PUT IN WRITING

Where works are consigned for a show or for a limited period of time to a gallery, a representation agreement is not necessary, but there should be in writing an understanding that states (1) the specific works received, (2) that the work is consigned for a specific period of time, (3) the prices at which the work is to be sold, (4) whether or not the work is insured while in possession of the gallery, (5) the commission to be paid to the gallery, and (6) when you are to be paid.

The contract is not the essence of the artist-gallery relationship. You and your dealer must realize that your dealings with one another, with or without a contract, are determined by mutual understanding, trust, and shared commitment.

Nevertheless, I personally favor a contract with an artist because, if reasonably drawn, it informs the parties of their responsibilities and objectives with respect to each other. If you and the dealer work well together, the agreements will rarely if ever be referred to, for you will generally be able to reach a mutually satisfactory accommodation on most issues. The agreement should be little more than the skeleton on which you build the relationship. It should not be carried around in one's vest pocket like a road map. Contracts may identify problems, but only people solve them.

Your agreement with a dealer should be positive in tone and written in language you both can understand. As a lawyer, I am aware of my colleagues' passion for precision, but as a gallery owner I know how intimidating and incomprehensible a formal agreement is to many artists and dealers alike.

The contract should be short and sweet. If you need a lawyer to understand it, what good is it (unless, of course, you have a lawyer in the family)? In the paragraphs that follow, I discuss what I believe should be in the basic agreement.

POINTS TO CONSIDER

The Parties

The agreement should obviously state the names and addresses of the parties. If your dealer is a corporation—and most are—then the agreement should so state. (If you have any reason to doubt that a corporate gallery can live up to its financial commitments to you, be prudent and request the dealer to sign individually as well).

The Term of the Contract

Often the first agreement between an artist and a gallery will be for a relatively short period—a trial marriage. If you work well together, you will renew the contract as a matter of course. Often neither party gives formal renewal a thought, and both parties continue to abide by the original terms of the expired contract. I admire the mutual trust, but attention to the formal renewal is recommended. A term of two or three years seems most common in artist-dealer contracts. If you are an unestablished or less established artist, signing a longer-term commitment may significantly interfere with your career in the future. On the other hand, your dealer may prefer a longer-term arrangement. Negotiating renewals every one or two years is not high on anyone's priority list. Moreover, dealers spend considerable effort and money promoting the artists they represent and in making the public aware that their work is available through the gallery. A dealer is less likely to do so with enthusiasm if there is concern as to your staying with the gallery. Another material, although often unmentioned, consideration is that the longer contractual terms discourage poaching by opportunistic rival dealers with packets of promises.

Extent of Representation

The extent of the representation of your work by your dealer can be restricted in terms of media and geography. For those bi- and tri-media types, it is not uncommon to have one dealer handle your paintings and another dealer carry your drawings or sculpture. The arrangement may make eminent sense, but it is the kind of issue that you should discuss with your dealer. Dealers don't like surprises any more than you do.

The limitation of a dealer's agency geographically is a more complex issue. Dealer preferences aside, whether you wish to be tied to a single dealer will be determined not only by your own personality but by the nature and quality of your work as well.

The advantages of regional representation are obvious, the disadvantages less so. The more dealers working to arrange for the exhibition and sale of your work, the better. It's a big country. But there are also drawbacks of which you should be aware. Unless the regional dealers work well with one another, there will be the usual disputes with respect to the timing and content of your exhibitions, the question of who gets what work and when. This is not a major consideration if your work is produced in multiples such as prints and photographs.

But having two or more regional dealers raises other issues as well. The need to keep track of inventory, accountings, payment, insurance, consignments to yet other dealers, and other record keeping is only compounded by multiple galleries, particularly if you have a large amount of work. For that reason, you may prefer to deal with one trusted individual who can arrange for and coordinate relationships with other galleries on your behalf. This is particularly true where your dealer has a truly national rather than a regional clientele. A gallery with a national clientele may curtail its promotion of your work if its geographic area is limited. That could adversely affect the sales of your work. It undoubtedly would also affect the size of any guarantee the dealer would be willing to make on sales. Relying on your exclusive dealer to make arrangements with other galleries may require you to give a little on the amount you receive for your work, and you will have to determine whether such an arrangement is in your best interests.

I note that a number of form agreements specifically allocate territory to a dealer in terms of where the clients reside. That to me is an extremely difficult and troublesome way to handle this issue. Unless your regional dealers travel the country, posing the possibility that they may end up in adjacent suites in the Topeka Hilton pushing your work, it is much simpler to permit each gallery to sell from its location without regard to where the clients reside.

Exhibitions

The representation agreement should provide for periodic solo exhibitions of your work for a specified number of weeks. This is, of course, an important consideration. The frequency of the exhibitions will depend not only upon how productive you are but also, with some dealers, upon the relative marketability of your work. Whatever the provision, it must be realistically applied. As you know, artists are not machines. They work in cycles as do all other creative people. There will be times when your work merits more frequent exhibition and other times when the exhibition of your work as scheduled will do neither you nor the dealer any favors. I have seen instances where an artist insisted upon the exhibition of his work pursuant to the contract although the quality and quantity of the new work did not justify a show at that time. The exhibition was not only unsuccessful financially but was also an embarrassment to the reputation of a major artist. Avoid that situation if you can. If you trust the judgment of your dealer, be heedful in this respect.

Some of the form contracts you will encounter stipulate that the artists shall have a solo exhibition every year or every so many months, shall be entitled to a specified amount of wall space, and so on. Those kinds of provisions severely restrict an intelligent dealer's prerogatives. In most cases, your dealer is as interested in promoting and selling your work as you are, although it may never appear that way. The artist-dealer relationship is in many senses a partnership and you must work together for your mutual benefit.

I also note, from writings on this subject, statements to the effect that the artist should control the choice of the work exhibited and the manner of exhibition. Undoubtedly there are artists with sufficient clout to enforce these provisions, but, with an intelligent dealer, they are self-destructive. Of course, you should be consulted with respect to the exhibition of your work. That does not mean, however, that the dealer's wishes and instincts should be ignored. Artists are not always the best judges of their own work—and rarely of the gallery's clientele.

Equally objectionable to me are those form contracts that give the artist control over advertising and publicity. This is a matter between you and your dealer, and is rarely a trouble point. But since the dealer is the one who must foot the bill and who ostensibly knows how to market the work, the dealer should ultimately prevail on this issue.

The provision as to exhibitions should also deal with who pays for the preparation and installation of the exhibit, and for the shipping costs. The gallery should pay for matting and framing of photographs and prints, but, where standards materials are not used and substantial expense is involved, another arrangement may be necessary. To avoid unnecessary disputes, this issue should be dealt with either in the agreement or orally, well in advance of any exhibition.

Commissions

The percentage of the sales price retained by the dealer as commission varies considerably, dependent upon a number of factors, including the nature of the artwork, its price and marketability, the size of the gallery and its overhead, and the services that the dealer renders to the artist. Obviously, a dealer who promotes your work nationally and provides innumerable additional services, such as handling and fulfilling requests for your work in museum and other shows, will require a larger percentage than will those dealers who merely handle your show at your expense. It is quite possible for one dealer to do handsomely on a commission of one-third or 40 percent while another dealer will have difficulty maintaining its operation even with a commission in excess of 50 percent. The commission, however, generally will range between 40 and 50 percent. Within any one gallery, however, the commission to artists should be fairly standard, if the same kinds of work are involved, if for no other reason than elemental fairness and to avoid the inevitable bickering.

Dealers usually give discounts to established collectors, to museums, and of course to other galleries. You should be informed as to what those discounts are. It is not uncommon for a dealer to request an additional commission on your work to offset discounts given to other dealers. Such a procedure should be spelled out. It is quite possible that your dealer may simply take a larger standard commission and absorb all discounts to other dealers and to collectors.

Private sales by the artist is a subject that should be covered in the agreement. It is one of those areas that can be handled gracefully, or it can create such friction as to test the artist-dealer relationship. The subject should be dealt with openly and honestly. If your dealer has an exclusive, he or she may want all inquiries to be referred to the gallery. Fair enough, but what about sales to friends, to collectors who have been with the artist from the earliest days, to others who just happen along? That answer depends upon a number of factors. For example, do you work in multiples, in which case your dealer may feel slightly less proprietary, or has your dealer promised that next big painting to the Metropolitan? Both of you should express your concerns and work it out. It will be a lot easier if you agree to report your private sales, on the same basis as the gallery accounts to you, and to pay your dealer a fair part of the regular commission on the sale of your work. Remember, the gallery cannot truly perform when you are dealing actively in your own work. That activity, unless acceded to by the gallery, will eventually undermine the relationship.

Finally on this subject, the representation agreement should cover those obvious transactions where no commission, or a reduced commission, should be payable to the gallery, for example, lecture fees and honorariums. But don't try to anticipate every conceivable situation that may call for a different commission arrangement. Wait until the situation arises and work it out with your dealer. Otherwise, the agreement will be overloaded with useless provisos that will only complicate the agreement and perhaps your relationship.

Guarantees and Advances

The greater your bargaining power, the more likely it is that the gallery will offer you a stipend or a guarantee of annual sales. More enlightened dealers will on occasion offer young unestablished artists stipends as well, in the fond hope that they will become important and profitable artists. However, contrary to the perception of many, few dealers can afford to be patrons of the arts and in most cases are not independently wealthy. Budgetary considerations often inhibit their more ardent and supportive impulses. In negotiating a stipend or a guarantee, ask for a sum that places reasonable expectations on the gallery. To require a greater amount can only lead to tension and to disappointment. One dealer I know gave a major artist a financial guarantee that the dealer could not possibly fulfill through retail sales. To meet the guarantee, the dealer peddled the artist's work at substantial discounts to personal friends and others. Such tactics are not profitable to the dealer and, perhaps more troublesome, can affect the integrity of the market for the artist's work.

If you are paid an advance against income to be received, make certain that it is nonrefundable. It is not infrequent for dealers to satisfy unfulfilled guarantees by buying the artist's work. That is an acceptable solution as long as the gallery and the artist are not placed in a conflicting relationship. It would take the integrity of a saint to refrain from selling gallery-owned material rather than consigned works. Nevertheless, if the guarantee is reasonable, the problem can be minimized.

Price

Your agreement should stipulate the prices of your work, and who sets them. This is a matter of critical concern to you and to your dealer, and you both should mutually agree on the prices set. You obviously wish to ask the highest possible price—as a matter of income and pride, and the dealer will want to maximize your income—and his. There is, in the long run, little to be gained by overpricing work. On the other hand, selling it too cheaply only diminishes the importance of the artist in the minds of clients. Remember, your prices can always be raised, but seldom reduced. While a dealer's guidance is helpful, the decision must be yours. Price clearly affects the volume of sales, but it is not only a business but a personal consideration by the artist as well. Some artists can produce to meet demand while others, as a practical or philosophical concern, choose to produce less.

The agreement should also provide that if you make private sales you will do so only at established or gallery prices. Certainly this is to protect the dealer, but it also is to protect you and your market. If you sell at a lower price, you are making it extremely difficult for your dealer to maintain your market. Artists are often considered "easy marks" by art patrons with a soft line and hard cash.

Accounting and Payment

Your agreement with a dealer should also specifically deal with the ticklish issue of accounting. For sales of consigned work, every gallery seems to handle the issue differently. Complete openness is the best policy. The agreement should specify when you are to be paid and that you should receive, with payment, a specific record of sales, including the names of the works, the purchase price, and the names of the purchasers. I've heard it said that certain galleries will not disclose the names of clients, presumably in the fear that the artist will subsequently approach gallery clients and deal directly with them. Such a fear does not justify secrecy. It is far more likely that a gallery client will approach the artist directly, in hopes of wheedling a good price, finding an opportunity to obtain work that is not in the gallery, or fostering a friendship. Again, these are matters that cannot be dealt with in a contract, but they are central to the underlying trust and respect between artist and dealer. If either you or your dealer undercuts the other's efforts, the relationship necessarily is a fragile one.

Galleries make accountings usually on a quarterly or a semiannual basis, although I understand there are some that account once a year. Dealers, of course, are reluctant to alter their accounting schedules to accommodate the wishes of an artist. Where substantial sales are involved, preparation of periodic accounts can be costly and time consuming. You should receive payment for the sales of your work a reasonable time after the conclusion of the accounting period. What is a "reasonable period" depends upon the amount of bookkeeping involved. Sixty to 90 days should be the limit.

You should also be aware that many clients and other galleries that purchase your work may take an unconscionable time to pay. The dealer understandably is reluctant (if not unable) to pay you for unpaid sales. If a substantial amount of money is involved, it is not unreasonable to insist that your work not be delivered to the purchaser until your dealer has received payment of at least your share of the proceeds. The slow-pay situation can be dealt with by requiring payment on all sales within a specified time after the sale. If payment is not received, it becomes the gallery's problem to collect. Although few galleries are in a position to be a bank, such a provision does keep the pressures on your dealer to collect on outstanding invoices. You will not, of course, endear yourself to your dealer with such an arrangement! Any dealer can regale you with sad tales of clients lost and work returned when they hassled clients for payment.

Artists will always be fearful of dealers in financial matters. The dealer has your work *and* your money. One way to ease some of the concern is for the dealer to furnish the artist with a copy of each sales invoice involving the artist's work. If your dealer is willing to comply with this seemingly reasonable request, you will at least know what is going on. Bulk invoices without breaking down individual sales should be avoided, as should the inclusion of the work of more than one artist on an invoice. Be cautioned, however, that a sales invoice is not money in the bank, so refrain from spending "proceeds" that haven't been collected. On all too many occasions, payment of the invoice is delayed, or, worse yet, the sale is subsequently voided. Nevertheless, with copies of invoices you will be saved the anxiety of wondering how the sales of your work are going.

It is also important that the dealer account for the works he or she is holding on consignment. The frequency of such accountings will depend upon the number of works you have with the dealer and, obviously, the ease with which that information can be provided. Nevertheless, both of you should feel comfortable that all the work is accounted for.

Insurance

Insurance is becoming a very sticky area in the artist-dealer relationship, as fewer insurers are willing to write art-loss policies, and premiums are escalating. While insurance is vital to any business, dealers are having to reconsider the extent of the coverage they obtain. Your agreement should provide that your work is insured by the dealer at least to the extent of what you would receive on its sale. The policy should also cover the damage or loss of your artwork in transit. (Public carriers are not renowned for their reverence of art.)

Be aware that not all damage is insurable. Many an insurance claim has been denied on the grounds that the nature of the damage constituted "ordinary wear and tear" and was not covered. This is especially true of prints and photographs and other works that are taken out of and put back into print drawers again and again and eventually show the effects of constant handling. Apportioning the loss for such uninsured damage is often the source of friction. The gallery should not solely bear those losses where the work has been handled expertly and carefully.

As the price of insurance rises, galleries raise the deductibles on their policies (the amount of the loss that is not covered) to contain costs. That, of course, means that in the event a less expensive work is lost or damaged, the insurance proceeds may not be enough to cover the artist's share of the loss. Who picks up the difference? Where it is clearly the fault of one party or another, no problem. But many losses result from the carelessness of others. Some galleries and institutions to whom work has been consigned for exhibition or sale have returned it in tatters, all the while denying any lack of care in handling or shipping. In those cases, it is often impolitic and sometimes impossible to recover on those losses. Your agreement can't deal with such problems, but common sense can, and you should be prepared to deal with them when they occur.

Change of Director or Dealer

Finally, you may wish to provide for your right to terminate the agreement in the event circumstances change and you are no longer transacting business with the dealer or director with whom you have established a close working relationship.

THE ARTIST-DEALER RELATIONSHIP

So much for the formal aspects of the artist-dealer arrangement. Other issues, not articulated in the agreement, are equally important to a strong working relationship. Don't let pride or ceremony inhibit you from "keeping in touch" with your dealer. If you feel neglected, don't be petulant and resentful, pick up the phone. But remember that you are not the only name on your dealer's dance card. That communication is vital to the relationship. If you are working on something exciting or new, your dealer should want to know. If you are approached for a museum show, let your dealer know. And don't feel as many do, "Why do I always have to do everything?" There is no room for pettiness or oversensitivity in this business relationship. You should be working together. Keep your dealer informed about anything that might make him or her more effective.

And make certain that you keep very good records concerning your work. As the art market has burgeoned and connoisseurship has declined, art as big business has had its share of "consumer problems." As the untutored have entered the marketplace, those who live off the ignorance of others have also dicovered a new opportunity. The result is growing concern on the part of the government to protect the consumer.

All this has had an effect on you and your dealer, and you should be aware of your responsibilities as an artist. Statutes are there to protect the unwary, and the art community can no longer be cavalier in what it does and does not tell the public. The specific provisions of the laws are not as important as is your realization of your responsibilities.

Artists have always used whatever materials suited them, and they have often been inattentive to the irrelevant details. You may not be interested, but the collector wishes to know what materials were used and whether they are stable or permanent. Newsprint, for example, is a popular contemporary material, but it does not react too well when exposed to sunlight. Nor do certain color photographs, watercolors, or drawings. That in itself is not a problem, but if the purchaser is not told, it could be. Furthermore, is the work a multiple? If so, who made them, how many were in the edition, is the edition limited, and how many artists proofs were made?

You should give all this information to your dealer. Pertinent information on the work itself is also helpful.

The artist should also be aware of certain other intangibles that play upon your relationship with your dealer.

The definition of the ideal artist-dealer relationship is as elusive as that of the perfect marriage. It is simply a matter of what works, given the extraordinary diversity of artists' needs and temperaments. Dealers, too, are a disparate lot. The relationship is often a deeply personal and subjective one. With artists' livelihoods in their dealer's hands, it is not surprising that many artists view dealers with guarded distrust, if not disdain. Some artists see dealers as primordial antagonists, insensitive bullies who employ their mercantile wiles to exploit artists and debase Art in their single-minded pursuit of commercial gain. It is a base canard, but, alas, few relationships can withstand such antagonism.

One reason for artists' distrust is that dealers control the walls; they have the power to say yes and the power to say no. What is perceived as dealer "power" is, for the yet unestablished artist without ready access to galleries, difficult to accept. In reality it is a misperception. Dealers have "power" as long as they have a choice among artists. But talk to a dealer about "power" in terms of successful artists! When a Jasper Johns takes a walk, for example, it's role reversal time. Paranoia is not the sole burden of the artist.

I don't intend for my remarks to read like a manifesto for the Society for the Prevention of Cruelty to Dealers, but it is important to understand the dealer's dilemma. Good artists make art for themselves, not for the "market," and dealers are wont to echo that sentiment. But the dealer's tastes, such as they are, must accommodate the need to survive. "Commitment," a favored word among artmongers, is a cherished ideal, as long as the rent is paid. An artist once told me that paying the rent was "my problem"; true enough, but it was also his problem. No gallery, no shows. Some successful galleries are fortunate enough to be able to carry a number of promising artists who have yet to establish a market, but the grim reality is that many cannot. Galleries are not museums, although that role is often wished upon them.

A successful gallery, as opposed to a "profitable" one, requires more than wall space and artists; a dealer must have or develop a strong clientele that buys the work. The market is not limitless (have you ever watched dealers squabble over a client?) and the temptation to bend to commercial considerations is fairly overwhelming. It is a regrettable, albeit certain, fact that there is a larger market for mediocre art, for post-post-post–impressionist paintings and wall decoration, than there is a market for interesting but untried new work that has yet to find a market. The dealer succeeds or fails on his judgment as to what is good *and* what will sell—a very subjective matter. It is understandable that artists will, for their own reasons, fault the judgment of dealers in that respect and, from time to time, consider dealers to be uninformed and insensitive cretins. The decisions are not easy ones, and doubtless some of them are made for all the wrong reasons. The occasional practice of giving shows to "well-connected" but marginal artists, or to prominent art patrons who also dabble in painting or photography, is indefensible, but our contempt surely won't change it. And few of us are in a position to cast the first stone.

The frustration of "the competition" also, I believe, underlies the occasional but strident complaint that galleries exclude women and minority groups. While I do not presume to speak for all dealers, I find it difficult to believe that any gallery

17 | The Integrity of the Artist, Dealer, and Gallery

Tibor de Nagy

TIBOR DE NAGY escaped from Hungary in 1948 and came to the United States via London in 1949. In 1950 he established the Tibor de Nagy Gallery in New York City. The gallery deals with contemporary painting, sculpture, and works on paper.

Art is a personal expression no matter how much or how little it covers of the universe. Whatever it encompasses, it has to be a sincere vision. The technical skill with which it is created is essential for its success. I see, in every artist, a priest of his own religion who wants to deliver his sermon in order to collect his believers. The places where he exposes his beliefs are art institutions and galleries. There are many priests but hardly any saints within a given epoch.

I believe in complete freedom of expression. You have to choose your own god and interpret him in your own way. But you have to be sincere about it if you want your prayers to be appreciated and remembered.

The brilliant mechanisms built in our heads are glorified computers. The creator must have constructed a great variety of such computers to try them out on so many animals. They registered only what was needed for their survival and reproduction. It was only when he attached to the computer a channel that had a direct spiritual contact with him that the human brain was completed and he announced, "Ecce Homo!"

Once this computer is fed with the history of art and absorbs the influences of numerous works of art, soaks in beauty and horror, past and present circumstances and experiences, the result may be a mixture that is an intellectual production—or there may be only a copy of something that has been done before. When the artist is capable of associating with the spirituality of the universe—that is to say when his soul feeds the computer as well—then the miracle happens. A striking balance of intellectual and emotional experience makes a great artwork. An original artwork will delight the responsive viewer.

THREE GALLERIES

Then the priest starts looking for a temple that would expose his sermon. He will have to face three types of possibilities:

1. The pioneering galleries, of which there are very few because they are rarely self-supporting.

228

2. Galleries that work only with well-established artists because they are out to make money.

3. Interior decorator galleries, of which there are many. They deal in pretty paintings with pleasing subject matter, or else with art that is very much in fashion. Often they will exhibit only with payment of a fee.

My gallery—although in existence nearly 40 years—still belongs in the first category and always will. It is, therefore, more interesting in my case to write about the coming-out period of the debutantes, than to concentrate on the high-geared business activities going on in the other two categories. The "Jus Prime Noctis" is a rather exciting experience. The virgin is so modest and yet so full of hope that one feels embarrassed even to talk business. The artist-dealer game starts!

THE ARTIST-DEALER GAME

The dealer-artist relationship is a rather complex one because it does not involve just commodities. It is rather like bringing up and exposing one's own daughters to society and then marrying them off as successfully as possible. Both parents will work together just as artists and dealers do for the best possible result.

Often even between the parents there are conflicting opinions as to what would be the most advantageous set of circumstances for solving the future of their offspring. Is the financial angle the most important? Or is it the moral standing and social position of the future husband (the place where the artwork finds its final home)? Should they expose and promote their daughter in a discreet, disciplined, and most dignified way, or just do it without restriction and hesitation?

When an artist ties himself or herself down with an art gallery, its reputation should give a clue about the handling practice of its artists. The artist can then decide whether or not it appeals to him or her.

The real and most common danger that threatens a lasting good relationship is where the two parties' mutual interest drifts apart, where the sharing of the burden of expenses and the dividing of sales price is at stake—who pays for what and how much and how to split up the money received for the artwork.

Agreements and legal contracts may help the relationship over a short period, but a lasting and good relationship depends on the basic philosophy and integrity of the matched parties. If the artist feels that the amount the dealer gets as his share from the sale is not a "necessary must," but a well-deserved cut for the services the gallery renders, the relationship will be pleasant and will flourish. The artist has to be convinced that for all the dealer's promotional work, advertising, printing expenses, exhibitions and placing of artworks in other shows, and—last but not least—the tremendous expense of the overhead needed to keep the gallery going, he has to take such a cut.

The artist has to see clearly that, once his name is becoming known and a demand is established for his work, it would become more and more difficult to decide whose merit it is when a sale or commission comes through in the artist's studio. It is no doubt the result of previous combined efforts. It happens because customers and agents think that, through a direct purchase from the artist, they may get a better bargain because the percentage to the gallery in commission is avoided. This is often the key factor in the breaking-up of relationships. It can be avoided only if the artist refuses to sell from his or her studio and directs the party to the gallery, or else gives an agreed-upon share to the gallery of every studio sale. If that procedure is carried out with honesty, the relationship will not suffer and no paranoia will start poisoning the atmosphere.

ART ADVISORS

It has been interesting to see how our rapidly growing art market has brought along with it a new profession which has squeezed itself in between the art dealer and corporations, banks and even smaller business offices—the art advisors. Some of them are well qualified; some of them quite ignorant but charming people. Some of them have established in the course of time a good vision but some cannot help remaining interior decorators. The quality of the corporations' art collections depends on them. Some of the art advisors are daring and ambitious and will want to educate the taste of their employers. But unfortunately the majority want to please unlettered executives with pretty, happy artworks—works that best fit the space and colors of the surroundings, just like a costume.

They not only take away business from dealers but also bring in much business which would not have happened without them. Whether they are salaried or not, they want a discount. Such discounts vary between 10 and 30 percent, thereby adding another problem to be worked out between the dealer and artist. Unfortunately, it is mostly the poor, not yet successful artist who has to share most of this added expense—not the rich ones who are in a position to dictate their terms.

Greediness will ruin a relationship. Therefore, in the long run, it will not benefit either the artist or the dealer. Sometimes marriages survive crises when adultery is confessed and the relationship gets back to normal. It is easier to forgive than to tolerate.

As a rule, artists are difficult—to say the least! Their emotions are more intense. Their egos are either enormous, or just the opposite, but they are never well balanced. Artists love and hate, and hardly ever feel neutral. Their enthusiasm is exaggerated. They recognize beauty faster. They are more sensitive in connection with other peoples' suffering. Their intellect keeps them from ever being boring to other people. Their jealousy tortures them day and night. They give more than they consume. In short, if you want a smooth existence, keep away from the art world. But if you want to really live—meaning suffer and burst out of joy—become involved with artists! You will never fade away; you will just die of exhaustion.

Generalizations are like statistics. They very often distort or even lie. The truth of the matter remains expressed in Goethe's *Faust:*

> He wants from the sky the fairest star, from earth the highest joy that's to be had: everything near and everything far can never satisfy his deeply stirred desire.

PART FOUR

EXHIBITING

Artists are responsible for the best and the worst they have to live out. We can't assume for a second that because we associate with a dealer or any kind of a system, we transfer the responsibility to somebody else to cover our act.

Larry Bell

18 | New York: A Dealer

Ivan Karp

IVAN KARP is the founder and president of O. K. Harris Works of Art in New York City and the unofficial mayor of SoHo.

It has been observed by those of us who care, and who are constantly alert to significant developments in American Art, that since the mid-1960s, and especially in the 1980s, there has been a dramatic growth in the number of mature and innovative artists working in painting, sculpture, and the related arts. This enrichment of the visual arts culture has occurred throughout the country, and a network of commercial enterprises known commonly as art galleries has grown in reasonable proportion to both the increase in the number of serious artists at work and the enlargement of the collecting public. This is particularly noticeable in the Soho district of Manhattan, and remarkably so in parts of Los Angeles (which had functioned as a kind of sleeping giant of the arts in the postwar years).

An explanation for this exciting evidence of a flourishing culture might well reveal that an increase in prosperity and leisure, and the growth of enlightenment as to the importance of the artist's contribution to a progressive society, have permitted persons of imagination to venture beyond the outlines of labor and commerce so vividly apparent in our brief but robust history. Yet the subtle and myriad factors that generate a visual culture in a particular place and time are never totally apparent, and remain a part of the very mystery of the creative process and the fabric that it generates.

All artists seek fame and fortune, preferably as soon as possible, and hopefully before they are 40. It has become evident that the quickest method of achieving this wholesome ambition to begin with is to have your work exhibited in a clean, elegant space that is populated by rich, intelligent collectors, enlightened art critics and museum officials, and presided over by a brilliant and generous art dealer. To have your work exhibited under these superlative conditions, you should have some evidence that your work has achieved a high measure of technical maturity that has struck, to some degree at least, an innovative chord.

"Evidence" implies that a majority of the "informed" have acclaimed your work and have included it in professional exhibitions, or referred to it in the press, or purchased it for a significant collection, or awarded it a meaningful prize in a rated competition. If your mother, father, spouse, or lover celebrates your artistic achievement, this would not necessarily be considered competent appraisal. To qualify as one informed to make judgments of works of aesthetic merit, one would also have to have been adjudged to be so qualified. This is a rather mysterious process since there is no known instrument that can measure a person's visual perception or, for that matter, what constitutes a work of art. It is only a matter of opinion.

It is therefore important to understand that some owners of art galleries have felt obliged to develop credentials through scholarship, regular collecting, or simply intense involvement in the art community. But there are many other persons operating galleries, who are simply burdened with leisure or money, who commence an art dealership because it is a clean and dignified profession which often brings media attention, community respect, and invitations to colorful social events. However, the judgment such amateurs may bring to a new artist's work may be far from accurate, and you must try to understand this in advance. There is no state law that requires art dealers to take a test to prove their expertise.

EXHIBITING IN NEW YORK CITY

Assuming that you, the young, ambitious artist, have convinced yourself, or have been convinced by others alleged to be informed, that you are ready to present your recent production to an established art gallery, New York City might well be your destination, since this great metropolis retains its role as the Biggest Apple for the visual artist.

This does not imply that you are obliged to take up residence in the city or open a studio, which is near impossible at this interval. But to inaugurate a career, one must circulate in the fine arts arena for a period of time and become acquainted with its method of functioning; make friends, whenever possible, with exhibiting artists; and attend pertinent social events, particularly gallery openings.

New York City has over 500 galleries, of which about 300 specialize in the works of living artists. Of these, about 75 exhibit work of a high professional standard on a regular basis. Of the 75 galleries so described, the majority have but one main exhibition area where 10 or 11 one-person shows are given every year, and perhaps one group show or "invitational" where promising young artists are shown with one or two works by each. If a gallery so described has a complement of 15 or 20 "affiliated" artists, it is unlikely to be assiduously seeking new talent. "Affiliated" means that the gallery expects to exhibit particular artists on a regular schedule—perhaps once a year if the artist is especially productive, and certainly every other year if the artist provides a body of work for the occasion. It would therefore appear that only a handful of openings for new talent occurs during the exhibition season, and artists are wont to discover that many of the dealers will not even review the slides of applicants. Such dealers are apparently unconcerned with the elation of making a "discovery" but will take recommendations concerning talent from their own successful artists or those they consider to be members of the art establishment.

PRESENTING YOUR WORK

When it comes to confronting the owners or directors of galleries for the first time, you must be in possession of the ability to survive repeated, and not always tender, rejection; in other words, you must have emotional resiliency and some perfectly intelligible evidence of what your work is about. This means a packet of 10 to 20 slides—or better still, large transparencies of current work—all properly marked as to topside, material, date of production, and size. A voluminous body of slides presented to the dealer may fatigue her in advance, or make her skeptical of your ability to sort out the significant portion of your work. Restraint in the presentation makes a good impression. It is sometimes permissible to show a painting or an object to clarify the images conveyed through photos. But most dealers will not enjoy your deploying a number of works around the exhibition area or in the private office, and he or she is likely to express physical or audible agitation if the work you show is remote from the gallery's exhibition concept. It is therefore imperative that you make a full survey of current exhibitions in the various galleries to try to determine, from what is shown, the approximate style of art the dealer prefers. Documentation of your previous exhibitions, achievements, and criticism may be offered. But a dealer with strong convictions about what is important art is not likely to be impressed by such material.

There are less than a dozen dealers in all of New York who will grant an interview to inspect your work upon your unannounced appearance. In most places an appointment must be made by mail or on the phone. Slides or photos sent in the mail should always be accompanied by a return envelope with proper postage and packaging. Dealers of good conscience will review the work and respond with commentary. Others may be distracted or uncaring and return your photos without any evidence that they have actually seen them—or they may not return them at all. It would be both stupid and irrational for a dealer to reject an artist because of race or gender, since the progress that a gallery makes in its fame and prosperity is primarily dependent upon the objects exhibited and not the person who produced them. There are, however, several cooperative enterprises that show the work of women exclusively. If a female artist prefers to be shown under their auspices, the selection process of the cooperative is generally through the consent of the membership.

Those who are made to feel utterly defeated by continued rejections should find a friend or relation to carry in evidence of their achievement. The various dealers really don't care who brings in the evidence since they exhibit not the artists but their production. A dealer who finds the work engaging may ask to see it in person—that is, to visit the artist's studio. In most cases the dealer will not invite the artist to ship works to the gallery for various reasons—such as the lack of uncrating facilities. In this event, artists who are not residents of New York City, and have found some measure of interest in their work, should locate a place in the city to set up some of their work for the dealer to see at his or her convenience. Since it could be burdensome for an artist to make such an arrangement, it makes sense for the artist to try to interest several dealers in his or her work so that the effort involved in transporting it will be more likely to prove worthwhile.

As in much of human endeavor and in many professions, physical beauty and/or intense and repeated proclamation of one's achievement may bring success of merit sooner than deserved. Fortunately, the majority of prominent art dealers possess some subtlety of mind, and are capable of resisting duress, if not beauty. There are also many artists who are identified by critics or curators as harbingers of a brave new vision, whose work is shallow and merely fashionable. There is nothing for an artist of integrity to do about such injustice but to persist in his convictions that his work is of transcendent importance and to try to get it shown.

All this may lead to nothing except an accumulation of praise and vague promises which may add to the artists' courage to persist or, conversely, to despair, or to pursuit of endeavors removed from the arts. It has been suggested that creativity, surely an overused and often misapplied description of a singular human attribute, is its own reward, and that personal serenity results from its possession. However, as an art dealer with more than 30 years of experience, I have rarely found this to be true. People who make things strictly to be exhibited are dedicated to the hope that these objects will be seen in their lifetime and eventually, but certainly, applauded. Fortunately, there is currently a sufficient number of enlightened observers to prevent an artist of consequence from being totally ignored.

19 | Los Angeles: A Dealer

James Corcoran

JAMES CORCORAN owns and operates the James Corcoran Gallery in Los Angeles (Santa Monica), specializing in contemporary painting, sculpture, drawings, and graphics.

Today the visual experience of painting has evolved into a complex business, the business of art. As Andy Warhol once said, "Business art is the step that comes after ART." So there it is, in just a few words; my business follows art. And business art concerns the artists (both living and dead) who create art, as well as the audience or market (nearly always alive) that desires and acquires art. My role, in terms of dealer and gallery, is to act as liaison between the artist and his audience.

The chairman of Twentieth Century Art at the Metropolitan, William S. Lieberman, has described artists as "the only superior beings of the art world." Obviously recognizing this, the contemporary artist Billy Al Bengston has further pointed out, "All great artists have sexual magnetism." Sounds awfully nifty, this role as artist, wouldn't you say? Quite exclusively, these superior sexual magnets create art. Yet it is easier for some than others: Robert Rauschenberg can, with some authority, proclaim, "It is art because I say it is." Statistics, however, show that in the state of California alone there are 50,000 art students who will eventually seek representation from a mere handful of dealers representing contemporary work in Los Angeles. Adding to this predicament, I have heard it said that at a generous estimate, perhaps one-half of 1 percent of contemporary painting and sculpture made and sold today will have any market value at all in 30 years' time. Statements such as these point to the sad situation facing new artists today.

As for the dealers—well, it has been rumored about the best of them that they know the predilections of every important collector in New York and perhaps a half-dozen other cities as well. So the story goes, they can or should be able to tell you the whereabouts of seemingly every modern work in private hands. Whether this is in fact an accurate observation of the mass of us or not, it describes the role assignment. The dealer provides a perspective of the art market. His or her knowledge about collections, collectors, transactions, and the finances involved—particularly in the present inflationary economy—must reflect a consummate day-to-day awareness not only of the art world, but of the international business world as well.

THE "VALUE" OF ART

"Nowadays people know the price of everything and the value of nothing." That was Oscar Wilde, yesterday. Today, specifically in the art market, he might have said, "Nowadays people like the price of everything new and the value of everything old." It is a fact that dealers who exhibit the work of living, contemporary artists have often subsidized these exhibits from transactions involving the work of dead artists. In my experience, no contemporary dealer is going to turn away a Rembrandt if one is offered to him. Such a reaction is due primarily to the large profit margin involved. Few living artists can generate enough profit to keep contemporary art dealers in a robust business. Also, my clients who invest in art are not particularly interested in experimenting with the potential of the younger artist. For the most part, they look for sound track records and established names.

Is all this just a matter of finances? From one viewpoint, it can appear to be. A successful businessman might insist that making money is art, and working is art, and good business is the best art. However, intrinsic to the good business of ART is the market's appreciation of and desire to own art. A former chairman of Sotheby's, in an interview for the BBC, noted, "Without covetousness you are not going to have an appreciation of art. And I think that if covetousness by some magic was destroyed art would come to an end. It's very rare to be able to appreciate art without wanting to own it." It is quite true that those of us who are involved in the art business do stand at attention in front of the art and covet it. This is not all based upon the dollar. There is something more to all the looking, evaluating, appreciating. As the market fluctuates, collectors and dealers do take note, but basically art retains a bottom line of its own—beauty.

I believe it is what George Santayana called "emotional consciousness" that separates the ordinary from the exceptional viewer. As Santayana noted, "Expression depends upon the union of two terms, one of which must be furnished by the imagination, and a mind cannot furnish what it does not possess. The expressiveness of everything accordingly increases with the intelligence of the observer." It is this aspect of expressiveness that keeps art a controversial commodity all its own, despite its value as an investment.

THE FUNCTION OF THE ART GALLERY

The fundamental qualities of art itself do not change. It is the art business, in reflecting economic pressures and intense internal competition, that has become increasingly more intricate as an industry. Galleries function to confront this intricate business of art. It is their job to set up shows; handle clients and inquiries; and process, filter, and organize miscellaneous data relevant to both the art they sell and the business of selling it.

Although galleries exist to relieve the artists they represent of these problems, in L.A. as elsewhere, there are simply not enough galleries and collectors to go around. The existing surplus of art school graduates and art initiates have no choice but to accept this as part of their reality.

There are a few alternate support structures in Los Angeles: Los Angeles Institute of Contemporary Art (LAICA), Los Angeles Contemporary Exhibitions (LACE), new galleries burgeoning especially in the downtown area, and academic-sponsored exhibitions. These developments provide a degree of exposure to the community of artists. Contemporary art dealers such as myself do look for new faces as far as our gallery is concerned, but we need artists who have clearly demonstrated themselves over the years. Occasionally I have been fortunate enough to encounter such new artists. But all in all, it is a generous approximation to say that in Los Angeles we have 10 established galleries representing 20 artists each. That's only 200 artists receiving representation. And, supposing an arbitrary law of attrition in California stipulated that between 10 and 20 percent of these artists leave the area each year, only 20 to 40 new names could be absorbed into the system. A depressing fact, but that's the game.

I continue to be astonished at the number of artists who come to me unsolicited. Politely, many of them bring slides in and leave them overnight so I can take a look at them at my leisure. One artist came to me with photographs depicting "Artist Undergoing Surgery." She was having holes drilled into her head. Some enthusiasts desiring to surprise me with examples of their work pounce on me outside of my office. This cat-and-mouse aspect of the Artist in Search of a Gallery is by no means unimportant for the artist. The need for representation, particularly among newer artists, is a real need. The problems are obvious.

> He was interested in my pictures, he said bring some more into the Marlborough, and I did, and they HATED them. Harry Fischer thought they were awful, and told Kas, "These are dreadful; what are you doing with this junk?"
>
> —David Hockney

But this search for a commercial outlet plays a minute part in a bigger picture—the relationship between the individual artist and the process of creating his art. While I find this relationship impossible to evaluate in any precise way, I offer the following which may shed some light: in June 1943, Mark Rothko and Adolph Gottlieb, with the then unacknowledged assistance of Barnett Newman, collaborated on a now well-known letter (written in response to a negative review). It begins, "To us art is an adventure into an unknown world, which can be explored only by those willing to take risks."

It's not a simple situation to understand. If you're a superior being, a sexual magnet, the art world may be for you. If you follow art around and covet it intensely, you may qualify as a dealer. If you take risks, you might be the next Mark Rothko. But keep in mind the philosophy of Andy Warhol: "If you say that artists take risks, it's insulting to the men who landed on D-Day, to stuntmen, to babysitters, to Evel Knievel, to stepdaughters, to coal miners, and to hitchhikers, because they're the ones who really know what 'risks' are."

20 Washington, D.C.: A Dealer

Christopher S. Middendorf

CHRISTOPHER S. MIDDENDORF founded the Middendorf Gallery in 1974. The gallery specializes in twentieth-century American art and represents the work of outstanding artists currently working in Washington as well as the work of many nationally known contemporary artists.

THE WASHINGTON D.C. SCENE

In the last 15 years Washington has boomed as an art center. Its art market has thrived as well, but does not have the critical mass to be an active market. Instead, the Washington art-buying public breaks down into pockets of collectors, each focused on its particular area of collecting. In terms of historical painting, sculpture, prints, and photography, these groups of collectors are some of the most knowledgeable and astute in the country. They collect at the very highest quality level, using Washington's tremendous museum resources as their guide and standard.

As one looks to contemporary culture and to collecting contemporary art in Washington, the issue is more complex. For the young or developing artist, Washington is a generous and supportive art scene. The best young artists quickly gain local followings. They are actively collected by collectors, and the strong presence of corporate collections contributes to the possibility of additional sales. As soon as artists reach a certain price limit, however, their market cools off. This is the crucial point for them. They can stay in D.C., get good teaching jobs, and survive well off their local following. But in that position it is extremely hard to make the necessary step into the New York market. If artists choose to stay in D.C., they can enjoy the high quality of life, but may always regret not having tried to make it in New York.

For the collector buying contemporary art in D.C., one can be an active collector in the local scene, but it is extremely difficult to collect the best contemporary art. Such art is rarely shown in the Washington galleries, so it is necessary to travel to New York to see the art that is considered "world class."

One might well conclude that, for the working artist, Washington is very supportive of its own to a certain point; then it becomes the responsibility of the artist to move on and make his or her mark in the national marketplace. For the collector, there is an excellent opportunity to buy extremely good artwork of younger artists in Washington, but the marketplace for the best new artists is in New York; to collect this level of artwork, one must develop a presence in New York to get access to top work.

For the dealer, there is great satisfaction in getting young artists going in their careers, selling their work to the strong local following, and slowly building reputations for the best of these artists outside of Washington. But that may well be the extent to which the dealer's efforts have an impact. If local Washington artists desire to be a part of the national marketplace, and a Washington dealer desires only to handle work that is viable on the national or international scene, the only choice left to the Washington dealer is to help the artist develop representation in New York. The Washington gallery must then consider itself the "parent" gallery, and that D.C. dealer, who may have represented the artist in the important developing stages of his or her career, must now take a back seat.

When the artist has established himself or herself in the New York scene, the D.C. dealer can then become one of the galleries that exhibits the artist's work outside of New York. As a dealer, it can be frustrating to watch this phenomenon take place, but as the real art market is in New York, D.C. dealers cannot compete from the outside. The D.C. dealer must then become established in areas that may provide some economic protection. Some dealers have found that the best way to offset the economic impact of New York on the contemporary D.C. art scene is to handle historical objects in the stronger areas of collecting, in addition to contemporary art. Such a business decision may seem more conservative, but the D.C. art audience—from museums to law firms to corporations to collectors—is less conscious of fashion and more likely to buy works of art that have historical importance.

I have represented and exhibited the work of contemporary artists for 15 years. During this time I have made mistakes about artists, represented some of them rather poorly and others rather well. But during this period, I have been keenly aware of what sort of relationship I wanted to have with artists, how I felt they should be promoted, and to what ends I wanted to reach for their work.

I have also been approached in business by many artists in ways that have sometimes been difficult and painful for both the artists and for me. In the following pages I will discuss certain things the artist may do to facilitate his or her entrance into a commercial gallery, some of the pitfalls that may occur, and some of the things I feel are and should be the responsibility of the artist in the development of his "career." I am speaking as a commercial art dealer, however, so some of the things discussed pertain to the dealer's perspective in the artist-dealer relationship. Together I hope that these pages will help to illuminate what must ultimately be a fine balance in the inevitable partnership between the artist and the art dealer.

OBTAINING SLIDES

First and foremost, you as an artist must obtain a high-quality set of slides or, even better, 4- by 5-inch transparencies. These should be accompanied by a complete list of what the slides represent: media, dimensions, date, and edition

size, if applicable. You should have slides of about ten of your most recent pieces and have available a short slide history of your earlier work. Concentrate on this. A beautifully printed resume means nothing, nor do reviews of your accomplishments. They may aid the dealer later in trying to promote your work, but keep in mind that the dealer is himself or herself a promoter and a salesperson and is most likely not going to be sympathetic to a sales pitch from you. Remember also that it is the work that counts. Presenting it in a clear and well-documented way is of the utmost importance.

You are now equipped and ready to begin the process. Unless you already have connections to a nationally known gallery, you must first concentrate on your own geographic area. There you will be able to build a local reputation most easily. The important thing now is to learn everything you can about the local galleries. In Washington the most established galleries are members of an organization called the Washington Art Dealers Association. The Association publishes a directory of its member galleries and is a clearinghouse for information regarding the galleries. You should know the types of exhibits the galleries have, the artists they represent, and the kinds of people who work in the galleries. Follow the galleries for several months, being aware of the visibility of their shows in the community, their advertising, the size of their openings, and the sort of press coverage they get. However, the most important qualification, as far as you are concerned, is the quality of artists represented by the gallery. The better the artists, the better the collectors frequenting the gallery and seeing your work.

CHOOSING THE RIGHT GALLERY

You should then choose the gallery that seems to fit your work best, so do your homework about what type of work each gallery exhibits. (Many galleries show a wide spectrum of work.) Try not to waste your time or the dealer's by showing your figurative work to a gallery devoted to abstraction. Also choose a gallery with space compatible to the size of your work. After you have made your choice of the gallery in which you are most interested, make a list of the other galleries.

Now you are ready to approach the gallery of your choice. You must first understand how rarely a dealer will take on an artist walking in the door with slides. "If he is so good, what is he doing out pounding the pavement?" You must be more subtle. Treat your own work as the dealer would treat it if he or she takes you on—as something special, something rare and important.

Begin by putting the dealer on the list for any shows in which you are participating. It is also a good time to begin putting together a mailing list of your own. At first, this list will be mostly friends and relatives, but as you continue, it will grow to include collectors, curators, and critics. Probably the dealer will throw away your announcements, but quite possibly he will remember your name. Try to get to know the artists in the galleries' stables. They are your best avenue for access, as dealers tend to listen to their own artists. As you begin to make these contacts, put them on your mailing list as well. Drop them short notes asking them to stop by and see your work if they get the chance. Try to build up a groundswell of enthusiasm about your work. Operate under the assumption that all galleries are booked two years in advance, so you have plenty of time to get the ball rolling. Of course schedules do open up, but you are best off if you are not in a hurry (another aspect of being subtle, since you certainly *are* in a hurry!).

But your main goal during this period is just to make the dealer aware of your work. Dealers are always in need of something new and good to sell, and if your work catches their interest, they will make the advance. It can also be beneficial during this period to get to know the dealer. Now this can be difficult and embarrassing, especially if you attempt to become friends at an important museum opening. The dealer will drop you like a stone if his best client walks by as you are introducing yourself, and you should try to avoid this situation. But getting to know the dealer can be a tremendous asset, even if he chooses not to handle your work. If the dealer respects your work, his contacts and knowledge may help you later. If the dealer does end up representing you, you will most likely be spending a fair amount of time together, and it helps greatly if you get along easily together.

Now you have reached the stage where you have been rebuffed and have gone on to the rest of your list or, through some of your subtle maneuverings, you have enticed the dealer to your studio. The first thing to realize is that although the dealer has been to hundreds of studios, he is just as uneasy as you are. First, he is out of his gallery, and second, he knows that his reaction to your work is making you nervous. You are the host, so do what you can to put both of you at ease. Try to have your best work hanging, as this may help to get the conversation going. Also have readily available five or six of your best works. Do not show the dealer thirty works, unless he asks. Showing thirty works will tire you both, and if the dealer has not responded to the first six, he is not likely to be swayed by the additional paintings. Make sure the dealer has time to really look at your best work, as most dealers will agree that first impressions are not always correct, and it is to your benefit to give the dealer time for careful analysis. Try not to talk about your work unless it is something pertinent to a particular piece; it rarely works, and most often will put him off immediately.

There are some dealers who will wax poetic right off the bat, but for the most part they will not say anything other than a few brief comments. They will want to let the work sink in, and if it is good work, they may want to go back to the gallery and savor it, and decide what to do about you later on. Do your best not to put the dealer on the spot by asking him how he feels about the work. If the dealer does not say anything about giving you a show, or getting back to you later on, then you have struck out. But it is at this point that you want to turn on the charm. The dealer may not be able to do anything for you now, but there is always the possibility that he may have a group show in the future that could include your work. Or he might be working with a client who may want something like your work. You want to leave these doors open. Do not ask for recommendations either. If the dealer feels your work is good, but not up his alley, he will make recommendations on his own. It is sad to say, but in this situation (the dealer coming to visit the artist), it is a dealer's market. Although it is potentially a humiliating experience, you must have confidence in your own work. You must realize that if the work is good, there will be a dealer who will appreciate it, and recognize the talent you have.

ALTERNATIVES TO COMMERCIAL GALLERIES

If you have been rejected with no open doors, in addition to moving down your list you should begin to look at the other types of shows besides commercial gallery situations. In most cities in this country, there are alternative spaces of all kinds. They will be the most receptive to your work as they are supported primarily by the community and should in turn be supportive of local artists. Also, be aware of juried shows at local museums. These can be great ways to gain local exposure to get other dealers to see your work.

Although it may be hard at this point, keep doing your own legwork and promotion. Although you may have a friend or relative who would love to take your work around to galleries and museums, this can often do more harm than good. For the most part these well-intentioned people correctly feel you are best off in your studio. But you must take responsibility for your own work and realize that although well meaning, these friends are often quite naive. The reaction they may cause with dealers and curators can do irreparable damage. Let them promote you to their friends, even let them sell your work to their friends, but if you are going to have an agent of any kind, it must be someone who knows what he is doing.

If the dealer has responded to your work and offers you a show, the relationship now changes dramatically. Suddenly you will be working together for the same goal: to promote you to the fame and riches you have deserved for so long! But you are about to enter a relationship that is very important, with a person whom you may see only three or four times a year. You must achieve a balance of proximity and distance, business and friendship, dependence and independence. This relationship will be based on responsibility—the responsibility that the dealer has to you for your work, the management of your career and promotion, as well as for the more practical things like sales and insurance. Your responsibility to the dealer is to continue to do good work and to support him in what he is trying to do for you. This will be hard to determine, but as you become accustomed to the way in which your dealer works, it will become clear.

SHOULD YOU HAVE A CONTRACT?

As the relationship begins, you must try to clear up as many of the areas of responsibility as you can. Certain dealers will present you with a contract. This should spell out exactly who pays for what, and when, who covers insurance, when you should be told if a sale has taken place, and how long you will have to wait to be paid. These contracts are usually pretty straightforward, but it is worthwhile to have an attorney look it over. On the other hand most dealers do not have any sort of contract. The art business is a business based on trust, and as things are drawn into a contract this trust can slowly change. It then becomes a relationship based on a contract, not a relationship based on trust. Contracts can be very effective, and do protect all parties mentioned above, but there is much more to the artist-dealer relationship than can be put down on paper and signed. In adhering to a contract, one tends to do what is required, and no more. But the promotion of an artist, especially a young or developing artist, takes much more time than most contracts require. It takes enthusiasm on an almost constant level, and you gain this most often by having a good relationship with the dealer, not necessarily by having a good contract. Contracts are basically irrelevant in this situation, as there is no way in a contract to spell out what a dealer really must do to promote an artist or to require how that dealer should feel about the work.

It is important to note, however, that there are dealers who take advantage of this no-contract situation and may cause you to lose your work without being paid for it. If you have done your research on the galleries, this should not happen to you. But if you are an artist from another town, with no way of keeping in easy reach of your work in a gallery, be advised to have some sort of agreement between you and the gallery. The artists who usually get themselves into this sort of bind are those who so hungry for exposure and for a gallery they do not think carefully.

With or without a contract, you should make sure always to get receipts for your work. You should pay enough attention to what goes on in the gallery to know if any of your pieces have been missing from the gallery premises after six months, and why you've not been told.

WORKING OUT THE DETAILS OF THE
ARTIST/DEALER RELATIONSHIP

The first thing you and the dealer will probably discuss will be the timing of your show. Although you are dying to have your work shown, it may take a certain amount of time to get the momentum going. Also, the lead time for advertising and other forms of promotion can be three or four months. Thus you are best off if you give the dealer and yourself plenty of time to get ready.

During this time the details of your relationship should be worked out. First and most important to both of you will be the setting of the prices and the commission for the dealer. However, here again it may seem like a dealer's market. If it is a good gallery—one that is respected in the artistic community for its exhibits of living artists, and one that has been in business several years—the dealer will know exactly where he wants to set the prices. This can be based on the price of your work in the past and also on the prices of work by other artists in the gallery and area. The commission the dealer will take will be around fifty percent. He may want even more if he is buying the work outright. This can be a mutually beneficial thing for the dealer to do. First, it exhibits his confidence in you in a significant way. Second, it may allow you the money to frame and present your work professionally.

This situation may also be damaging to you, since the dealer may buy all your great works for less than the going rate. You should be careful to protect your interests; in the long run you are best off keeping as good a selection of your work as you can. Thus the way to keep yourself and the dealer content is to sell off a limited number of pieces at a time, being careful to retain some of the very best for yourself. Another alternative to this situation is to set up a certain commission for the dealer if he takes your works on consignment, and an even higher commission if he purchases the work outright or mounts an exhibition of your work. The costs involved in putting on exhibitions are tremendous, and the extra percentage can be a significant difference in making certain it is done right.

Once the hurdle of the commission schedule is surpassed the other aspects of the relationship are fairly simple. Any works the dealer takes on consignment from you should be covered by his insurance against almost all forms of loss. The insurance coverage should be worded so that in case of loss you will receive your commission as if the work had been sold. You should take all precautions to protect your own work as well. It should be your responsibility to make the dealer and the gallery staff aware of any necessary special handling techniques. Also the quality of materials for your work and its frames should be the best you can afford. It is important to note that when a dealer sells one of your works, be it for $500 or $5000, he then becomes responsible for the lasting quality of your work—physically, not aesthetically. If the work falls out of its frame, or the stretcher is warped, or the paint chips off, the upset client will call the dealer, not you. Also, and more important, if the dealer is selling your work as something special, he wants it to last. As the price for good contemporary art rises, it is reassuring to a potential buyer to know that the work is made to last.

In addition to the quality slides you used originally in discussion with your dealer, you should supply him with the best master set of slides or transparencies you can put together. This, combined with a complete scrapbook of your reviews and catalogues, will be not only a valuable tool for the dealer in the promotion of your work, but also a valuable visual record for you. This sort of accurate documentation may seem like a tremendous hassle, but in the long run will be extremely useful to you and the dealer. The expense for this material should be borne by the artist, but any additional copies of slides or written material should be paid for by the dealer.

PROMOTIONAL EXPENSES

The gallery will also be responsible for several other expenses. The most costly of these is advertising. The budget for advertising should be discussed between you and the dealer. The amount of money that can be spent on ads is tremendous, but the artist should realize that the amount and size of ads should be balanced against the current sales price of the work. As the prices rise, so then can the budget for advertising. Also included in this budget will be the cost of invitations to the opening, mailing expenses, and the cost of the opening itself. These costs should all be borne by the dealer. At first, simple postcards and cheap wine will make economic sense to the dealer, but with luck, as time passes, catalogues, posters, and an open bar will be your standard.

The budget for ads and invitations, the costs of frames and openings all are part of the fine balance that has to be worked out. Resolution of these simple problems in an easy way without either party feeling he is getting the short end of the stick is very important; not as important as the quality of the artwork, or the quality of the representation shown by the dealer, but nevertheless something that can damage a relationship based on trust and responsibility.

The final link between the dealer and the artist must be respect. The dealer should sincerely respect the work he is handling, and if this changes in any way, then you as the artist are in the wrong place, and the dealer will probably have a difficult time selling the work. But if the dealer is sincere, he will continue to respect you and your work as long as he represents you. Also his respect for you will begin as soon as he responds to your work. The respect you show to the dealer will come much more slowly.

In the early stages of working with a dealer, it is quite easy to treat the situation as an adversary relationship. You hope your work will be shown and promoted in a certain way, yet you have to have these discussions about commissions and costs which are very difficult for you, especially since you may not understand how the gallery works. But as the relationship strengthens, framing costs, advertising expenses, and commissions will become less and less important. The more important issues will be placement of your work in the right collections and shows, and your gaining more national and international exposure. These are the areas where a good dealer will earn your respect.

GALLERY OWNER VS. ART DEALER

These are the types of issues separating what I call the gallery owners from the art dealers. A gallery owner will put on exhibits of artists every month and that is all. Of course they will try to sell the work as best they can and even promote you in a certain way. But an art dealer will do much more, and will always be thinking of much more. Someone once told me that being an art dealer is a terrible way to make a living, but a wonderful way to get rich. By this I have always assumed he meant that if you are able to support, show and purchase works by a group of artists who interest you, eventually, if you have done a good job, you will have a tremendous art collection. A good art dealer, although he will always be concerned with the short run, will more than likely be looking at your work as something he will be promoting for a long time. For this reason there will be situations where he may sacrifice a sure sale in order to be able to do more with you and your work. An artwork is not something that should be indiscriminately sold. Objects sold to someone who does not care deeply about the work might as well not be sold at all. For an artist who has limited production, the dealer may be able to sell all of his work without making an effort. But the good dealer will be more concerned with where the work goes; whether it will be seen again and cared for; whether it is becoming part of a collection that means something.

A good dealer will be of great assistance in reaching galleries in other cities to handle your work. You have already gone through this exercise once, and the last thing you should be doing is trying to do it all over again in another city. Your dealer should write you letters of introduction to dealers he respects but might not know, or convince dealers in other cities that he knows of your worth as an artist. Now the tables turn, and it becomes the dealer's turn to be subtle. Getting your work into fine collections, museums, or other cities will most likely be done by word of mouth. It will be up to the dealer to build on a larger scale the type of enthusiasm for your work I recommended for you earlier.

Also, as your real talent as an artist begins to surface, the dealer's talent in his craft will emerge also. The dealer's talent will not be simply in selling, as he would probably be better off selling cars, but will appear more in his ability to assess the whims of his clients, the strange quirks in tastes of the people who frequent his gallery. It will be knowledge of the collections of the clients with whom he works that will enable him to bring your work up at the moment when it might actually do some good. It will be his ability to earn the respect of your artistic community in order to better convince them of your true quality as an artist.

These are the types of qualities in a dealer that will be hard to judge until you have worked together for a while. But they are the types of things to look for in a dealer, and the types of things you will want him to bring to the fine balance of your relationship. Your paintings, sculpture, or whatever media you work in must come first and be of a certain quality. If they do, then you are in the position to demand an equal level of quality in the representation of your work.

THE WASHINGTON, D.C. SCENE

As far as the actual marketplace goes, Washington has evolved from a sleepy southern city of ten years ago, to an active almost thriving art center. Beginning with the Kennedy Center, Washington has seen the arrival of the Hirshhorn, the East Wing of the National Gallery and the new Air and Space Museum change, enhance and pick up the pace of the cultural activity in the city. At the same time new commercial galleries have sprung up all over; hundreds of artists have moved here and collectors are now starting to come as well.

Even with this frenzy of new activity, Washington is a tenuous art market. The major collectors have always chosen to go to New York to buy, and rightfully so, as there were not major pictures for them here. Now there are, but it is difficult to break them of their old habits. But the new collectors and the increased interest in collecting by corporations have stimulated the art market here. This combined with the tremendous influx of foreign and American visitors has caused many galleries to thrive, and made Washington an exciting and visible place for any artist to exhibit.

Yet it is still true that the market for art is created in New York. It is possible for an artist to survive and thrive in D.C., but to expand his or her market, to gain a national following and reputation, and to achieve major prices, the artist must be represented and shown in New York.

21 Chicago: A Dealer

Rhona Hoffman

RHONA HOFFMAN is owner of the Hoffman Gallery in Chicago.

Since the first edition of this book in 1982, enormous changes have taken place in the world's art market. There are more artists, dealers, galleries, museums, alternative spaces, as well as more collectors—private and corporate—on every continent and in almost every country.

For America, 1982 may well have been a water-shed year vis-à-vis the attitudes and habits of collecting. American dealers, collectors, and museum curators went in greater numbers than ever to Dokumenta in Kassel, the Zeitgeist exhibition in Berlin, and the Venice Bienalle, returning home with a greater understanding and interest in contemporary European art, a broader under-standing of what was being created in America, and, importantly, the connec-tions between them. The chauvinism regarding "American-only art" was over, replaced in part with a refreshing and more intelligent openmindedness and acceptance of plurality of style and concept. Neither figuration nor abstraction enjoy supremacy one over the other. High art and low art, architecture, painting, and sculpture can be co-joined and appreciated.

The economy in America (and the rest of the world) has generated a staggering number of people with expendable incomes and an almost equally impressive thirst for acquisitions of all kinds. Newspapers and magazines, focusing on and giving more prominent space to art, enforced the urge to collect. Seduced by the cache of collecting and armed with money, more people started to buy. Other people, for different reasons (genuine interest in art and its history as well as the enrichment possibilities for their lives) stepped up their buying. At certain aesthetic levels, this activity generated a marketplace, with more buyers than art for sale, and the result was a steep rise in the prices of certain artists involved in national and international markets (particularly on the secondary market level). Unfortunately one of the by-products of the public's interest in investment buying is damage to the health of the art market aesthetically (although certainly advantageous for selfish short-term gain): the search for the new in the race to catch a rising star, or beat the market and look smart, could, in the end, ruin the possibilities for certain serious collectors to "stay in the game." After all, many wonderful collections have heretofore been put together with modest means. Moreover, many well-deserving artists not on the "hit parade" list will continue to have trouble finding galleries and collectors. Nonetheless, it is still *easier* today for artists of real talent, be they looking for immortality or simply an income, to find some gallery or agent to represent and sell their work.

The art world in Chicago has greatly expanded, in part due to the world just described. Well-known "big" collectors in Chicago, as well as younger ones, expanded their interest (vision) and enlarged their collections. People who had previously never thought about collecting, but had friends who did, went to museums and galleries and also began collecting. As a result, there are many more galleries in Chicago to feed the larger population of possible consumers.

By 1983 most galleries had abandoned the Michigan Avenue area for cheaper rents and better (larger) spaces to the west, in a neighborhood now alternately dubbed "SuHu" and "River North." Restaurants and boutiques, in predictable fashion, followed the galleries and generated the doubling and tripling of rents by 1988. Always in search of low rents in underdeveloped but interesting places, galleries old and new found the near Northwest side. On Milwaukee Avenue, between North Avenue and just south of Chicago Avenue, one may now find a growing number of galleries—there is already a Near Northwest Side Arts Council.

There seems to be a gallery for every type of art, at every level of taste and financial level. The *Gallery Guide* is proof positive, with over 80 galleries listed within the Chicago city limits and over a dozen in the outlying suburbs. Some galleries still reflect eclectic programs, but more and more specialize in particular types of work and specific media—painting and sculpture, prints, photography, glass, ceramics, fiber, neon and light, naive and primitive, video, performance, furniture, architectural works, art clothing, jewelry and accessories, and decorative arts. East/West Contemporary Art focuses on Chinese art. Isobel Neal shows only black artists, and the Latino Arts Gallery speaks for itself. There is also a growing list of spaces which regularly, if not exclusively, exhibit younger artists' work: Robin Lockett Gallery, Feature, and Ricky Rainer Gallery to name just a few.

Despite this positive situation, it is still difficult for some artists to plug into the exhibition world. The only way is still the hard way—researching the possibilities; sending slides, bios, and return envelopes; and following up with phone calls. More important, artists should try to get into group exhibitions, with their peers as curators, since art dealers make efforts to go to such exhibitions in search of new talent. With the growth in the number of galleries and the continuing development of alternative spaces many more artists will find the opportunities they seek.

22 Houston: A Dealer

Janie C. Lee

JANIE C. LEE opened her gallery in Texas 20 years ago. Through it, she introduced to Texas many of the major artists of the 1960s, such as Johns, Stella, and Frankenthaler. Although the gallery continues to exhibit sculpture and paintings, its primary focus now is master drawings of the twentieth century. Ms. Lee recently opened a second gallery in Manhattan which is devoted solely to twentieth-century master drawings.

Ms. Lee has been on the Board of Directors of the Art Dealers Association of America since 1980, serving as vice president since 1984. She also is a member of the Houston Art Dealers Association.

The Houston art scene is a healthy and active one. It is an exciting art community to be part of, for it is still emerging, maturing, and changing. If an artist is talented and willing to work ridiculously hard, he or she can and will succeed in Houston. Artists who become immersed in the Houston art community will probably shortly find themselves contributing to its development.

One reason for the health and growth of Houston's art scene is its museums, university exhibition spaces, commercial galleries, and nonprofit spaces. Each institution has a different goal and/or set of tastes, which contributes to the variety in the community.

VARIETY OF HOUSTON'S ART SCENE

The Museum of Fine Arts has a superb permanent collection which includes the John and Audrey Beck Collection of Impressionist pictures—in itself an excellent teaching tool. In addition to the fine permanent collection, the museum continues to initiate and receive exhibitions like the recent Schnabel show. In 1987 the museum opened the Cullen Sculpture Garden, designed by Isamu Noguchi, with a growing collection of important twentieth-century sculpture. The museum continues to acquire important masterpieces from every period and has recently purchased paintings by Johns, Polke, and Kiefer.

The Contemporary Art Museum gives the Houston community a superb overview of what is happening in the art world today. The contributions of the Museum of Fine Arts and the Contemporary Arts Museum, which are directly across the street from one another, are a perfect complement to each other: one institution concentrates on exhibitions and acquisitions of the past or the proven present, and the other creates excellent large and small exhibitions of every description, informing the public about the best new work of living artists irrespective of age or geographic location.

The Menil Museum opened in 1987 as a permanent exhibition space for the extraordinary collection of Dominique and the late John de Menil. Housed in a two-story building designed by Renzo Piano, the collection reflects the excellence of the founders' acquisitions. Installations change as works are rotated from study areas to exhibition galleries in the museum.

The University of Houston and Rice University both have active exhibition galleries—the Sarah Campbell Blaffer Gallery and the Sewall Art Gallery, respectively. These spaces have good educational exhibitions as well as student and faculty exhibitions. The Blaffer Gallery is host to an annual Houston Artists Exhibition, and the Contemporary Arts Museum is now sponsoring a Texas Triennial Exhibition.

Among the nonprofit organizations, the Lawndale Annex functions as the exhibition space for young artists who have had few or no prior exhibits and also for artists who have shown extensively in Texas, the Southwest, and elsewhere. Under the auspices of the University of Houston Art Department, the Lawndale Annex has organized comprehensive group exhibitions and has hosted traveling exhibitions. Lawndale also provides a forum for multimedia and performance events. Another alternative art space of note is Diverse Works, which has enlivened the art community of Houston with exhibitions and performance art of great vitality.

LIVING AND WORKING

It is possible for artists to find studio space that is good and relatively inexpensive, and there are several groups of younger artists who have banded together to share large warehouse spaces. Art-related jobs, however, are difficult to find. There are good art departments in the colleges and universities in and around the city and in the Glassell School of Art of the Museum of Fine Arts, but teaching appointments are highly sought after. Well-trained and experienced art handlers can usually find work, although it might be part-time work, for the commercial art galleries, the institutions, and the established art handlers in the city.

Once involved in the Houston art community, artists have relatively easy access to the curators in all the museums and nonprofit art spaces. The curators are generous with their time and devote considerable energy to young and/or emerging artists in the community.

COMMERCIAL GALLERIES

Houston has a variety of good, respected commercial galleries, unequaled in this part of the country. Most of them have an area in which they specialize, such as nineteenth- or twentieth-century art, Texas art, Southwest art, photography, prints, and so on. The large number of professional galleries and the variety of their tastes are tremendous assets to the community and the young artists.

At the time of this writing, the Janie C. Lee Gallery has been in Texas for 20 years. During this period there have been many changes in the Texas art community and in the gallery itself. Our basic premise, however, remains the same. The gallery is interested in, and committed to, exhibiting the best quality mature work we can find. The work we usually show is from established artists. It is not our objective to show primarily New York artists any more than we set out to show Houston artists, but the artists to whom we have been committed for many years—Johns, Stella, Frankenthaler, and Motherwell, to name a few—happen to live in the Eastern part of the United States. The gallery exhibits artists from Houston, Dallas, and other areas because their work is also of high quality. Our goal is to find the best quality art and to exhibit and sell it.

Our format is a little different from that of other galleries. We have very few major exhibitions; instead, we usually have a gradually changing installation of works on paper, sculpture, and paintings. We work with and exchange work with our New York gallery, Janie C. Lee Master Drawings, which mounts a general or theme exhibition approximately twice a year accompanied by a major catalog.

We try to have a diversity of works in our gallery. For instance, there will be work from our "stable" of artists, individual well-known pictures consigned to the gallery for sale by collectors, pictures by artists we want to observe more, and work by artists we believe are talented but with whom we have not made a gallery commitment to exhibit. We commit very slowly in taking on an artist; however, if we do take one on, we feel a great sense of responsibility toward him or her.

We should note that though we continue to work with certain paintings and sculpture, the galleries both in Houston and New York primarily work in twentieth-century drawings.

Much of our time is spent caring for the art and artists we represent. This means working with the artists to obtain new work, curating and caring for their work, setting new exhibitions, selling the work, keeping the artists informed by regular reports on the activity of their work, and maintaining records for the artists in the gallery. Another part of our activity is looking for new art. This means looking for new art by our established artists and also by younger artists.

The manner in which we approach new artists usually follows the following sequence. First, information comes to us via an artist, curator, art historian, or dealer for whom we have great respect and whom we know personally. That person calls us or sends us information on an artist whom he or she considers unusually interesting. Following receipt of such information, we definitely want to see slides of the work. If we like the slides, we then follow up by making an appointment to meet the artist to see his or her work.

Artists who arrive at the gallery without an appointment will be asked to leave their slides or send them to us. If they arrive with actual works of art, we will request that they submit slides instead, for preliminary review. As is the case in many galleries, we are understaffed and overscheduled and usually can't stop what we are doing to give unannounced artists the time and courtesy they and their work probably warrant. We regularly allocate time to study slides sent to us to be able to give them our full attention.

The community in Houston that collects and purchases art is still relatively small. It has, however, grown consistently, which is a productive, positive working situation. With the economy in our area gradually improving, we are confident that this growth will continue.

A collector does not say that he has no more space on his wall. A collector buys a work of art because he loves it and feels it is of great quality—then he worries about wall space.

One major facet of a healthy art community that is lacking in Houston is in-depth press coverage of the art being exhibited, or, for that matter, of art that should be exhibited. The local newspapers attempt to cover the scene and in some cases have excellent people who do a very good job, but are given inadequate space to write on the subject in depth. It would be a tremendous asset if Houston had an arts magazine, staffed by people who understood the visual arts. Such a magazine could include articles from art historians, museum curators, and artists living in the area, as well as art critics. The city, with its community of museums, galleries, and artists has proven itself worthy of such a publication.

I believe that artists need representation. If a gallery represents an artist, it has a tremendous obligation to assist the artist in every way it can. After all, the gallery is only as good as the artists it represents.

THE NEW YORK CITY EXPERIENCE

Emerging artists have a very real and difficult problem in bringing their art to the attention of those who can recognize its quality and want to acquire it. I think that the gallery should help such artists—it is to the gallery's advantage to do so. I must also mention that I believe artists need to spend time in New York City. I do not mean that they must make a permanent residence in New York, but I am deeply committed to the results of the experience of a few years in New York—the art in the museums, the dialogue among one's colleagues, the advantage of seeing art that is being shown in the hundreds of galleries. All the advantages New York City offers, in addition to the foregoing, are an intrinsic part of the artist's development. I am not suggesting that it is easy to live in New York, but then it's not easy to be an artist either. But somehow, even though it is difficult, many people have done it. Most of those who are recognized as our greatest artists today have managed to live in New York City at some point in their lives. I believe the New York experience is pivotal to the maturity of the artist and his or her work.

SUMMARY

In reviewing the Houston art scene, I find the activity, the variety of galleries, museums, exhibition spaces, and cooperative galleries are what make it an interesting artistic community. Had we but one museum, or one or two good galleries, or one university art department, I believe it would be a much less viable place for young artists. There are good artists who have had to leave Houston to become recognized, but they are not the majority.

All the people I've met connected with the art scene in Houston genuinely want to make it better, myself included. We may differ as to how to make it better, but that too can be productive.

I can think of very few professions more difficult than that of an artist. It is so hard, one must be a little crazy to want it at all, but it can also be very rewarding.

Houston is not a city suffering from feelings of self-sufficiency. It still respects nothing as much as it does the best talent. It welcomes it. It is not important where you came from; it's what you do and how you do it when you arrive. If you're good in medicine, finance, or any field—including art—Houston will give you a chance. Then it's up to you.

23 Artists' Spaces

Jenny Dixon

JENNY DIXON has been involved in the New York City nonprofit arts community since the mid '70s. She was affiliated with the Public Art Fund for 9 years, serving as executive director for 6. Since 1986 she has been executive director of the Lower Manhattan Cultural Council. Over 150 arts groups fall within the geographic jurisdiction of the Council.

In many guises over the years, artists have created situations—guilds, salons, co-ops, stores, clubs, and galleries—to exhibit their own work, and that of their contemporaries, while creating a place for the exchange of ideas. Much in this vein, alternative spaces were founded throughout the country during the early 1970s, primarily in major urban centers. Once the idea caught on and, for the first time, government support kicked in, such spaces began to evolve in smaller cities as well.

The first national meeting of artists on "alternative" spaces was held in 1977 in Los Angeles at LAICA (Los Angeles Institute of Contemporary Art). Most of those in attendance represented visual arts organizations or multidisciplinary art centers, where fine arts, as opposed to the performing arts, functioned as the point of departure for programming. In 1982 at a similar meeting in Washington, the National Association of Artists Organizations (NAAO) was founded. There were new spaces represented at the March 1988 meeting, and other formerly strong voices were notable in their absence; particular among these was one of the earliest alternative spaces, AND/OR from Seattle, which had gone out of business. NAAO now has over 200 members. The visual arts alternative spaces comprise one part of the membership, and equally well represented are those groups primarily involved in performance.

Alternative spaces, both those that survive from the early 1970s and new ones that continue to evolve, are committed to providing an exhibition area for artists' work. The work may be anything from video installations, to painting by vocational artists living in the community, to performances and performance installations. Spaces may be committed to one kind of art, such as drawing, sculpture, or video, or a combination of art forms. Similarly, spaces may be committed to one kind of painting. The now-defunct Artists Choice Museum in New York City was committed to realistic work. AIR Gallery shows only work by women artists. What these "alternative spaces" have in common is, for the most part, their commitment to showing work by emerging or not-yet-commercially recognized artists.

Another common characteristic is the fact that most alternative spaces are not for profit. Being not for profit, particularly when arts funding was more prevalent, provides a mechanism to give artists exposure in a noncommercial context. Artists are able to take risks with their work. Nonprofit alternative spaces function as an early door to pass through on an artist's way into the art world and eventually into the commercial system. However, there are other variations to the concept of alternative spaces, and, as in the past, these have been, are, and will be developed by artists.

For six years I produced and moderated a weekly radio program "Artists in the City," on New York's municipal broadcasting station, WNYC. In 1982, I interviewed two young artists on the program who had recently founded Nature Morte and Guerilla Warfare, commercial galleries in Manhattan's East Village. When I asked what had motivated them to start galleries in the East Village, they spoke of coming to New York out of art school and of naively thinking they could "get shows" in Soho galleries. They went on to say how they soon learned the difficulty of becoming affiliated with a gallery as an unknown and, thus, began to explore possibilities with downtown alternative spaces. They reported that many of the alternative spaces had also proved to be inaccessible to them. They wanted to show their own work and that of their peers, so they opted for running their own spaces, renting cheap storefronts and initially taking outside jobs for financial support. The alternative space ABC No Rio had already established a presence in the East Village, and the two artists cited it as being somewhat instrumental in their locating in that area.

During the early 1970s, alternative spaces were founded in part as alternatives to the gallery system. At the time, there were relatively few contemporary commercial galleries in New York, and a great number of young artists felt the need to expose their ideas and work, if only to each other. Ironically, ten years later a number of artists were finding alternatives to the alternative spaces: small no-glitz commercial galleries. One of the first to open and first to close was Fun Gallery. An artist friend told me it has closed because the founder Patti Astor wasn't having fun anymore. Five years later, commercialism and escalating East Village rents caused many of these small galleries to move to Broadway in Soho and also caused equally as many to close.

While Guerilla Warfare is out of business, ABC No Rio remains very much a part of the East Village community it pioneered. The annual budget is modest, and by being noncommercial it is able to continue to take risks. Government funding, however helpful and attractive, can compromise a space. Because of the "hoops" a grant applicant must go through, some nonprofit artists' spaces become "risk adverse" and, therefore, stale.

In my mind the best alternative spaces are run by highly creative, energized people, who function like entrepreneurs with no capital. The alternative space itself is the product that these people are constantly seeking to capitalize, not themselves beyond the space.

ABC No Rio was founded by a few artists who had been affiliated with Colab (Collaborative Projects). The Colab artists had been interested in working with the texture of the city and had not found the venues they sought for their work in traditional galleries. Neither did alternative spaces, with the exception of Fashion Moda, located in the South Bronx, hold much allure. Five years later, similar steps would be taken by the founders of Nature Morte and Guerilla Warfare: their point of view and fresh energy was most visibly seen in the Times Square show they organized during the summer of 1980. Collectively this group of artists, which included such people as Jane Dickson, Charlie Ahern, Becky Howland, Christy Rupp, Keith Haring, Tom Otterness, and Walter Robertson, took over a decrepit building in Times Square, transformed it and hung a show. Trying to gain access to the art world in a noncompromised manner, and defining new environments for art, they were interested in creating nonelite work, reflective of their urban experiences. The majority of the original Colab artists are now enjoying commercial success.

Artists have historically found and defined alternatives to the world of galleries, institutions, and profit motives in seeking exposure for their ideas within the context of the art community and the community at large. A symbiotic relationship exists among all venues available to the artist to get ideas into a public arena. Alternative spaces are a relatively new arena. Perhaps the notion of actual physical spaces has usurped the notion of alternatives. Colab, Fashion Moda, ABC No Rio, and even the early East Village galleries were, and in some instances remain, strong alternatives to the more directly commercial venues. Skirting a raw edge, taking risks, allowing different points of view to be exposed which may either enter or not enter the commercial mainstream, are ideally what alternative spaces should be doing. The fact that an idea is not considered valid in terms of current art trends should not be definitive in terms of alternative spaces deciding who will and who will not have a show, a performance, a chance to curate, or the opportunity to make an installation.

The alternative spaces which were initially founded by artists are now often administered by nonartists—by professional arts administrators, who have, out of necessity, become well versed at the funding game. In becoming skilled, they have brought in the funds to change what are initially spawning grounds into small institutions in their own rights. The notion of alternative spaces as originally conceived in the early 1970s, soon after the founding of the National Endowment for the Arts, may be obsolete. In New York City there are few alternative spaces that have had the same director since their founding.

Beyond the self-perpetuating funding cycles of a kind of "dog chasing his tail" scenario, alternative spaces have changed, at least in New York City, as the art community has changed. There are a great many more galleries in the city than there were in 1970. There are people coming out of art school who are far more interested in so-called commercial success than the realm of ideas and need for exploration initially afforded by alternative spaces. There are more people collecting art and paying more for it. Many more artists are being given major museum retrospectives before the age of 40.

While the alternative spaces and artists have functioned as cost-effective ways to develop neighborhoods (e.g., Soho, Tribeca, and the East Village), rent escalation causes them to leave the areas they defined. The sense of community among artists that alternative spaces helped to nurture is becoming obsolete. Nevertheless, in newer communities, alternative spaces still function as a nucleus for artists. In New York, one of the newest spaces is Minor Injury. In Brooklyn, where Minor Injury is located, one finds a community where many artists have moved to because prior artists' neighborhoods are no longer affordable. In the 1987 NAOO Directory, Minor Injury lists its annual budget as $14,000. Conversely, The Institute for Art and Urban Resources, Inc., which includes The Clocktower, the oldest alternative space in the Tribeca community and P.S. 1 in Long Island City, Queens, lists its annual budget as $1,155,000.

TWO NEW YORK CITY ALTERNATIVE SPACE SCENARIOS

White Columns

A group of artists including Gordon Matta Clarke, Tina Gerard, Dicky Landry, Richard Nonas, Jeffrey Lew, and later Ned Smyth were involved with the founding of the 112 Greene Street Workshop in the early 1970s. They worked separately, supported both themselves and the space through the restaurant FOOD. Holly Solomon, a collector, became interested in many of the artists from 112. Real estate interests pushed 112 out of its location by 1980. With the assistance of the Lower Manhattan Cultural Council, 112 moved to a Port Authority—owned building five blocks west of Soho, changed its name to White Columns, and hired a director. Josh Baer, who subsequently became a private dealer, Tommy Solomon, son of Holly, and then Bill Arnig served as directors. The space functions as an exhibition space for visual arts and has a film program. The director is known to have a specific point of view.

Franklin Furnace

In 1976 Franklin Furnace was founded by performance artist Martha Wilson, then a recent faculty member of the Nova Scotia School of Art & Design. Founded as an archive for artists' books, the Furnace was among the first settlers in the Tribeca community.

Innovative exhibition and performance programs continue under Wilson's direction. Artists such as Laurie Anderson, Michael Smith, and Eric Bogosian received initial New York exposure at the Furnace. It remains open and accessible to artists working in performance and "fourth-dimensional" art forms.

PART FIVE

BUYING AND SELLING

My work was very popular for about two or three years and sold like crazy. There was a waiting list and everything. Then I changed what I was doing—the work went through a radical change, and so did my popularity. Everyone wanted paintings I didn't want to do anymore, so you never know when you're going to be able to make money.

—Joan Snyder

24 Museums: The Artist and the Museum

How to Crack the Sight Barrier

Tom L. Freudenheim

TOM L. FREUDENHEIM is the assistant secretary for museums at the Smithsonian Institution. Former director of the Museum Program at the National Endowment for the Arts, Mr. Freudenheim also served for eight years as director of the Baltimore Museum of Art.

The artist-museum relationship seems eternally strained—a reflection of the outsider trying to get in, with those on the inside closing shades and shutters (or eyes?) to keep the outsider an outsider. The exception, of course, is in those instances when a living artist *is* shown in the museum. In this case, the ranks of outsiders have been diminished by a single unit, not assuaging the feelings of those left out. Moreover, the outsiders generally are convinced that some highly illicit relationship lies behind the fact of the exhibition and the choice of the artist.

Like all simple-minded explanations, this one probably contains a certain amount of truth, even as to the questionable relationship between exhibited artist and exhibiting museum. But it also explains nothing. If it contains some truth, it is nevertheless not actually true. The artist-museum issue is complicated, cannot be simply stated, and depends greatly on which artist and which museum one is discussing. But this is not to say one cannot attempt to clarify matters or even advise artists on how they might relate to museums.

MANY KINDS OF MUSEUMS

First of all, the artist must realize (as he or she presumably already does) that there are many artists and that each one (or almost each of them) is trying to be seen somewhere—in studio, gallery, museum, or collection. Knowing that one is not unique is probably small comfort, but it ought to provide some sense of perspective. On the so-called other side—that is, the museum—there are a number of factors which must be understood. All museums are not alike. Some range widely through the history of art and may have little or no interest in the work of living artists (this extreme is relatively rare). Other museums specialize in modern and contemporary art. In between lie as many variations as there are museums. And in these museums there are people working (directors and curators, to name some that may be of interest to the artist) who may also vary in terms of personality, interest in living artists, time to spend seeing artists or slides or studios, and even ability to make judgments. The artist sees himself or herself as a major figure, but may not be. Why should not the same be true for those people who work in museums and make decisions about what art is shown? It is a field of human relations and personal choices (we would hope informed choices, but nonetheless personal ones); it is not a field of litmus paper tests for quality or eventual impact on the history of art.

DIFFERENCES IN ATTITUDES

Adding to this mix of museum type and staff type is the matter of institutional policy. Even among those museums that do exhibit the work of living artists, there are many variations, based on opinion or official policies. Thus, one museum may be interested only in established contemporary art that has met the test of audience and critical viewing in commercial galleries or art publications. Another museum may take special interest in local or regional artists. The artist has a responsibility to understand these issues and factor them into any view of museums. It makes no sense for an artist to spend a great deal of time trying to be shown in a museum that has never shown any work similar to his—not so much in terms of style, but in terms of being local or relatively unknown. Many artists work in vain in such situations, and it is heartbreaking both for the artist and (believe it or not) for the people working in the museum who somehow share in the sense of the artist's frustration.

And it is from these kinds of tense beginnings that adversarial relationships begin, in spite of the fact that artists and museums ought to have at least one thing in common: art. After all, the direction of art has been changed on occasion because of the impact on artists of an exhibition. Historically, artists have enjoyed looking at the work of artists who came before them (or even those working at the same time) and have found this information a source of energy, inspiration, or reaction. From the museum's point of view, the artist is in some ways the ideal visitor-viewer. The artist knows how to look and can use visual information creatively; those are goals that many museums set for all viewers. Therefore, the notion that artist-museum relationships should be adversary relationships is somewhat absurd and ought to be fought or rejected.

TIPS FOR APPROACHING MUSEUMS

As a general guide to artists, one can suggest a number of simple approaches to the museum.

1. Don't start out resenting the idea that the museum's prime interest is not in your work. The museum has numerous tasks and obligations; seeing new work may be only one of them.

2. Find out about the viewing policies of the museum. Some museums have viewing days for seeing artists' work. Others accept slides through-out the year. Some will see slides but not warm bodies. There are many policies, and a call to the museum should tell you that institution's approach. (Some don't want any new work brought to them; those are the breaks!)

3. Along with formal policies (where they exist), it is important to find out the interests of the staff. By looking at a year's exhibition cycle, you can sometimes get a sense of taste and directions and interest of directors and curators. Read their catalogs or other published writings to grasp how they might relate to viewing your work. (You may end up psyching it out incorrectly, but it's worth a try.)

4. Try for other visibility first. A museum is seldom the place for your first exhibition or group show. Museums are not the same things as galleries. Most contemporary art curators see other exhibitions in their area—at commercial galleries, schools, banks, or other such places. Sending an invitation with a personal note can't hurt, but may not help at all. Being noticed by your local paper's art critic might assist visibility in general, but not necessarily as far as the museum person is concerned. Museum people have their own strong convictions and will frequently be unmoved by the comments of the critics (except when the critics are praising their own exhibitions.)

5. Enter regional and local juried exhibitions when they come around in your area. Those exhibitions are frequently juried by notable museum people from around the country, and the best of those people take notes on what they have seen. You may end up being discovered through a juried exhibition, just as you may be asked to pick up your rejected work the next day. The artist has to be prepared for that, too, alas.

6. If you do find a museum willing to accept your slides for viewing, try to be sensible about the number of slides you submit. Try to get some distance from the material—perhaps have a friend help you make the most judicious selection of your work. The artist is seldom the best judge of his or her own work, and you want to make certain you have submitted the best.

7. If you are represented by a gallery, it never hurts to have the gallery try to show your work to the museum staff. Gallery people often have their own special relationships with curators, and thus can promote work more easily.

8. There is no evidence that socializing with museum people is of direct assistance in the system of showing contemporary art, but there is also no evidence that it has hurt too many artists. So whatever opportunities

the so-called "art world" affords for developing personal relationships are probably worth pursuing. If the result is not useful for exhibitions, you still might develop some friendships, or at the least a better mutual understanding of the world of the artist and the world of the museum-worker.

9. Try to understand that the museum director or curator may have literally hundreds of artists like you wanting to be viewed and shown. Even the interested and willing museum person has other things to do (like directing or curating) and cannot spend all day seeing artists, visiting studios, and viewing slides. In a few instances, there are museums with curators assigned to do mostly or exclusively that, but such are exceptions, and even those curators eventually have to spend time writing the catalogs or installing the exhibitions of the work they selected from slides or studios.

The artist who *does* manage to arrange for museum exhibition, having conquered the so-called heights then has a new set of concerns to deal with. There ought to be some kind of formal written agreement stating the fact that the museum has agreed on the exhibition, with dates, if possible, and whatever other formal arrangements are involved. It is not unusual for an artist to believe that an agreement has been reached, while the museum may have only the most tentative of plans. Staffs change occasionally, and commitments are either not met or are not even seen as commitments. Formalities may seem intrusive, but they are appropriate and businesslike, and they protect both artist and museum because they clarify the relationship.

Having overcome the general problem of the exhibition's really taking place, there are many other details that ought to be worked out formally. Will there be a catalog? Who will write the essay? What else will it contain (bibliography, list of exhibitions, biography)? Will it be sold? For how much? Will the artist get any free copies and how many? Who will pay the costs for production? (The museum ought to do this.) But is the artist expected to supply photographs and research materials, and at whose expense are the photographs taken? Such costs are generally the responsibility of the museum, but taking it for granted does not make it so, and the cost of photography alone can be quite expensive. There ought to be clear understandings on the size of the catalog, number of photos reproduced, and number of color plates, if any. Design decisions can also be an issue. All these matters should be mutually understood and agreed on, if the artist-museum relationship is to be sound.

Another issue that can and does arise involves the identification of gallery spaces in the museum. The artist may believe that the museum is using one space, while the museum is planning quite another space for the exhibition. Agreements about sales of works in the exhibition should be made, since the museum may want to take a commission for sales of works sold while on display, and the artist ought to know this in advance. Loan forms should be issued for all loans, with the museum providing wall-to-wall insurance. Packing, shipping, travel, conservation questions should all be answered in advance, lest the project be underway and the artist find that the responsibilities are not clearly assigned. Museums generally have conventional ways of dealing with these situations, and the artist has a right to be treated with the same respect as any other lender to an exhibition, just as the works ought to be handled carefully whether they are from another museum or "just" from a local artist.

It may be excessively cautious to suggest that the artist use legal advice to make certain that all such items are carefully covered. But in some instances it is the lack of such advice that creates situations for which the artist later needs legal assistance, so it might not be a bad idea to start out with the best advice.

There is no easy route, but that doesn't mean there is no way at all. In any given year, hundreds of new artists are shown in our museums—not just the same old names, but artists totally new to the museums where they are being seen. The museum must be understood as only one part of the complex world with which the artist deals. And while it may superficially appear to be the most important, the museum as a factor in the artist's career goals should be kept in perspective.

25 Art Advisory Services
The Age of the Art Advisor

Jeffrey Deitch

JEFFREY DEITCH is a professional art advisor with clients ranging from individuals to corporations throughout the world. With experience as a museum curator, art critic, and gallery executive, Mr. Deitch helped to create CitiBank's Art Advisory Services program within the Private Banking Division and now is president of Jeffrey Deitch, Inc., an organization devoted to acquiring and selling art as well as related services for its clientele.

THE AGE OF THE ART ADVISOR

When I started out in the art business in 1974 as an assistant at the John Weber Gallery in New York, the gallery had more artists than collectors. I think it was only once during my two years with the gallery that someone who we did not already know walked in and actually bought something. John Weber represented many of the most influential artists of the decade including Sol LeWitt, Carl Andre, Robert Ryman, and Richard Long. Their impact on the art world was enormous, but the market for their work was small. The regular purchases of Count Guiseppe Panza di Biumo, the great Italian collector, and a few others basically supported the gallery.

In the mid-1970s very few people thought of art as an investment. It was hard to imagine that there would ever be a booming resale market for Sol LeWitt wall drawings and fluorescent tube sculptures by Dan Flavin. The contemporary art world was an intimate international community of about 2,000 artists, curators, dealers, and others, of whom maybe 50 people were active private collectors. Very seldom did news of the contemporary art market appear in the mainstream media.

Several economic, demographic, and cultural trends began to converge in the late 1970s to change the art world almost beyond recognition. First, there was the coming of age of the heralded "baby boom" generation. There were thousands of well-educated young professional people who had studied art history in college, and who had benefited from the popularization of the art museums. American society in general was becoming more "Europeanized," more conscious of fine cuisine, fashion, and fine art. However, it was the inflation panic of the late 1970s—early 1980s that was the real economic fuel behind the new vitality of the art market. This newly prosperous, aesthetically oriented generation, and their parents as well, saw their cash eroding in value and rushed to put their money into tangible assets such as art. Business magazines began to promote the booming art market, and the auction houses began their remarkably successful marketing blitz. A fundamental change of consciousness took hold in the art market. Buying art was no longer perceived as a pure luxury. It actually made business sense. A whole new generation of collectors emerged, who perceived of buying art as buying solid assets, not merely an indulgence.

It was just as the art boom was taking off, in 1979, that I thought I might be able to parlay my newly minted M.B.A. from the Harvard Business School, and my background, as a museum curator and art critic, into a position as an art market advisor with a major bank or financial institution. I had long been interested in the economics of art and had decided to attend graduate school in business rather than in art history to sharpen my understanding of the economic structure of the art world. This was in addition to the purely practical reason of being able to find a job after graduation! I had numerous interviews with officers of major banks and brokerage firms, who loved talking about the idea of starting an art market department, but were not really ready to do anything about it. I finally was offered a position in Citibank's Private Banking Division to help manage their soon-to-be-announced "Sotheby's/Citibank Art Investment Program." Sotheby's had been hoping to set up an American version of its art investment program for the British Rail Pension Fund, which had channeled tens of millions of dollars into the art market. It soon turned out, however, that there were not tens of millions of dollars sitting in Citibank trust accounts waiting to be funneled into art.

Even though the program's original intention was a bit off the mark, we were at the right place at the right time. New collectors were rushing into the art market and badly needed someone they could trust to help them understand the often mysterious issues of quality and value in art. Why was it that one Picasso painting was priced at $100,000 and a similar looking work was priced at $300,000? If an Andy Warhol painting was estimated at $30,000/$40,000 in an auction catalog, how much should one bid, or would it be better to buy a similar work in a gallery for $50,000? We slowly began an art market advisory business where we combined our backgrounds in museum work with an understanding of the market.

At first, the art world was very skeptical about a bank being even remotely qualified to give competent art market advice, and it was quite an effort to win over our first few customers. Word of mouth travels fast in the art world, however, and as collectors began to see that we were increasingly active in the marketplace, we began to get more and more inquiries. Within a few years Citibank's Art Advisory Service was representing many of the most active buyers and sellers in the international art market. The growth of the art advisory business had a lot to do with the growing role of the auction houses. Until the recent auction boom, many, if not most of the important works of art that came up for sale were handled by private dealers or galleries. The potential buyer usually had plenty of time to return again and again to the gallery to contemplate the work and could usually have it sent home on approval. There was ample time to ask the opinion of friends and of specialists in the field. Now, with more and more of the best works being offered at auction, a collector may have only a few days to make a purchase decision involving millions of dollars. An auction catalog comes out two or three weeks before the sale, and the works are on view perhaps five days prior to the auction. A discreet professional service to scout the market, to preview the auction offerings in advance, and to analyze the quality, condition, rarity, and value of potential acquisitions definitely filled a need.

Our customers at Citibank were not pure investors, but dedicated collectors who believed in art as an excellent long-term asset and were comfortable making a substantial commitment to the art market. They realized that the supply of great works of art that are potentially available for sale is slowly shrinking and the number of potential private and institutional collectors is slowly increasing. From the late 1970s to the present, we have seen substantial new interest in the art market coming from areas where there was more limited interest before: Japan, Korea, the Middle East, not to mention California. The increased competition among buyers, and the vastly increased speed of the art market, has led many of the most active collectors to employ professional art advisors to help them sort out the opportunities and help them make decisions.

It is probably fair to say that the majority of active art collectors now have one or more formal or informal art advisors. Sometimes the art advisor is also an art dealer with whom the collector has a close relationship. Sometimes the art advisor is the local museum curator who hopes that the collector will donate one of his or her acquisitions to the local museum. Then there is the growing bank of professional art market advisors, some of whom are former professors or museum professionals, some of whom are former auction house staffers, and many of whom have no real qualifications at all except for an ability to get along well with wealthy people who buy art. The tradition of advising art collectors is actually quite long and distinguished, however. The great art advisors include not only famous connoisseurs like Bernard Berenson, but great artists like Marcel Duchamp. Duchamp may in fact have been the most influential art advisor of our century, helping to build the collections of the Arensbergs, Katharine Drier, and Peggy Guggenheim.

As the auction houses continue to consolidate their role in the art market, as increasing amounts of capital become necessary to compete as an art dealer, and as good museum jobs remain scarce, it is likely that more and more people with a talent for connoisseurship and a flair for the market will find their calling as art advisors. As the art market becomes faster and more complex, more collectors will need them. As they do with their lawyers or investment bankers before completing business deals, collectors will increasingly want confidentially to discuss the merits of a contemplated art purchase with a well-informed professional advisor.

Connoisseurship is developed by seeing as much art as possible, good and bad. In fact, it is only after studying bad works by an artist that one really begins to understand what makes their best work great. It involves a tremendous effort to keep moving around the world to the various art fairs, auctions, and museum and gallery exhibitions to keep up with the market and keep sharpening one's connoisseurship. It is essential to get to know some of the great collectors, dealers, and curators personally and to look at works of art with them in order to understand how they make their judgments. My greatest education has come from visiting museums and galleries with some of the great "eyes" of the older generation. One of the most satisfying realizations of participating in the art market is that the learning experience is cumulative. The more one sees, the sharper one's eye becomes, and the deeper one's understanding develops of the work of art and *how* it fits into the unfolding of art history. Art connoisseurship eventually becomes not just a profession, but a way of life. To stay on top of the fast-moving art market and to keep abreast of the latest insights of the art historians, one has to be consumed by the whole process.

I have had the opportunity to do all sorts of extraordinary things in the course of advising my customers at Citibank, ranging from taking Andy Warhol to China (filmed by Lee Caplin, the author of this volume) to curating one of the first large exhibitions of international contemporary art in Athens, Greece. I had the thrill of acquiring two of the greatest works of contemporary art to have come on the market in the past decade, James Rosenquist's "F-111" and Jasper Johns's "Diver," but also hid in an upstairs office at Sotheby's and bid on the telephone to execute orders for works of art that I was embarrassed to be seen buying!

After almost a decade at Citibank, I decided to build on my experience and open my own international art advisory firm. I will remain affiliated with Citibank as a consultant as I develop my own venture. I have faith that whatever the state of the economy, art market expertise will remain a rare and desirable commodity. Some collectors feel that prices are so high, and there is so little great art left to buy, that traditional collecting is over. I would strongly disagree, pointing out that even in the priciest art collecting fields such as post-Impressionism, many opportunities remain to buy significant works by lesser known, but still important, artists for reasonable prices. One has to have imagination and look at the art market creatively. Even today, there are still areas for collecting where there are more great works of art for sale than great collectors to buy them.

The artist himself or herself is one of the major beneficiaries of the changing art market. The diminishing supply of important historical works that are available for sale will increasingly direct institutional and private collectors to the art of the present. The market's globalization will enormously expand the audience for the best contemporary work. The admirers and collectors of young New York artists are already starting to extend from Athens to Tokyo. All this means a much more challenging and interesting role for art advisors like myself. We will have to keep abreast of the latest developments on at least five continents and subcontinents and work very hard on our language skills.

26 Individual Art Collectors

The Role of Art Consulting in the Art of Collecting

Barbara Guggenheim

BARBARA GUGGENHEIM heads a firm of art consultants, Barbara Guggenheim Associates, Inc., has a Ph.D. from Columbia University in Art History, has been a lecturer at the Whitney Museum, taught at the New School, headed departments of American Art and Primitive Art at Christie's, and founded Art Tours of Manhattan, a company providing art tours and lectures.

A peculiar aspect of the fine arts as a profession is that it enjoys the participation and interest of a general public which is necessarily lacking in the knowledge and experience to make decisions for themselves. That is, art collectors can be characterized as intelligent, self-assured, highly successful in their own professions, and, above all, very busy people. They rarely can spare the time that art collecting deserves in terms of a devotion to the study and observations required to make intelligent choices in acquiring works of art. The new buyer/would-be collector who has confidence in his own business and thinks he can translate that acumen into the area of art collecting goes to auction, and not understanding, is the one who pushes prices up at auction. Those who recognize that art, the art market, and art history are highly complex subjects seek help from an art consultant. Connoisseurship, as well as taste and an understanding of art history, develops only over decades of time and experience with thousands of objects of art, and a professional art consultant can help the collector, especially the beginning collector, hasten the process and prevent disasters along the way.

People know when they need a doctor or a lawyer, yet it is remarkable how few realize that they need an art consultant. More than ever, however, people are realizing that art is a complex, formidable subject and cannot be entered into lightly; much money is involved, as there is an awareness that the buyer of art is placing his own taste on the line. It should be a relief to know that there are professional art consultants whose job it is to provide immediate enlightenment of the mysteries of art collecting and professional assistance in dealing with objects of art. Art consulting is thought of by many as a new business, if not a new discipline. Actually, for centuries it has not been uncommon for collectors to engage the help of connoisseurs in forming collections. It is the purpose of this essay to discuss what role an art consultant plays in the art of art collecting and the problems intrinsic.

The simplest way to explain what an art consultant really does is in the form of a recapitulation of a conversation with Mr. Smith. Actually, "Smith" is not his real name (art consultants dwell in a world where discretion is sacred), and it is actually a consideration of ten or so "Mr. or Mrs. Smiths."

Mr. Smith	Betsy's just come home and she's getting on the extension.
Mrs. Smith	Hello, I'm really excited about getting involved in art.
BG	Betsy, your husband tells me that you like modern art. By this, do you mean Picasso and Pollack or young artists?
Mrs. Smith	I like young artists, but I also like Lichtenstein and Helen Frankenthaler.
BG	When you come to New York we'll visit studios. In the meanwhile, I'll send you some magazines to go through. Please cut out photos or write down the names of the artists you like.
Mr. Smith	A friend of ours just bought a Rauschenberg painting at auction, and Betsy would like to have one like it.
BG	Do you remember what the piece was called and what year it was made?
Mr. Smith	I don't know. Is that important?
BG	Do you drink wine? The year a painting is made is as important.
Mr. Smith	How does it work financially between us?
BG	Since the art consultant represents you, the collector, our arrangement has to be mutually agreed upon. As you know, as a professional art consultant, I own no inventory and receive renumeration only from the buyer. Some of my clients prefer paying me a fixed monthly retainer, others choose to pay me on a fixed percentage basis.

After visiting New York, it was easy to see that Mr. and Mrs. Smith are typically successful and intelligent and possess a very individual point of view and taste. Probably the biggest problem is that some Mr. Smiths are not accustomed to taking advice. The collector and art consultant together have to solve the problems intrinsic. Consider the old expression: "I don't know much about art, but I know what I like." Many novice collectors who pursue this simple point of view without getting help succeed often in embarrassing themselves by showing that they like the wrong kind of art, which is as evident as dressing or behaving badly.

Another observation which can be made from looking at the conversation with the Smiths is that there is an evolution of taste. Collectors begin on a certain level and with education can develop. Those wanting to collect nineteenth-century art often come with either one of two strains: either they love the

Bouguereau candy-box mentality or the Monet-Renoir axis. It is not unusual for a novice who wants to collect young artists to sight Lichtenstein (hard-edged line) or Helen Frankenthaler (soft-color school) as artists they like. It takes time before the collector understands that these are not the kind of work being done today and to adjust to what is being done.

The term "art consultant" has taken on a certain pejorative meaning since every "Park Avenue lady" who ten years ago called herself an interior decorator now calls herself an art consultant. A professional art consultancy is another matter. It brings to the situation conversancy in all periods of art and exposure to tens of thousands of works. It is this reservoir of knowledge, experience, and a perspective upon which the collector can draw in making decisions. The education of the client is primary. The art consultant is the ultimate griot: a cheerleader conveying enthusiasm about art—helping the potential collector to decide on the area of interest by taking him or her to galleries and museums, going through catalogs, books, magazines, and so on. But this is just the beginning.

After the client decides upon an area or areas of interest the consultant goes into high gear. To find the best examples of work which fit the needs and pocketbook of the collector, the search begins in major and minor auction houses, galleries, private dealers, other collectors, and artists' studios. Collecting is a full-time job, and the consultant becomes the eyes and ears of the collector telling him or her on a regular basis what is going on—trends, who is buying what, exhibiting where, prices, and so on. Often on a first large purchase there may be some degree of "hand holding" through the psychological trauma which can accompany the client who suddenly realizes with horror that he or she is about to spend a fortune on a painting of an artist he or she had never heard of two weeks prior. The client must be told the facts of life, with such reassuring reminders that buying art is not spending money—it is merely converting it from one form to another, and art collecting will do this—and that the greatest likelihood is that this will be a money-making transaction and even has the possibility of being a get-rich-quick scheme.

Logistical details follow: checking authenticity, provenance, condition, arranging for framing, restoration, insurance, and final installation are all the functions of the art consultant. Even then, the art consultant's job is not complete. It is also important to help the collector maintain a presence in the art world and making certain that his or her buying interests are generally well established. Ultimately, there is the change in the focus of the collection, the upgrading, selling, and perhaps even the "cashing in of the chips" which are part of the evolution of a collector. A professional art consultant, to do all these things, must maintain a sizable staff of professional art historians and others to attend to the enormous amount of research and followthrough. In my organization there are three Ph.D.s (myself included), two M.A.s, and four B.A.s all in Art History.

A good art consultant makes the difference in a collector's forming "a collection" or a "good collection." For every auction there is a buyer for most of the 300 or 400 lots. Of these, 5 to 10 are really good, and only 2 or 3 extremely interesting. The art consultant is able to guide the collector to the masterpieces available, given his or her interest and budget, guide him or her toward a great collection as opposed to an attractive assemblage of the obvious.

Apart from making certain the collector picks only jewels, the art consultant realizes that every good, successful collection reflects first and foremost the personality of the collector. A less good collection might reflect the taste of an art dealer on whom the collector might rely, and whose point of view is reflected in the purchases from said dealer. Translated, Park Avenue is lined with apartments "done" in the taste of various dealers. A collector may build a collection around a certain subject of interest. For example, a client of mine who is a land developer collects paintings of buildings between the wars—what he calls "real estate" art. Another of my clients who is in farming collects panoramic landscapes. Sylvester Stallone, a client of mine, collects larger than life sculptures that reflect the theme of the triumph of virtue over vice through physical development. Not surprising, is it? These may be exaggerated examples, but it is the job of the art consultant to bring out and analyze the motivating personality traits. A client of mine who feels comfortable with his Rolex and Jaguar collects name brands—Picasso, Leger, and so on. Another who has a job that is cluttered with the most minute detail collects black and white minimal art.

Once the collecting personality begins to emerge, the art consultant exposes the client to different periods of art, different categories of objects that might satisfy his or her taste, interest, and pocketbook. In essence, as opposed to a dealer, the art consultant is in the education business, being a teacher and psychologist wrapped into one. In the beginning, not that an art consultant wishes to impose his or her taste, but the primary job is to prevent terrible errors in purchases and every once in a while, if the situation demands it, to "force" a client to buy something he's not ready to acquire. "Buy this, you'll learn to love it."

It is hoped that collecting stems from a love of art and one's need to surround oneself with beautiful objects—paintings, sculpture, decorative arts, and even furniture (why should you put your rear parts on something less than perfection?). There are collectors who deny that they are, saying, "I'm not a collector, I just buy things I like for my house decor." Apart from the obvious satisfaction of owning beautiful objects, collecting also provides a variety of "by-products." It is the fastest route to participate in the world of conspicuous cultural consumption—one doesn't have to sit through concerts or read and wait for the subject to come up in conversation. The result is instant. Art provides status of a sort different from that of yachts, houses, and fast cars.

Some people want an instant collection; others like the process of searching and learning and never want it over. Collecting can quickly become a hobby, keeping more marriages together than any hobby I know. It can also turn into an all-consuming passion if not obsession. True story—one morning I got a call from a new Texas client who had been in New York with his wife the week before and had seen a beautiful painting by William Merritt Chase. He screamed at me, "I didn't want to do this. It was our twentieth wedding anniversary, and I promised my wife we would find a new activity we could do together, and she picked art collecting. Anyway, you know those books you sent me? I was up all night reading about Chase. I can't believe that that dude painted that painting." I knew he was hooked.

The art world has rules other businesses do not have or follow. It is a disorderly market in the way that the real estate market is disorderly. One month a painting may be worth X and six months later X times 2. The art consultant can help the client put smart money in art by identifying areas of collecting out of fashion, but about to return to favor, or by identifying contemporary artists who are about to become more popular. Collecting "futures" appeals to many collectors, and it is to individuals in this group that, when asked, "How do you become a collector?" I answer, "Rent a warehouse."

And one must not forget the psychic income art collecting affords. Not unlike the stock market which enables one to know his or her net worth at any given time without having to sell shares, there are always sales in the art world which offer the owners of works of art by the same artist an idea of what their pieces are worth. I actually have a client who carries in his breast pocket at all times a list of the paintings he owns, how much he paid for them, how much they are worth now, and a grand total of his psychic income. And so you see, Mr. Smith, art collecting has everything.

27 Art Collections in Corporations

Mary Lanier

MARY LANIER is president of Mary Lanier, Inc., an art advisory firm specializing in the creation and care of art collections in corporations. She is currently advising Becton Dickinson and Company, BMW of North America, Inc., Dow Jones and Company, Inc., and Metropolitan Life Insurance Company, among others. Formerly, she was the director/curator of the Chase Manhattan Bank Art Collection.

THE ART OF ART IN BUSINESS

Support of the arts is a burgeoning activity in American business. Corporations have poured millions of dollars into one form or another of arts support. It is difficult to determine exactly what percentage of corporate support is applied to art acquisitions, given the fact that art collections serve the symbiotic purpose of decorating corporate facilities as well as creating a market for artists. Some corporations record their collections as capital assets, thereby making figures readily available to stockholders. Others lose their art acquisition statistics in furniture and PR budgets, where it is impossible to evaluate art collecting as a separate entity. Nevertheless, one need only set foot inside any modern corporate headquarters to see the evidence of a new consciousness about art in the workplace. Sophisticated selections create challenging dynamics in office facilities which might otherwise be hopelessly sterile.

Realizing that it is difficult to determine precisely which corporations are buying what, it will be useful for the artist to understand as much as possible the realities of corporate art collecting to have a clear picture of how to approach this growing market. Indeed, a knowledge of these realities may serve to guide artists toward audiences and settings that are hospitable to their particular kind of work. The most important thing to understand is that corporate art collections are only as good as the people who select them, and while one corporation may have a reputation for volume buying, another may be quietly acquiring a small number of superb examples from a defined medium, period, or style.

While the best collections have a point of view and an experienced advisor, others utilize art to perform the artless function of Muzak—as an environmental tranquilizer. This color-coordinating, mix-and-match approach to art in the corporation does not recognize the difference between serious art and decorative framed objects which serve only as visual background music.

WHAT MOTIVATES CORPORATIONS
TO COLLECT ART?

It should be understood that business is business and, fundamentally, that corporate interest in the arts is self-interest. Corporations need to know that there is a purpose in becoming involved that goes beyond helping artists. After all, art is viewed as a luxury, not a necessity of life in the workplace. Keeping in mind that all of life's endeavors contain self-interest, it behooves the artist to determine just how enlightened that self-interest is in order to evaluate the possibilities for entering the corporate marketplace.

For the corporation, the challenge is to create a collection of art that measures up to the highest standards while addressing the needs and style of its own corporate personality. Unfortunately, this must often be accomplished in a bureaucratic context in which art can be expected to fill many needs beyond the pure enjoyment of it. For many artists, this is difficult to accept. Corporate needs that must be addressed when collecting art include the need to

- Improve corporate image.
- Decorate walls and public spaces.
- Provide good investment.
- Satisfy a percent-for-art law.
- Challenge thinking, please people, boost morale.
- Improve productivity.

While most companies do not ask their art programs to fulfill all these functions, at least two of them are operative in every corporate collecting situation. In almost all cases, corporate management is intent upon improving the work environment. At the same time, it must answer to both stockholders who question the appreciability of art expenditures and to employees who might feel that the art budget should be applied to salary increases or other financial benefits.

Given all these cross-purposes, it is still possible, with the courage of conviction, good advice, and a decent budget, for the corporation to become an important catalyst between the artist and the public.

WHICH CORPORATIONS COLLECT
ART?

Some major corporations, such as the Chase Manhattan Bank and the First National Bank of Chicago, have had serious art programs for at least 30 years. The number of large companies with significant art holdings is growing rapidly, and one may assume that most major companies have some kind of art activity. Such well-known companies as American Express, Prudential, Chemical Bank, Citibank, Bank America Corporation, Equitable Life Assurance Society, Readers Digest Association, and First Banks Minneapolis, to name a few, are known for the high quality of their art programs. There are many other companies, however, that are quietly active—many of them smaller companies—and it is the task of the artist to identify these and to learn whether his or her work applies to any of these situations. *The ARTnews International Directory of Corporate Art Collections* provides a full and excellent resource for particulars on the many companies that collect art. Keeping one's eyes and ears open to news of corporate art buying is very important. One good method is to obtain the names of collections from the biographies of artists whose sensibilities are similar to one's own. Another is to follow the annual fall surveys of *Art & Auction* magazine, which lists specifics about America's most active corporate collections. Information can often be obtained from the switchboard of any company thought to be involved in collecting. Getting the name of the art director, public relations manager, corporate communications director, or even the architect or designer, as well as inquiring into the nature of the program and the appropriate way to make one's work known, often yields valuable information. After determining who is in charge of the art-buying activity, the next step is to contact that person with a cover letter, slides, resume, and a self-addressed, stamped envelope.

These suggestions apply to companies that have established or are beginning art programs. The artist may also learn which companies are building new buildings and determine ahead of time whether art will be required. Getting in touch with interior designers and architects may be a method of approaching the subject of commissions as well. It is helpful to know which communities have established a percent-for-art law and to learn which companies are planning facilities in these places. In any case, a brief, polite letter, with accompanying slides, is the best way to approach architects, corporations, art advisors, and even galleries. Being able to address the key people by name is, of course, useful. Obviously, a personal recommendation from someone should be used when possible.

"CORPORATE ART" AND THE "ART CONSULTANT"

The phenomenon of corporate collecting has created two distinct yet unfortunate concepts that threaten to separate corporate collecting from more serious, meaningful collecting. One of these concepts, "corporate art," is an unhappy term that implies that which is facile, easy to live with, uninspired, and not of museum quality. "Corporate art" is decorative fluff made for offices and touted by its distributors as "great for bank lobbies and offices." One sees it everywhere and forgets it immediately. It is not intended to be noticed, and yet its presence often makes people believe that they have art around them. Such people are willing to pay dearly for these worthless unlimited objects. Much "corporate art" is finding its way into corporate settings as a result of peddlers who often call themselves "art consultants." The challenge for the qualified art advisor is to help companies discern between art and corporate art.

The untrained art consultant is the second negative aspect of the new industry and can be held responsible for perpetuating mediocrity. When corporations began to spend large sums of money on art, the so-called art consultant appeared on the scene to help them do it. Many art consultants were unqualified, and their corporate customers did not know what to require of them. Being an art consultant often meant simply selling large editions and worthless reproductions. In the last ten years, however, public consciousness has begun to be raised. Professionals have been identified by their qualifications and experience, and organizations have emerged to articulate standards of practice. Many professionals have eschewed the term "art consultant" and call themselves art advisors to unburden themselves of past connotations. The job of the art advisor is to counsel the client on the acquisition and/or programmatic use of fine art without reference to any particular inventory, gallery, or artist, and the art advisor assists in the client's understanding and appreciation of such fine art objects. The Association of Professional Art Advisors was incorporated in 1980 to devise standards of conduct so that artists, dealers, and corporations could work together more effectively. The Association has determined that an art advisor should be a full-time professional who is paid *only* by his client and not by the artist or seller. The art advisor does not sell art, but rather time and knowledge. If an art advisor keeps an inventory, takes commissions, or sells art to a corporate client, then he should be considered an art dealer and not an art advisor per se. The Association recognizes the integrity of the art dealing profession, but it wishes to keep the two—dealing and advising—professionally separate. When an art advisor arranges a sale to a corporate client, he or she will often negotiate with the seller a discount and ask that it be passed directly to the client. This assures the client and the seller that the advice is conflict-of-interest free. In addition, the client enjoys a reduced price that is the result of working through a reputable advisor.

Art advisors are go-betweens in the realms of art and business. Other types of go-betweens include commercial galleries and private dealers who buy directly from the artist and resell at a markup to the client. In addition, there are consultants who sell to corporations and want a commission from the artist or dealer as well as a fee from the client. One should be particularly wary of those who "take it from both sides."

An artist should evaluate a consultant/advisor by his knowledge, forthright-ness, and reputation. Art prices are higher than necessary because of the various costs built in to "cover" commissions to go-betweens. The Association hopes that the terms *wholesale* and *retail* will someday be eliminated from the art market and that added-on costs will be reduced because more consultant/advisors will be working on a fee basis with their clients and not on a commission basis from art sellers. In any case, the key person in the selection process is the advisor/consultant, whether he is in-house or independent. This person will either make the selection himself or will advise someone within the company to do so. Sometimes there is a committee which deliberates on the advisor's recommendations. It is difficult and usually unnecessary for the artist to know how decisions are made internally.

WHAT DO CORPORATIONS BUY?

The answer to this question varies as much as do the eyes, sophistication, and budget of those who make the selections. Earlier, in discussing why corporations buy art, it was determined that the main concern is usually the visual quality of the environment. That being so, it is reasonable that most corporations want art that has a visual presence. This basic need limits the acquisition of conceptual and minimal objects (although there are collections such as that owned by Gilman Paper Company, which have concentrated specifically in these areas). There are important collections specializing in constructivist art, landscapes, abstraction, photographs, and sculpture. One would do well to determine which corporations are focusing on particular points of view. Yet, for the most part, corporations are collecting "eclectically," experi-menting with all media, periods, and styles. It makes sense that unless a corporation begins with a particular focus, the quickest way to introduce a wide audience to the broad possibilities of contemporary art is for the advisor to present examples of a wide range of the best available. (Still, looking at corporate collections, one is aware of the scarcity of art bearing political, religious, or erotic messages.) The fact that many corporations are hoping to improve their working environment by having a variety of work opens doors for emerging and lesser known artists.

Beginning collectors do not want to spend vast sums on art that is untested in the marketplace, and at the same time, they do not want to invest in blue-chip items. Therefore, budgets are often modest, and they are willing to consider things that are of interest in their own right. This thinking does not require "big names" and represents a market opportunity for lesser known artists.

The kind of corporate thinking described here presents advantages for the artist who wants to sell and for the company that wants art. This kind of symbiosis should provide a way to keep the art community alive, and enrich the lives of the millions who work and do business within the corporate setting.

The challenge, of course, is to do it well. Artistic energies should be applied to the work itself. Marketing of this work presents a different problem; yet we are now seeing a tradition emerge—the corporate art collection. There are indications that a structure of communication exists that will enable the artist to reach that market.

28 | Contemporary Art at Auction

David J. Nash

DAVID J. NASH, senior vice president and member of the board of directors of Sotheby's North America, is in charge of all the fine arts departments at Sotheby's in New York. He is also a member of the Art Advisory Panel of the Commissioner of Internal Revenue.

The market for contemporary art at auction has a relatively short history. The first sale devoted exclusively to postwar and contemporary paintings was held at Sotheby Parke-Bernet in New York in 1970. Predictably, it received considerable attention from the art world and the journalists, but the results were mixed. At the time the common wisdom was that this was too experimental a market to hold regular and successful sales on a sustained basis. Before 1970 a few important abstract expressionist paintings had appeared at auction, but always in company with earlier nineteenth- and twentieth-century European paintings. The highest price by this time was $45,000 paid in 1965 for a Jackson Pollock painting of 1946, and very few works by living artists appeared for sale.

The first sale in 1970 contained a mixed selection of works by American and European artists, most of whom were living at the time. The highest price paid was $60,000 for a painting by Andy Warhol called "Campbell Soup Can with Peeling Label," but a major Lichtenstein of 1964 entitled "No Thank You" failed to sell at $35,000. The total of the sale was $450,000. Nevertheless Sotheby's remained committed to achieving success in this field, which was considered risky and not likely to prosper widely. It was felt that the market for an artist's work had to be promoted and cultivated by the dealer who represents him and that prices at public auction were unlikely to match up to these carefully maintained levels. Two more sales were held in 1971 and 1972 with varying degrees of success, but in October 1973 the public market was firmly established by the courageous decision of Robert Scull and his wife to auction 50 paintings and sculptures from their renowned collection of postwar and pop art. This sale, which contained major works by the leading American artists of the 1950s and 1960s, had a profound impact on the course and the structure of the contemporary art market.

The total of the Scull sale was $2,200,000, far exceeding the results of any other sale of contemporary art. The highest prices were for works by Jasper Johns ("Double White Map" of 1965 sold for $240,000) and for de Kooning ("Police Gazette," of 1955 sold for $180,000). Paintings by Franz Kline, Barnett Newman, and Andy Warhol also passed the $100,000 level, and a Jasper Johns sculpture of two Ballantine Ale cans sold for $90,000 to a German dealer.

The consequences of this sale were far reaching. No longer did it seem dangerous to put contemporary art up for sale at auction. Collectors began to be comforted by the reassurance that they could resell their paintings on the open market. Probably the most important influence of the Scull sale, however, was the realization of the enormous potential profits that could be made by an astute collector. Robert Scull's investment for his 50 paintings was repaid many hundreds of times, although there is no doubt this intention was farthest from his mind when he acquired these works. For many collectors, however, the possibility of buying contemporary art and at the same time profiting from shrewd purchases was very tempting. Dealers, too, could point to the resale potential of their artists' works when showing new paintings to a client. The public market for contemporary art had finally matured.

It is important at this stage to understand what is meant by contemporary art. As far as auction sales are concerned, this designation generally applies to works painted since the days of Jackson Pollock and the abstract expressionist school in the United States, and since 1950 in Europe. Although Picasso, Chagall, and Miro were all alive and painting well past this date, they are generally not included in the classification, nor is the early work of Dubuffet. Furthermore, it is important to understand that the number of artists included in this category is still relatively small and, on the whole, is confined to those artists who have already achieved a reputation and enjoy a market in one form or another. The foundation for this reputation has already been established by the dealer who represents him or her, through exhibitions, sale, and critical notices, and most commonly by discussion among collectors and professionals such as museum curators and art historians. The ideal moment to offer a work by a living artist at auction for the first time is when (1) the demand in the primary market (from the artist's dealer) outstrips the supply and (2) if a work were to appear on the secondary market (such as auction) there would be several bidders in competition for the work. Works offered through the auction process with the intention of creating a market for an artist who is not established with a dealer have invariably failed. The auction rooms cannot give the same specific attention to an individual's development that a dealer can through one-person shows, individual catalogs, and the careful placement of works in collections and museums. The first work by a truly contemporary artist to come to auction that filled the criteria just described was a work entitled "Notre Dame" by Julian Schnabel offered at Sotheby's in May 1983. The demand for Schnabel's work at that point far exceeded the supply. The work was a characteristic one in every respect. It was also of exceptionally high quality and fresh to the market. It therefore had all of the ingredients for success in the auction room. In view of the fact that Schnabel's work had no precedent at auction, the initial estimate for the painting had been "in the region of $50,000." The interest elicited from contemporary collectors was enormous, and at the auction there was fierce competition. The painting fetched the then unprecedented price of $93,500. The ramifications of such a price for a painting which would have originally sold a few years earlier for well under $10,000 were enormous. It both validated contemporary painting as a sound financial investment as well as raised the possibility of speculating in the field.

The sale of May 1983 marked the outset of the most startling increase in the dollar volume of contemporary art sold at auction. In the following five years to the end of 1987, sales at auction were to increase 427 percent. During this period there were a number of unique masterpieces offered for auction. They included Mark Rothko's "Maroon and White" offered in November 1983, which fetched $1,800,000 from the collection of Ben Heller. In 1986 Sotheby's offered Mrs. Ethel Redner Scull's painting by Jasper Johns, "Out the Window," which broke the $2 and $3 million marks, selling for $3,600,000. The following spring in 1987 Sotheby's sold de Kooning's masterpiece, "Pink Lady" of 1944, for $3,600,000 in a sale in which two other paintings exceeded the $2 million mark. Million-dollar price tags were now commonplace: the May 1988 sale including six works which fetched over $1 million in a sale topped by another rare master-piece—Jackson Pollock's "Search" from 1955, for $4,840,000.

Over the same five-year period the contemporary art field broadened enormously, with a greater number of private collectors entering the field than ever before. The traditional role of the auction rooms as the wholesale market-place where dealers come to buy inventory was replaced as greater and greater numbers of private collectors came and bought for their collections. The aggressiveness shown by collectors in the sales led frequently to unprecedented prices, which themselves influenced the dealer market.

What accounts for this explosive increase in the popularity of contemporary art among collectors? No doubt one of the contributing factors is the huge growth of interest in art in general. Attendance records at museums and at exhibitions have multiplied dramatically, and looking at art is no longer the preserve of an aesthetic elite. New museums have opened at a rapid rate, not only in the United States, but also in Japan and in Europe. Several of these new museums show only contemporary art, such as the Saatchi Museum in London and the Museum of Contemporary Art in Los Angeles. In addition there are numerous private collections being formed around the capitalist world, and many of these collectors have plans for a permanent public museum for their artworks.

Another important factor in the development of interest in contemporary art is its availability. It is hard to form a collection of Old Masters or Impressionist paintings today. The prices are high, and the supply is limited. Buying contem-porary art does not require such an art historical education as is needed, for example, to collect Old Masters. Authenticity in contemporary art is seldom a problem. With a few obvious exceptions, hugh sums of money are generally not required for the formation of a collection. And last, contemporary art speaks to its own generation as it never has before.

The sales held by Sotheby's and Christie's represent only the visible tip of this market. Their auctions of contemporary art include the work of no more than perhaps 800 artists. When seen in the context of the enormous number of professional artists working around the world today, this is a very small number indeed.

How easy is it to control or manipulate this market? Sometimes it seems as though high-powered promotion counts for more than talent in the establishment of an artist's fame. Can a well-financed and powerful dealer create a demand for an artist where such a following did not exist before? Are artists influenced by dealers to paint what is more commercially acceptable? These are questions to which there are few categoric answers, except to say that some of these concerns might be true in the short term. In the long term the artist's reputation will stand, slide, or fall depending largely on his or her talent and creative inspiration. If the world perceives the work to be second rate or without meaning, in the end it will cease to be collected with enthusiasm, and the auction block is virtually indifferent to manipulation.

29 | Commissions

Helen and Newton Harrison

THE HARRISONS are a collaborative team, working across media. Essentially they are conceptualists and story-tellers. Their subject matter often deals with reclamation and environmental and social issues. They work variously with performance, large-scale murals and massive proposals, which often take humorous and ironic turns. They live in Del Mar, California.

Editor's note: Conceptual artists Newton and Helen Harrison individually discuss their early experiences with commissions and then reflect on their experiences together.

Newton: There is great romance surrounding commissions as well as many peculiar expectations. My early experience with commissions began in 1946 when I was an apprentice to a sculptor in the National Sculpture Society. I was 14 years old at the time and got the job simply by going to the studio and knocking on his door. He hired me, because I modeled horses better than he had when he was 14. I worked for him for three years—casting, chasing bronze, making models, pointing up small figures, and the like. He did commissions and earned his living by making medallions and reliefs with industrial and war memorial themes. He had himself apprenticed to master sculptor Lee Laurie, who had designed the Atlas figure in Rockefeller Center. As did my teacher and his before him, I experimented with the neoclassical themes of giant horses being restrained by giant men with oversized forearms and thighs, until I eventually found myself in an aesthetic wasteland.

However, the apprenticeship experience was illuminating, in part because of the skills I gained, and in part because of the image I formed of studio as shop, sculpture as profession, production as craft, and commission as business. The business of it followed a rather standard format. An architect would send plans of a wall needing a relief, or an open space needing a fountain or figure. Often the subject matter was predetermined. My boss would then make a model, scaled at 1 inch to the foot, submit it, and receive a modest fee. If the model was accepted, an agreement was reached on materials and price. Then the sculptor would make a quarter-sized model in plaster, which, if approved, was followed by the full-sized piece in plaster. The model was then either cast in metal or concrete, or transferred to stone, usually by someone else. After it was installed, there was an unveiling ceremony, and the sculptor received his final payment. The experience, in retelling, sounds quaint.

Most art isn't like that anymore and, since the passing of the Academy in the nineteenth century, many artists find the restrictions of meeting requirements for professional commissions appalling.

Helen: My first experience with a commission was for a university gallery for an exhibition called "In a Bottle." The exhibition director requested—commissioned—all participants to do works in bottles. No contracts were given, no scale models were viewed for approval, no quarter-sized models were made, and no full-sized models were made in plaster and transferred to another material. There were no preliminary, intermediate, or final payments. In fact, the piece cost me $75 and several weeks' work once I had decided on the concept. The work was well liked, was well received, and was shown several other times. My gain was the work itself.

THE VARIETY OF COMMISSIONS

Newton and Helen: These two examples of our personal experiences with commissions we perceive as opposite in poles, two ends of the spectrum of commissioning. After all, what is a commission in art but a request by somebody to a somebody else for a something to be done? The variations of agreements, outcomes, gains, losses, and possible misunderstandings are endless and amazing.

To us there is an inherent contradiction in an artist becoming a "professional." According to our definition of art, the value often appears in a work's spontaneity and risk. Risk means an artist cannot always deliver the goods. A professional, on the other hand, is expected to deliver the goods on time and in a prescribed manner. A corporation wants the risk eliminated and the outcome predictable, and to the extent that the outcome is predictable, any spontaneity, improvisation and pursuit of a vision, wherever it may lead, is lost. But someone who commissions a major artist—because of that artist's unique vision—may run into quite a problem. It can be quite a problem for the artist as well.

We were once commissioned to do a water piece for the backyard of an elegant Spanish-style house in North Hollywood. The cost was to be about $8,000, the design fee, about $3,000, and we were to be the overseers. The work was to be subcontracted. We agreed that if the cost overran $12,000 we would give up the design fee. The work was inspected by the building inspector half-way into completion. The inspector insisted that we add a complex concrete support system dug into the adjacent hillside in order to secure the work. As a result of this decision, the piece had to be done over again. Its cost went up by a factor of three. We ourselves lost not only the design fee, but about $5,000 in expenses as well.

However, the money problem alone was minor when compared with the human misunderstandings that grew from conflicting expectations and desires that both we and the man who commissioned the work encountered along the way.

Our water piece was in effect a crab farm. We were doing cannibalism experiments in it as part of an ongoing work on art, ecology, and habitat reclamation. One of our incentives and conditions for agreeing to proceed at so low a fee was the information we would gain in the process. However, we believe the client saw the piece more as an investment which, if successful, would give him the opportunity of patenting a crab-mating process and ultimately cornering the crab market. Thus, when we asked for our information, he perceived it as his possession to use as he saw fit, and refused to give it. We then refused to offer more information on habitat control. His net product was a few crabs in an elegantly conceived pond, along with a business loss. Our net product was a lot of experience in making outdoor ponds, but no additional ecological information, and a business loss to boot. After that, we made the decision to be as specific as possible in our requirements before accepting any future commissions; specific not only as to costs, but also as to expectations, desires, and intentions of everyone concerned. In the case of commissions, human interaction is more important than any contract. But the bottom line may be the letter of the contract, even though with trust and good faith, contracts can be easily changed or adjusted.

The stories of artists' experiences with commissions abound. For instance, during the 1930s depression, artists were commissioned by the WPA to do murals in public buildings. The pay was minimal and varied from job to job. Artists responded in their own way, depending on the deal. If the pay appeared too low, an artist might choose to paint people only in profile, or as figures whose hands were in their pockets in order to complete the work quickly.

Another type of commission can emerge from a circle of friends. Matthew Rothenberg is the 14-year-old son of Dianne Rothenberg, an anthropologist, and Jerome Rothenberg, a poet. Walter Munk, an oceanographer, and Judy Munk, who is involved in community planning, are friends of the Rothenbergs. The Munks heard that Matthew and a small group of his friends had done some murals and went to see the 8 × 10 version of the Mona Lisa that Matthew had done in his room. They commissioned Matthew to do a 14-foot mural in a large room in their house. They agreed upon a Rousseau-style image for the mural, to be done on various walls with special treatment for doorways. An agreement was reached: the Munks would pay for the materials and a fee on top. (This arrangement is one that industry calls "cost plus.")

Matthew assembled his team of two friends. They had worked together before and were confident of their abilities. The trio worked for about five months, averaging three days' work per week, which totaled 180 workdays. The work was completed to everyone's satisfaction. The team received its fee of $500, or about $2.79 per day per person. If Matthew and team had worked out an arrangement with the Munks on the basis of materials, wages, and overhead (that is, cost of travel, the bus or parents driving them), and as beginners charged $3.00 per hour, their 180 days of work would have cost about $4,320. Had this been the case we doubt the Munks would have wanted to invest about $5,000 in three ambitious but untested 14-year-olds. They, in turn, would not have gained their first and very valuable experience in taking on such a major project.

CORPORATE COMMISSIONS

As we all know, the great commissions in the Renaissance came from the church, the kings, and the city states, which, with the newly emerging banker/merchant class, began the great collections of art. Along with the emerging middle class, these remained the chief sources of commissions or patronage for several hundred years. However, the forms of these sources changed. Public and private museums were founded and often commissioned works. In recent years corporations have also become involved in commissioning art: sometimes to build an image; sometimes for investment, tax, or other benefits. We argue with the treatment of art as a commodity, with prices that can be inflated or manipulated. This is ultimately to the disadvantage of both the artist and the art community. However, when strings are not attached, a corporate commission can be as viable as any grant that is relatively economically and politically neutral.

Four years ago Metromedia commissioned us to complete a large work in which we were already deeply involved. We had expected the work to take another ten years to finish at our own pace. The work is called the Lagoon Cycle. It has about 50 panels, each 8 feet high, and altogether it will cover about 350 running feet of wall space.

The few stipulations made by the company actually turned out to be very useful. The contract, however, was astonishing in its scope and detail. It was ten pages long and treated our work as a physical property.

Their lawyers proposed, for example, that we do no other Lagoon Cycles. We agreed. Further, they proposed that we do the best possible Lagoon Cycle we were capable of doing. Naturally, we agreed enthusiastically. The idea that anyone might assume we would work below our best capacity had never occurred to us. However, they also stipulated that any material used in the Lagoon Cycle was not to be used in any other work or referred to in any way. That is to say, they assumed we would turn over to them not only the images, but the ideas that generated the images. At this point all other negotiation stopped. We explained that all artists—authors, moviemakers, whatever—often cite prior themes in new work. If a work were completely new, communication would come to a standstill. Moreover, the Lagoon Cycle itself was derived from prior art and experience and contained understandings which even cited earlier works. Finally we arrived at a satisfactory agreement, and the contract was signed in sextuplicate. Actually, the contract as a model is a unique and valuable document, and at some point it might be useful to publish it.

Now, for our problem: Metromedia did not bargain or haggle with us. They asked for our price and our justification for it, and they paid us exactly what we asked. Our price, however, was based on the costs of materials and labor—both our own and our assistants'—in 1977. We calculated our overhead to be 20 percent and added another 10 percent as a hedge against inflation. As a result of not accurately factoring inflation into our calculations, each year we work on this piece we lose about 15 percent more. Yet, if we hurry in any way, we risk debasing a project which has taken up a good part of the last ten years. So our profit is rapidly evaporating, and our empathy for all people on fixed incomes is growing.

How to summarize. . . . We think commissions fall into a number of categories. There are corporate commissions, architectural commissions, museum commissions, government or public commissions, private and individual commissions (which, if they are not done for professional collectors, often evolve from friendships).

CHARACTERISTICS COMMON TO ALL
COMMISSIONS

We have found all commissions have two common properties: (1) request and (2) expectation of gain by all parties involved. Museum commissions rarely entail financial profit, but they do advance careers. Generally, if a museum asks us to do something substantial—an installation, for instance—they will pay for the cost of production, shipping, installation, travel, per diem, and occasionally a modest honorarium. This is not unfair since we keep the installation. However, we feel that a wiser choice for the future might be for museums to pay artists either fees or wages and keep the installation, since these are often created for a specific site and are therefore unsalable.

With museums, and with other types of commissions as well, we regard the essential precondition to be that the artist's work has evoked critical discourse among other artists, dealers, collectors, and museum directors. Thereafter, personal preference, friendship, or the "buddy system" may speed things up. Conversely, clashing personalities, hostility, and antisocial behavior may slow things down. In all events the likelihood of obtaining commissions is not great even under the best of circumstances.

We regard any invitation to do a work we would not normally do, or any request for a proposal that is not self-generated, as a commission. We tend to treat these as opportunities to experiment. Generally, the lower the fee, the greater the freedom to be playful.

Art Park in Lewiston, N.Y., regularly commissions artists to do temporary work—mostly on a 40-acre flat area, which is a former quarry refilled with rock from the Niagara Power Project. The area is called a "spoils pile." An honorarium, per diem, and a materials budget are offered. Artists are expected to do their work in the open, and part of the bargain is direct interaction with the public.

Having been invited to do a work there, we proposed to transform the whole 40-acre spoils pile into a meadow surrounded by trees. Our plan was to persuade the various towns in the area, who by law had to rebuild their sewer systems, to dump all excess dirt and all compostable material on the spoils pile site. Art Park agreed; the clients agreed. The contractors would save money using close-by Art Park as a dump site instead of others farther away. The work proceeded. We saw the piece as particularly simple and direct. It was congruent with ideas of joining art and reclamation, and art and utility, which have been our chief preoccupations since the early 1970s.

However, again there was an unexpected conflict: this time between Art Park's vision of our proposal and our own. By the time 3,000 truck loads had been dumped, the scale of the work infringed on the Art Park's notion about how much space a work, even one such as our own, should take up. The director called off the dumping, and finally we settled for a 20-acre meadow instead of the 40 acres originally planned.

Other stories we've told exemplify the various forms of commissions and the pitfalls awaiting the unwary. Contrary to expectations, we find that the benefits of being unwary have outweighed the disadvantages, since overcontrol limits freedom of invention. In this game every commission has its original problem. Each piece is one of a kind and is finally valued for its uniqueness and quality of expression.

In conclusion, we wish to mention a type of commission that has no name—where the outcome is a surprise to all parties. This type of commission involves utility, play, social change, and community—both within and outside of art. Often this kind of commission does not have the expected objectlike outcome. After all, one may be commissioned to do anything, and one thing leads to another.

In the spring of 1977, we were approached by the president of a small San Diego–based company that does Environmental Impact Reports (EIRs). He had read an article about us, describing us as environmental artists with social and political concerns. His company was competing to do the EIR for a particular project in the center of the downtown area of the city of San Diego. We reviewed the qualifications of his people, and he reviewed ours. Finally, we agreed to do the aesthetic section of the report. Since we had no idea how to do an EIR, we began by looking at similar sections of earlier reports. Mostly the EIRs were done by architects. Mostly they seemed underconsidered, with the definition of aesthetics narrowed down to simply whether the project looked good or not. Generally the EIRs said "yes" to the plans, if this or that small change were made. Requesting a small change was called "remediation." The project called for a scaled-down version of a suburban shopping center, two stories high, with a five-block solid wall offering one entrance and one exit. Elderly people would be displaced, and the views of the ocean would be blocked. The space above the city streets was not considered, nor were the city streets themselves—nor any interaction between them. An historic small park was to be made the entry to a bank. In short, the entire seven-square-block area was to be walled and devoured. We wrote a 20-page argument, which essentially pointed out the anomalies, and we called the plan irremedial. Our question was whether the people of San Diego wanted a single-purpose, fortresslike, suburban shopping center to be the metaphor for the "Center of the City." This question was picked up by the newspapers and made a cause célèbre. The redevelopment agency was furious and attempted to call the EIR illegal. The developer threatened to pull out. There were many meetings and much fuss. Finally the original plan was abandoned and a new architect was hired. The elderly people were included in the project's housing plans, and a more open design was adapted. Needless to say, since that time we have not been asked to do any more "aesthetic EIRs" in the San Diego area! We were paid $1,600 for what was to be four days' work for the two of us. We estimate our actual pay at about $60 per week. We consider it a bargain.

Fortunately, information travels in odd ways, and life is enhanced as much by serendipity as by design. Our plaza critique came to the attention of an East Coast arts administrator, whom we met by accident at a sculpture exhibit. He commented on our critique and asked if we would like to criticize the Baltimore City plan, with an eye possibly to proposing an alternative. We said we would, and the plan was sent. We visited Baltimore and found ourselves in conceptual agreement with the city planners. We proposed a work called Baltimore Promenade, based on the concept that the promenade is a universal urban form, central to the well-being of urban ecology. Our ideas were accepted in general; a plan for action and a design fee were agreed upon, and the actual work began.

This most recent of our commissions will, from one point of view, have no "object outcome" at all. From another perspective, the object and transactional results, if our design is put into practice over the next decade, will be rather complex. We are actually proposing to set up a promenade network that will make Baltimore a place where walking is a central means of experiencing the city. Our art, if successful, will simply be a background to everyday life.

We feel that anyone who hopes to live entirely off the proceeds of commissions while maintaining his integrity as an artist is likely to have a hard time of it. But from our own experience, our recommendation to those who want to engage in public art is to regard their work as a form of public service, and then simply to put one foot in front of the other.

30 | Craft Fairs

Carol Sedestrom

CAROL SEDESTROM is president of American Craft Enterprises, Inc., the marketing subsidiary of the American Craft Council, an educational organization with a national membership of 35,000. The Council publishes *American Craft* magazine bimonthly and maintains the American Craft Museum in New York City, as well as sponsoring marketing events for craftspeople.

The opportunities to exhibit and sell handmade objects appear virtually endless in the late 1980s. More and more galleries that specialize in crafts open every day. Craft shops are doubling and tripling their floor space and "mainstream" retailers are including more and more handmade objects in their inventory mix. Although there are no reliable statistics on the growth of the "industry" in general, sales volume has increased by quantum leaps. The Winter Market of American Crafts held annually in Baltimore, Maryland, by American Craft Enterprises, the marketing arm of the American Craft Council, reported sales in February 1988 of over $12 million—the highest sales figures ever reported at a craft event. A.C.E. produces five events annually.

The majority of all craft sales take place at craft fairs. There are basically two types of fairs: one geared strictly to the "trade," that is, one for the general public, and the hybrid type sponsored by American Craft Enterprises, Inc., which combines the two by opening for two to three days for wholesale buyers and the three days to the public. Most commercial gift shows now include a section devoted solely to handmade work, and there are public-oriented events in almost every city every weekend.

An artist who produces work that qualifies for sale in a craft event need only determine what direction he or she wishes to follow—the opportunities are enormous.

ADVANTAGES OF CRAFT FAIRS

From the customer's point of view, craft shows offer several interesting advantages. Only at a show does one have the opportunity to meet and get to know the artist who made the unique piece of work that is about to become part of one's daily life. At shows, visitors have the chance to see artists working and learn about the skills and expertise that are required to create a piece of pottery or an enameled brooch. Shows offer an enormous variety of choices not to be found in any other shopping opportunity. Furthermore, many craft shows feature interesting food booths and occasional music and casual entertainment, thereby offering a cultural experience for the whole family. Craft shows have become an important addition to the leisure activity alternatives of the American public.

From the craftsman's point of view, participating in a craft show provides an excellent means of selling handmade objects. Being in one of the largest wholesale-retail shows is the fastest way to gain exposure and begin setting up one's business. Shows provide an excellent opportunity for feedback from potential customers, and are an outstanding way to develop custom work or commissions for unique pieces. Educational opportunities abound in shows, either for material in the form of seminars on pricing, promotion, packing and shipping, and so on, or even more important, in the form of "hand-me-down" information from contemporaries operating in the field. In addition, most craftspeople, who generally live very isolated lives, enjoy the social aspects of fairs: seeing old friends, making new ones, and being part of the warm camaraderie.

HOW TO SELECT A CRAFT SHOW

Shows vary in size, quality, and standards, and it behooves the newcomer to do some "homework" before signing up to exhibit.

The best way to assess a show and its potential as a means of selling your work is to visit the show personally. This will help you understand what kind of work is featured, what kind of clientele visits the show, and how the show itself is managed. If you want to be part of the event, ask exhibitors how they became involved, or ask for the manager's office or information booth.

Obviously, one can't visit craft shows all over the country. The next most reliable source for information about shows is other craftspeople who have been in them. They may not be able to assess whether your type of work would sell—particularly if they are involved in jewelry and you are in pottery—but they should have facts on the management policies, clientele, and general attendance of shows in which you may be interested.

Another source of information is your local craft shop. Most shop managers and owners attend numerous fairs every year, and are generally pleased to advise a newcomer on which ones they consider to be good resources.

If none of these avenues is available to you, it is possible to assess a show without recommendation. There are several publications that list shows—some even evaluate them. Three such publications are *Sunshine Artists U.S.A.; The Crafts Report;* and *American Craft.* Check your local library for addresses and telephone numbers.

Write to numerous shows for applications, and then compare the applications themselves. Scrutinize the requirements and standards set up by the show management in its material. It is generally considered that juried events produce a higher standard of quality than nonjuried events. A further tip to the wise: be certain the management publishes the names of the jurors in the preliminary material. Some shows charge a percentage of sales and are juried by the management—not on the aesthetic quality of the objects, but on the basis of what sells the best, thereby ensuring a profitable event for the management, rather than one that upholds the standards of the craft movement. Most craft shows with integrity require that the artist accompany his or her work to the show. They do not permit sales representatives or importers. This requirement generally ensures a legitimate craft event.

Events are sponsored by craft organizations and by promoters. It is generally felt in the craft community that events sponsored by organizations are more likely to produce results that are beneficial to the individual. Some promoters' primary interest is in their profit, not in their exhibitors. Craftspeople have been badly taken advantage of by this kind of promoter.

If you are satisfied with the general integrity of the show, its size, location, and philosophy, the next step is preparing an application.

The application material should inform you whether the show focuses on retail sales, wholesale or trade sales, or a combination of both. "Selling to the public" shows are generally shorter, are not as expensive, and do not require as much preparation as do wholesale or combination shows. To do a retail show, you need a certain body of work to sell and a booth or display from which to sell it. Wholesale shows where you would be dealing with buyers who are writing orders for future delivery require a commitment on your part to produce work for delivery in the future—as well as more extensive displays, price lists, brochures, order books, and packaging materials for immediate deliveries. There are very few "wholesale-only" shows; most wholesale events open first to the trade and then to the public for two or three days. The combination shows are generally longer than public shows, are more expensive to participate in, and require more professionalism from exhibitors. If, however, you are interested in developing your work as a business, they are definitely the best vehicle.

WHAT SHOWS COST

Fees range from as low as $10 at local bazaars to as high as several hundred dollars charged at the larger, more successful shows. The fees should be commensurate with the services offered. In other words, if you have to put your booth up every morning and take it down every night, if there is no security, and if there may be little or no publicity or advertising, you shouldn't have to pay much for the show. On the other hand, a show that guarantees services is generally worth the extra money.

HOW TO APPLY

Almost all craft events—whether they are sales expositions or museum exhibitions—select their participants on the basis of slides of your work. Your slide will become a surrogate for your work, and the preparation of your slides should be approached with the same degree of professionalism with which you approach the making of your craft.

The purpose of the slide is to focus the viewer's attention on the object. You should avoid the common problems of using a background that is too "busy" or too textured or too distracting, thereby diminishing the viewer's attention to the object. Your object should be framed in the center of the slide—not too small or too overpowering. Photographic problems like focus, distortion, over- and underexposure, hot spots, and incorrect use of film should be avoided. Choose a background color that will enhance your subject, use appropriate lighting, and frame your object well. Slides should be simple, accurate records—not cute or clever.

If you don't want to invest the time and money in learning how to take your own slides, then contract for the services of a professional photographer. Remember, though, that you must offer editorial guidance. Most professionals are used to "jazzing up" product shots and, while appropriate for consumer magazines or catalogs, that type of shot is inappropriate for a craft exhibitor. Writing to American Craft Enterprises for an application is worth the time if for no other reason than to receive their full-color brochure on how slides should look.

If your work is rejected from a show, remember, it is not the end of the world and does not necessarily mean that your work is inferior. It may be that your work is inappropriate for the show or that the competition that year was very strong. Don't be discouraged. Continue to apply, because most shows have a new jury each year. Perhaps the next year's group will be more favorable toward your work.

After you have been accepted for a show, the next consideration is what kind of display you plan to use. Most fairs that operate in an indoor or tent facility (an event where you can leave your booth intact at night) encourage their exhibitors to spend time and creative energy on their displays. Your booth is your most important marketing tool at a craft event. It is a showcase for your work and a vital factor influencing traffic and sales. It should provide an attractive and advantageous environment in which potential customers can view your work. One publication credited the original Rhinebeck Craft Fair as being "like a series of 500 individual boutiques, one more exciting than the next." ·

The temporary nature and diverse physical circumstances of fairs present a number of special display problems.

From an aesthetic point of view . . .

- Begin by thinking of your space as a total environment for your work. Keep it simple, uncluttered, so that objects are presented as dramatically as possible. Your most important objective is to enhance your work.

- The setting should be complementary to the work displayed. Think about color and texture that are in character with your work so that you create a harmonious whole.

- Be aware of scale. Consider the proportion of the displays (cases, pedestals, shelves, racks) in relation to your work. Don't let them overpower your objects.

- Pay attention to details of execution and finishing; your work deserves careful as well as creative presentation.

- Consider your neighbors and the appearance of the event as a whole; finish the back and sides of your booth. If possible, consult with your neighbors; often, people working together can arrive at extremely effective display solutions.

From a practical point of view . . .

- Display your work at an eye level that is comfortable for visitors. Displays that are too low cause backaches; those that are too high lose their audience.

- Build a secure structure that will stand the strain of crowds, curious young visitors, baby strollers, and other hazards of busy, eventful days. Avoid protruding shelves or dangerous support wires.

- Protect your work. Shoplifting is always a problem; display your objects so they are enclosed, attached, or anchored, or so they can be watched. Don't leave your booth unattended.

- When planning your booth, consider who will be setting it up at the fair. If one person will be setting up, design units that can be managed by one individual working alone.

- Secure your work. If it is breakable, anchor it in place as unobtrusively as possible. Visitors should feel comfortable in your booth; objects should seem accessible, yet not be precariously displayed.

- You are there to do business—provide an area where orders can be written and other business transacted.
- Make certain your booth is properly lighted. Some objects benefit from spot-lighting; other crafts look best bathed in a clear, even light.
- Bring a hand-truck, dolly, wagon, or other wheeled conveyance to move and carry your work and display materials.
- Be flexible when planning your display. Not all space assignments are exact, and sometimes the loss of six inches can be a catastrophe if your display is rigid. Adjustable units that can be used for various size spaces work best.

And don't forget to . . .

- Construct a display that fits easily in your car or van and that is comparatively quick to set up and break down. (Some craftspeople find that modular units that can be used together or separately in more than one situation pay for themselves many times over.)
- Provide space to display your name and/or logo, and room for business cards and display literature—and to store backup stock and packing materials.
- Keep your booth and the area around it neat and tidy. Boxes, papers, and packing materials can distract greatly from your display. A broom, dustpan, and garbage bag or wastebasket are very helpful. Build or set aside an area where these materials can be hidden from view.
- Consider weather protection gear if you are planning your booth for an outside event.

You might consider . . .

- Using part of your booth to educate the visitor in the processes involved in your craft. Or you may want to display your work in different stages of creation.
- Showing slides of a wider range of your work or of the processes involved in creating it.

Some craftspeople prefer to use commercial sources, such as Abstrata, for their displays; others prefer to rent drape and tables from decorators affiliated with commercial exhibit halls. Your most important objective is to present your work in the most favorable fashion.

BEFORE GOING TO THE FAIR

Once you are amid the hubbub and confusion of a big fair, it is difficult to determine policies and approaches to selling. So before you go, be sure to cover the following points:

1. Determine your policy concerning consignment: Do you consign, or only sell outright? If you consign, what are your terms? Ask about insurance of work while in the shop's possession. Establish the length of time the work is to be consigned. All arrangements should be clearly understood and be stated *in writing* and signed by both you and the shop owner.

2. State your minimum order, if you have one, either in the number of pieces or dollar amount. Many shops have expressed concern about what they feel are unrealistic minimum orders set by craftspeople. Sometimes a "number of pieces" minimum works better for everyone. Offer any guidance you can in helping a shop make a selection of your work, and try to guide the buyers in the most salable pieces for their kind of shop.

3. Please be sure your name and address are on your order pads, packing slips, and billing invoices. Be *certain* that any order you take is signed by the buyer; without signature, the order could be refused later. Some craftspeople reconfirm all orders taken at a marketing event, just to avoid unfortunate confusion.

4. State your business terms and payment terms. (Some fairs provide you a card on which to do this and which you can post in your booth during trade days.) If you make a service charge for late payment, this should be stated on your order forms and billing invoice. If you charge for packing and shipping, alert the buyer and state this on your order form. If your prices are subject to change, that should also be noted.

5. Business cards and/or printed information about you and your work are invaluable. These need not be expensive, and are extremely good for your business as a way of advertising. Craft events have a very high rate of "callback" business, and many exhibitors find themselves receiving new business for months after a show.

6. Establish a delivery date, and if you can't keep it, *notify* the shop that you will deliver late. If you cannot deliver at all, give the shop ample notice so they can fill their stock another way. Do not attempt to deliver orders that are very late; the shop has the right to refuse delivery.

There are other ways to sell one's work beyond craft fairs, but they are usually more time consuming, more costly, and generally less productive. Most people who plan to make their living from the sale of their work begin their careers at a craft fair.

PART SIX

THE POLITICS OF ART

Politics? Leave it alone. The making of art is one of the true areas where we have a chance to have a kind of independence and assert our own sense of morality. It is one of the free activities still left to some of us. So I say, use it. Use it and enjoy it."

Sylvia Stone

The Great American Art Game

Lee Caplin

The following quotations are from the CBS cable television show "The Great American Art Game," produced by Lee Caplin.* Included are thoughts and opinions of people from the five major groups comprising the art world: dealers, curators, critics, collectors, and artists.

In the art world there are forces that transcend the basic artist-dealer-collector business relationships. Many people refer to these forces as the "politics of art." "Politics" in this case reflects the comings and goings of the respected (or not-so-respected) and/or vocal members of the art world. The power they may have comes from their perceived ability to affect the public's taste in art and, consequently, the value of art itself.

Art dealer Mary Boone said that "taste is a combination of a thousand different things that are known and unknown." A simple translation of Ms. Boone's view may be that it is impossible to account for individual taste at all. As for how much art is worth, James Rosenquist feels that a work of art has little inherent value: "You just take ground-up minerals and oil, and arrange them on a surface into an illusion, and people pay money for that." If these statements are taken at face value, it could be the politics of art is unimportant as well, even though artists will acknowledge that the greatest acclaim is often bestowed on art that may not be the "best." While it is obvious that some artists value the acclaim itself and see it as validation of their work, other artists see acclaim as the antithesis of art.

In all events, the existence of "politics" in the art world is universally recognized. Art dealer Leo Castelli commented that "there is politics in every-thing that one does." Paula Cooper, another dealer, observed that "you can become successful in anything if you want to manipulate things and put all of your intelligence and energy in that. But that's being successful at something else—not particularly what you are supposedly being successful at."

To understand the politics of art, it is first necessary to understand the forces at work in the art world. Leo Castelli described it simply when he said, "The

---

* Excerpts are by permission of CBS.

important forces are the people around the artist, interested in art: the museums, the critics, the writers, and perhaps more important than all to really start an artist's career, the collectors." By leaving out dealers, Mr. Castelli may be suggesting that his profession merely provides what dealer Arnold Glimcher describes as a "service role." However, in fulfilling that service role, dealers have many choices as to what artists they will represent, how they will show the art they have for sale, the mechanisms by which they will set the price of art in their galleries, and in what way they will present their galleries and themselves to the public.

ART DEALERS

Mary Boone: Great dealers are always made by great artists. However, the inverse of that statement is not true. No matter how great a dealer is, you cannot make an artist. I would never take an artist on under the basis that I could sell them.

    The notion of building a career for an artist is a very accumulative one. By the time you see several of these so-called "young" artists, you're looking at about ten years worth of work. For me to establish what are all the connecting factors between all the artists that I represent is, in fact, a kind of intellectual distillation that I have put on top of what was essentially an intuitive response from the beginning.

    [As for selling an artist's painting to just anyone] Since there are so many people who want paintings and so few paintings that are available, it's very important for the artist that these paintings either go to museums or to collectors that have other substantial art . . . major collectors. It's not about snobbery. It's not a marketing technique. I don't feel that it is political. I mean, I know that that term's even been applied to me. But there are only three things that it takes to collect art: a great deal of enthusiasm and patience both together which is a rare combination, and then the kind of intelligence to be able to understand something new, and the last one is money.

Sidney Janis: We opened our gallery in 1948. Forty-eight, forty-nine, and fifty were pretty tough years. None of the big names that we know today of the abstract expressionists were doing anything at all. When we put on their one-man shows, for example, the Jackson Pollock show that we put on in 1952, it wasn't a smash hit, but it brought in a lot of people, and they began to look seriously at Pollock. And when we put on de Kooning's first one-man show a few months later, it was an exhibition of figurative paintings. Many of the abstract artists felt de Kooning was betraying them, and there was a great to-do about that.

[As for getting the public to buy the art at substantial prices] that happened in the normal way. In that de Kooning exhibition, I think the largest painting sold for $3,000, and the smaller ones sold for $2,500 and less. There was one picture in that group I sold to a wonderful fellow for $1,800, and his widow later sold it for $850,000. The first Rothko we sold was $1,800, and after five or six years with the gallery I think the highest price we got was $15,000. Sometimes the artists objected to the fact that we were a little moderate in our raising the prices, but it worked out better that way, I think. I think that an artist feels more secure when his prices go up gradually but steadily. There is the risk of an artist who is known for a year or two and who is getting $40,000 and $50,000 for his paintings, a risk that it can turn the other way. I don't price work for economic reasons. I do it because I believe in the artist. And I'm also confronted with the fact that it is a five-year pull before something happens.

I should imagine that there may be more self-seekers today. You see, the artists are multiplying like mad. Where there were 40,000 artists 20 years ago, today there may be 250,000 and some of them are ambitious. I find that an artist who has a lot of integrity about his work is one to be watched, rather than one who is interested in making a reputation overnight.

Leo Castelli: I was more interested in literature as a young man, drifted from one job to another, and finally I got some funds from my father-in-law (I was married to Iliana Sonnebend at that time), and so we started the gallery. My first artists are now very well known and made a great impact on the art scene: Rauschenberg, Jasper Johns, Cy Twombley, and Frank Stella.

I would not urge anybody to buy anything. People have to make up their own mind about that. They come for advice, but I don't know whether you can really give advice. The artists I discover are already, I would say, fully developed. If you start thinking about marketability, then you are sunk. You have to buy what you think is a great work. I myself have made bad choices. There are certain artists that I thought were important, and would be good, and then, well, they weren't exactly bad, but they proved to be disappointing, so that happens to everybody.

I have relationships with myriad dealers, not only all over the country, but also dealers in New York, odd as it may seem. We work very much together. Of course there's competition, but there is also a great deal of collaboration among dealers—planning, strategies, tactics, and so on. [As for selling a work of art to anyone who walks in off the street] I would want to have credentials about the collection. I don't want a good painting to get lost somewhere and never be seen again. Or in very bad company, you know?

Arnold Glimcher: We have an adjunct company so that a college student can buy a poster by Jim Dyne for $10 or $15, and later, maybe a print for $1,000 or $2–3,000, and then, eventually, a painting. Over the past 20 years, we've had clients come up with us from putting posters on their walls in universities to buying major works. I could double the prices and sell the pictures, but I think that's capricious. We don't want to cut out all of the collectors who can afford the works at this moment and go to the next level of collector who are much more rarified. There are fewer people to pay $1 million than there are to pay $100 for a picture.

When an extraordinary group of work happens at an artist's studio, before the exhibition, before the work is even here, very often we'll talk about it to museum directors or curators who are our friends, and they will go see the work. If I think that something is vital and should be placed in a museum, I'll contact the museum and say, "I have this extraordinary painting by Jasper Johns, and it is obviously a painting for the Whitney Museum." And that's the way the Johns sale was put together. It was my conception to place the work at the Whitney. I'm very friendly with the collectors who own the work, and I went to them and suggested that it would be a placement during their lifetime that they would be involved with, and I structured the deal. I was even involved with some of the collectors who donated the money to the Whitney for the acquisition of the painting. I don't think art is an investment at all. I think that anybody who invests in art is foolish. It's something to buy because it's part of your life-style, it extends your perception, it enriches your life and you can afford to do that.

Paula Cooper: A gallery is like a store, in a way, and it's also a public place where people can come. But representing an artist also involves being an agent, like an agent for an actor. It takes me a long time to make the decision to start working with an artist, because it's a tremendous commitment, and I don't want to have to stop working with the artist, if possible.

[Regarding selling art to just anyone] Number one, the person has to be serious. Number two, I would like, hopefully, someone who's not just buying art as an investment and is going to turn around and sell it in two years, or a year, or six months. Usually people that you know get preference. And we work with a great many institutions, museums and so on. It's to safeguard the work. It doesn't have to do with the people, although when you've been around a long time you know people, and you have an easy relationship with them. They're very approachable, and you're very approachable. Even with new young curators.

CURATORS

William Rubin (Museum of Modern Art): In the art world a generation ago, when the Museum of Art was almost alone in showing modern work, to be shown at the Museum meant more than it does now, when there are competing museums. There are 20 more times the galleries than there used to be. It still means something for an artist to be singled out by the Museum, but I don't think that any one singling out has the impact it used to. I'm a great believer that work finds its own level, so that if an artist is good, sooner or later it will be recognized and his chances will form. And if he isn't, he can have all the museum shows in the world, and it's not going to make any difference.

Thirty years ago when I was a student and a young professor, you could cover the art scene. It's not possible anymore. And so you depend on word of mouth from people you respect. You ask them what they've seen, and you go and see that. And then people that you know are good, you go and see that. There are some critics whom one respects. There are other curators. And, above all, certain artists. Being an artist doesn't give you a kind of automatic ability to judge, but I would say there are certain artists who have terrific eyes, not only for their own work, but for other people's work.

[In terms of today's artist superstars] I don't think they're really superstars myself. I think that there's a lot of hype, and there are quickly made reputations based in part upon the tremendous increase in intensity and speed of art communication. But it's precisely the absence of a superstar like Jackson Pollock or even like Frank Stella on the scene now that I think is characteristic of what is basically an eclectic scene in which there is not a universal consensus about any of these artists.

Patterson Sims (The Whitney Museum of American Art): When I was fourteen I realized that I wanted to work in a museum. When I graduated from college I took a job in the O. K. Harris gallery in Soho. About six years after I started working at the gallery I was offered a job at the Whitney. Ivan Karp (the owner of O. K. Harris) was very hard to leave as a boss because he was such a wonderful personality, and I learned just about 87 percent of what I know from him.

The contemporary art world is an immensely complicated and fascinating place. And it requires a tremendous number of personalities to make it work. All those personalities play very critical roles, none really more important than the other, except, of course, for the artist. Because the artist and his or her talent is at the basis of all our activities, in a sense all of us who aren't artists are service personnel for the artist.

The curator has to pick and choose and make very hard and fast decisions about what will be shown. In that process you have to decide what you think is best based on two things: one, your instinct, and two, that instinct being informed by experience. I spend most of my waking hours looking and thinking about works of art, and in that process I decide certain people seem to be making the thing that I call art better than certain other people. So I will go to the studios, alternative centers, other museums, galleries. It's the mix of experiences. Some artists can make a fantastic individual work, but then when you see the idea repeated 10 or 15 times, as it will be in a body of work, it doesn't hold up, it doesn't look so strong anymore.

We play a rather critical role in terms of the development of reputations for artists. I sense the responsibility I have as a curator to try to make decisions based on thinking about who are the dominant personalities, who deserves to be shown at a given moment. You can do a retrospective of an artist who's an absolutely wonderful artist, but if the timing is wrong, if you show that artist at a moment when there's been a shift in a consciousness about what's interesting, important, and significant in art, that show will have no impact. So you must have the show occur at the right moment. I look for visual impact. It has to be visually very, very exciting to me. Maybe a new way of thinking or to substantiate a group of artists who are working at that particular time.

There are people one turns to for advice. People who are very alert, who are looking all the time, who are very open to what's going on in American art. You have certain galleries that you select as being more interesting than other galleries. All this involves an extraordinary tightrope walk between professional and personal. Because in order to be open to what's going on, you have to establish certain kinds of personal relationships. You have to know artists very well. You have to know dealers very well. You have to know collectors very well. But in all those relationships you have to be able to decide when it's transgressing into something that's overly personal, where you can no longer make an objective judgment, and something that gives you access to that individual so you can have a certain degree of information that wouldn't be possible without a degree of friendship.

Artists are such exciting people. The way they think, the way they behave, the way they live is so tantalizing. When an artist says somebody else's work is extraordinary, you listen. Because an artist very seldom will be generous about another artist unless their work has fantastic impact on them. The politics of art is a fascinating topic because here we are all involved in this very exciting visual substance. The substance which seems to us to be almost like life itself, or maybe even better than life itself. Yet revolving around this subject is money. Tremendous amounts of money. Fantastic sums. And also an ability for the people who collect works of art, who are involved with artists, to have certain kinds of social prestige. There's no Securities and Exchange Commission in the art world. There very well might be because of the enormous amount of money passing backward and forward. There are very few regulations which govern it other than a sense of ethics, a substance which a lot of people say is in very short supply in the art world. You have to deal with a situation where you as a person who makes not that great a living in terms of what your salary is as a curator, deals with vast sums of money—when we were trying to decide about the museum buying the Jasper Johns for $1 million, it was a bunch of people who make about $20,000 a year deciding how to spend a million dollars.

But the power is just an illusion. It is something that comes from my position working at an important museum. If I lost my job I'd be out in the street looking for another job. I might be able to find a good job as a result of working at the Whitney, but I wouldn't have a tenth of the power that I have here. Artists often, as a manifestation of their feelings about you and the way you've helped them to make their work clearer and more accessible to people, want to give you something in return. Also, you can be aware of certain artists doing very good work by putting them in an exhibition. What will often happen is their work will go up in value and so you can quite unknowingly buy their work of art, then put it in an exhibition, and then discover the work of art has gone up in value. So you can be inside a situation, contributing to a situation where there's a fluctuation in the value of a work of art. We have instituted a policy whereby if you buy a work of art—which is completely legitimate, if it's your money and you want to do it—you have to report that fact so that the museum is aware of it and has the option to buy that work for the same price, or has the option to buy it at its market price if you bought it a number of years ago. I think we're all becoming increasingly sensitive to the possibilities of abuse that exist between the museum and the money part of the art world.

CRITICS AND WRITERS

Hilton Kramer (*The New York Times*): I've written rave reviews of artists whose exhibitions have been crowded, say, for three weeks, who never sold a picture. I've condemned other people to perdition, and they've sold out.

I mean, after all, we know there are artists in New York who are praying on their knees every night for a bad review in *The New York Times,* so long as it's long enough.

I go to very few openings. I see all the exhibitions, or as many as humanly possible. If there's an artist whose first show you may have seen, who had something interesting but not really good enough to focus on, but then you go to a second show and think "well, he's really made strides," it's important, you write about it. I don't know of any artist whose career I've broken. I suppose I've contributed to some reputations. But you see, an artist's reputation is really constructed of a great many different elements. I mean his age, the kind of attention the museum is paying to him, the kind of collectors who buy his work, the gallery in which he's showing, the relation of his style to what people seem to be interested in, what touches the sort of nerve of feeling at the moment. There are always people who can only function within a sort of main-stream, and then there are always eccentrics, always people on the margin, and they often flourish both economically and aesthetically. I mean the scene is so complicated and pluralistic and so contradictory that you can't pinpoint success.

I enjoy the scene a lot, but my art scene consists mostly of objects. I know a few collectors, but they're not, as you might say, my people. I know many artists, and artists are, in a sense, my people. But it's possible for a critic to have friendships with some artists but not with others, because, after all, what does an artist want from a critic? He wants to be praised, you know. I've lost artists who were friends—they felt betrayed or offended by what I wrote. I felt disappointed in them because I felt that they should be larger than that. But I understand it, and I don't have any illusions about it. I'm aware of the tremendous power that is attributed to those words. It's (the dealers') business to bring pressure on me to review their artists. I think it's perfectly legitimate, but we don't make a decision on the basis of how much pressure's being brought to bear. It has its amusing side. That's part of the scene. But mostly my scene is going to look at works of art and writing about them.

Fundamentally I write for my readers and myself. Sometimes in that order and sometimes in reverse order. I mean, I want to be very clear in my own mind what I think about what I'm seeing. [If a friend doesn't like what I've written about them] it's a matter of total indifference to me. One thing that's very important to understand about criticism is that it is not criticism in the long perspective that really constitutes the fundamental influence on what happens in art—even on what happens with reputa-tions. It's the way artists respond to what other artists are doing that really creates taste, creates value, creates reputations, and gives us a sense of hierarchy of values in art. I always think of that wonderful remark T. S.

Elliot made when asked if most editors were failed writers. Elliot said, "Well, perhaps, but then so are most writers." And that's true of artists too—I mean, most of them are failed artists!

Peter Schjeldahl (*The Village Voice*): I don't think I'm in the business of making artists either happy or unhappy. I get anywhere from 20 to 50 pieces of mail a day and telephone calls . . . a hundred shows. I guess I assume I must have some impact. But there are so many factors going into an artist's career. One thing you have to realize about art is that it is a handmade object. The most prolific artist in the world is turning out a product in a very primitive manner. There's no mass production. So the amount of art available from an artist is always limited, and it doesn't take very many people to want that artist's work to, in fact, create a seller's market.

The art gallery is a very complicated business. The dealer is the artist's agent, but also the artist's employer, in a way. The relationships between the dealer and the artist and between the dealer and the collector go on in the back room. My feeling is if you're too far outside, you don't know what you're talking about. If you're too far inside, you can't tell the truth. I would censor myself rather than hurt somebody's feelings. If you hang out in the inner sanctum of the art world, then, naturally, people tell you secrets. I mean there are all kinds of critics—who write for art magazines—who are writing more for people very close to the center. That's a very honorable thing to do, and the rules are different, you know. [As for collecting art] in a way I feel that maybe writing a check is an alternative to writing a review.

COLLECTORS

Richard Brown Baker: I never thought of forming an art collection. I look for a reaction in myself, I suppose. I consider it a visual phenomenon of a response. I do think artists are extremely interesting people. I've never much cultivated their company, but there are hundreds in my collection. I used to go to openings more when I was newer at collecting. I can recall so well in the old Castelli Gallery, walking down a corridor where there was a little shelf with a group of (Jasper Johns's) little "Number Nine" oil paintings, and one of them, "Number Three," kind of spoke to me. I went in and Ivan Karp was then at Castelli. I said to Ivan "I want that 'Number Three,'" and he said "All right, you can have it for three hundred. It's number three!"

I know I have bought scores, hundreds of works that will not be treasured, shall we say, by art historians and museum curators—ever—but, nevertheless, I feel a certain reluctance to winnow out in a way that

I wouldn't if I were collecting Matisses. I don't aspire to make money out of art, so I don't want to sell them and make capital gains. I realized that my interest is in the work of living artists, so I got this chronological formula that I would buy work created after the First World War. I don't think in terms of movement.

Nathan Cummings: I took a trip to Paris and saw this painting in a window. I didn't know anything about the artist. It was just a picture of a country scene, of a couple of haystacks. So I went into the gallery and asked the owner how much the painting was, and he told me. I asked him "Would you let me take this back to my hotel and let me look at it tonight and see if I really like it?" He said "I can't do that without asking my partner. A lady owns half of this picture, and I own half." So he phoned the lady. He didn't know I could speak French, and, apparently she asked him "Does he look honest?" He answered in French "He looks very honest." So I took the picture back to the Plaza and put it on the mantle. After looking at it for an hour or so I said to myself "But that's an awful lot of money to spend. I could start a store with that." I was a small wholesaler of groceries at that time. I nevertheless convinced myself "Oh, I'll take a chance and buy it." [It was a Pisarro.]

I look for something that appeals to me in the way of color, in the way of composition. Because when I was very young I studied show card writing—to dress windows in department stores—that's what I thought I was going to be, a window dresser in department stores. And I never forgot that I had the touch for the brush, as it were. I consulted art experts in the beginning, but afterward I found out that all they did was go home and read books about artists—and I could learn as much as they could if I'd read the books, so that's why I've got a pretty good library of art books. I study up fairly well on the artist, and then I've got a fairly good eye for what I like and can make up my mind almost in a matter of minutes whether I should buy a picture or pass it up. I don't think of the investment angle. If I like the picture and the price is within a certain range that I make up my mind I'll spend, I won't spend any more. I always set a mental limit as to the price that I want to spend."

ARTISTS

George Segal: I'm terrible at business, and I think I'm lucky to have an honest dealer who understands artists thoroughly. His relationship with me has been remarkably free of any kind of commercial pressure. Part of me is gregarious, you know. Another part is private. Sure I enjoy the parties, and I like to go home and work.

There may be too much emphasis on the business side of art. When my generation matured, we were introduced to art as almost a substitute to religion. I have no objection to making money, especially selling my own work. But it's not the primary reason, you know. I think it's too easy to forget the dreams and ideals that are in art.

Jennifer Bartlett: I was disappointed (dealer Paula Cooper) didn't instantly offer me a one-woman show. But she gave me three or four numbers to call and said to ask her back when I had more work. Then I had a small show at an artist's studio and (she) gave me her mailing list. When I had my first one-man show in New York, I asked her to go see it, because, despite a kind of business aspect, I would still like to know what she thought. At that time I had more respect for (her) than I had for my (then) dealer.

I know some critics—just long associations, or after they've written about me—but I would be depressed if I manipulated myself to some position of visability. I somehow want it to come for other reasons, rather than incredible political finesse, or skill. I've been known to become discouraged at times, plus violently jealous when anyone gets anything I don't have.

Chuck Close: I always knew, at least from the time that I was about four, that I wanted to be an artist. It never occurred to me that I would make a dime off my work. I thought I would have to have a profession to support my profession. If I had listened to everybody who told me what I ought to do to be successful, I probably wouldn't have been. I don't think anyone was more surprised that my paintings were purchased than me, with the possible exception of my dealer, who was really surprised. I found my dealer walking in off the street, throwing my slides on the desk, and saying "You wouldn't be interested in this, would you?"

I try to fool myself and make believe that there's no relationship between the pieces I make and the checks that come in. I prefer to think I'm on a stipend or welfare. I care a lot about art, and I like to know what's going on. I see a tremendous number of galleries every month, and I'm very interested in how other people who are alive and well and working today are trying to do—not to keep my finger on the pulse in order to alter what I do to make it fit any particular shift in the wind. I don't know that many curators—not that there isn't hustle going on, but I don't feel that that's the best way I can use my energy.

There is an aspect of big business to the art world, and there is hype and a lot of money spent for advertising. You can inflate something for awhile, you can support the prices at auction, but it's really a jury of your peers. If other artists don't consider what you do of value, it can't be sustained forever.

Index